# The Practical Handbook of Group Counseling

*(Revised and Updated)*

by
Sheldon D. Glass, M.Ed., M.D.

2nd Edition

Order this book online at www.trafford.com
or email orders@trafford.com

Most Trafford titles are also available at major online book retailers.

Printed in Victoria, BC, Canada.

ISBN: 978-1-4269-2071-4 (sc)
ISBN: 978-1-4269-2072-1 (hc)

Library of Congress Control Number: 2009912445

*Trafford rev. 2/19/2010*

 www.trafford.com

**North America & international**
toll-free: 1 888 232 4444 (USA & Canada)
phone: 250 383 6864 ♦ fax: 812 355 4082

# Table of Contents

# PREFACE

This book has been written to be a primer in group work with children, adolescents and parents. It has been designed so that an individual counselor can use it as a ready reference for practical information. It has been written with the help (and questions) of teachers, counselors, administrators and graduate students with whom I have had the pleasure of working. The first edition has been used by over 300 colleges, universities, and public school systems in the United States. It has been enhanced by several suggestions that educators have made. It has been refined by the successes and failures that these same educators have had in group projects. The book is not presented as THE model of group work; it is presented as a text that can challenge the individual's ideas and upon which the counselors can develop techniques that will fit their personality and meet the needs of their school. The text is a synthesis of the various problems and successes that a counselor may encounter and offers one model that may be useful in enhancing and/or resolving some of these issues.

In the interest of maintaining a gender fair manuscript, I have alternated chapters, using the masculine pronoun in all odd numbered chapters and the feminine pronoun in all even numbered chapters.

I would like to thank my research assistants: Ms. Allison Burns, Ms. Marquay Kirkland, and Ms. Carrie Vivien for working during their summer recesses to help me research and revise this new edition, Mrs. Beth Schlein for her attentive assistance in word processing, and Mrs. Ellen Gerber and Mr. Paul Sambol for their research contributions.

My special thanks to my wife Saralynn, whose patience and help have been above and beyond the call of familial understanding.

# CHAPTER I

## *INTRODUCTION*

The aim of this book is to present the practical techniques of group counseling in the school setting. It has been written to emphasize the skills necessary to know how to use group counseling, when to use it, where to use it, and when not to use it. The book has not been designed to review the theoretical concepts of group dynamics. Theory will be discussed in terms of group dynamics only when it is practical and applicable. The book is not meant to be a scientific document. It is based primarily upon the impressions and experiences of the author. The material presented has been obtained through extensive work at the Johns Hopkins Hospital, the Johns Hopkins University, and in the Baltimore City school system and throughout the Maryland region (MD, DE, and VA) where large group counseling programs have been initiated at every level of the school organization: that is, elementary, junior and senior high schools, as well as specialty schools – i.e., the vocational schools and the schools for adolescent pregnant girls.

Group counseling can be a very useful technique in the school program. It has been used in different school settings for various purposes. We have used it with above-average children with leadership skills, average children, potential dropouts, under-achievers, disruptive children, developmentally disabled children, adolescent pregnant girls between the ages of eleven and eighteen, and specialty groups such as peer counselors, fashion design students, and students with specific somatic problems. It has been used specifically for college orientations and vocational guidance.

One important fact that group counseling has shown is that it is not a substitute for the classical one-to-one or counselor-to-pupil relationship. The one-to-one classical approach is the basic foundation upon which the counselor works. Group counseling, however, can facilitate this one-to-one relationship and offer both the counselor and the student opportunities which individual counseling cannot. Sometimes the best way for the counselor or teacher to "reach" the individual is through a group. In other situations a counselor who has been working on a one-to-one basis may not have time to continue, but feels that the youngster still needs some type of counseling support and may elect to continue working with the student in a group.

## *GROUP IDENTITY*

In working with students educators are concerned with many goals, one of which is giving the youngster an opportunity to develop their own identity. Usually when the counselor considers the problem of identity, the counselor means self-identity, self-concept, or self-worth. The counselor should review, however, the entire concept of identity.

Identity can be separated into two related but separate parts. One is self-identity or self-concept, which is the way an individual looks at himself. The other is group identity, which is the way an individual conceptualizes himself as a member of a group. Although group counseling helps to reinforce and develop the self identity of the individual, it is the technique of choice for helping to reinforce and develop one's group identity. It is the interaction among peers and the development of the social processes within the individual that are stimulated by the process of group counseling. With many students the group approach accomplishes what the classical, individual approach cannot. For example, within a group of youngsters in the inner city there may be a youngster whose self-identity and self-worth are well developed. The student may have a desire to go on to college or higher learning, but the group pressure may be one of anti-college or anti-higher learning. In order to identify with his peers, the student must assume the same attitude as these peers. A one-to-one classical approach may or may not help, because it may be appealing primarily to the way the student views himself as an individual rather than as a member of a group. When the educator utilizes a group approach he is reinforcing the group identity of the youngster. The group approach may help the student to overcome problems that his peer group may be presenting. It is the substitution of a positive group identity (that is facilitated by group counseling) that may offset the negative group problems that a student may have with his peers, neighborhood, or family. By participating in group counseling, there is group support for the formation of a constructive attitude. The complement may also be true in suburban or perimeter areas where the group pressure may be to go not only to college, but to go to "big-league" colleges like Harvard, Princeton, Yale, Radcliffe, or Wellesley. The youngster who is just average and who may have trouble gaining acceptance into a junior college may have difficulty in handling this particular problem with his college-oriented peers. In this situation, group counseling would give the student the opportunity to share ideas with others, obtain the support of his peers in a group setting, and develop a more positive group identity. This will not offset the attitudes of the peer group, but will give the youngster a concept of group support and affiliation with others with similar problems with which the student can identify. The development of a more positive group identity is often more difficult to achieve in a classical one-to-one, counselor-student relationship.

Group counseling reinforces the youngster's estimation of himself by giving him an opportunity to see that he is not different, but shares the same problems as others in his own peer group, and that his reservations about himself and his expectations are not unusual. When the youngster is unusual, it gives him an opportunity to develop ideas that may help him, with the group support, to "work through" whatever difficulties he may think exist. Group counseling gives the student an opportunity to develop, present, and test original ideas (necessary for spontaneity and perhaps creativity) that many of our classical classrooms do not.

One of the single most important contributions of the group

approach to counseling is that in a given period of time the counselor can work with a greater number of students. In an era when the counseling staff in most school systems is understaffed, counselors must utilize any technique that will effectively increase their capability of working with a greater number of students. The modern counselor can no longer rely on the basic one-to-one approach to accomplish all of their many obligations. The counselor should be able to utilize the group approach, whether it be with the entire school, grade, classroom, or small group.

One of the interesting phenomena that have occurred with counselors who have started to conduct group work is that many children who were previously hesitant to talk to the counselor on a one-to-one basis have been presenting themselves to the counselor in groups. One rather dramatic example of this happened in a junior high school, where the teacher had notified the administration that if something could not be done to improve his particular classroom he was going to submit his resignation, because he no longer could cope with the situation. The children, not knowing about this ultimatum, had spontaneously approached the counselor, asking if he could work with them so that they might be able to resolve the problems that they were having in the classroom. The counselor did in fact work with the children, and worked independently with the teacher. The teacher remained and the children became productive students.

Another phenomenon that occurs when the counselor starts working with groups is that the teacher is more likely to present and discuss his classroom problems with the counselor, hoping to obtain concepts of group work to apply to the classroom. Chapter VIII is devoted to the basic relationship of the counselor to the teacher and the practical application of a group approach in the classroom.

During the last twenty years, group work in the schools and other organizational settings has received a great burst of sustained enthusiasm and activity. But the enthusiasm in a few schools was short-lived. Group counseling in these schools had a gradual demise. During the subsequent decade there were an increasing number of reports of group counseling being conducted in various school systems throughout the nation, but this work was not as active nor widespread as the reports would indicate. It is important to reflect on why in some schools the popularity of group counseling subsided so quickly. One apparent reason is that without specific guidelines and rules of procedure, group counseling can "get out of hand" because it facilitates spontaneity on the part of the child. Some types of spontaneity within the school setting should be encouraged, for it is helpful in facilitating the process of teaching and learning. Other types of spontaneity can be destructive to the school program. It is this latter type of spontaneity that the counselors were not expecting, and consequently they did not take the basic precautions that were necessary in order to avoid difficulty.

The second reason that group counseling has "sputtered" more than it should was that the orientation was to group therapy, not group counseling. The emphasis in this book is on group counseling. This is not group therapy.

There has been much written about the similarities and the differences between group counseling and group therapy. There have been many definitions of group counseling that have been presented in the various counseling texts. Most of these have been reasonable definitions but have not emphasized the difference between the two techniques. The basic difference between group counseling and group therapy can primarily be emphasized by understanding the dynamics of groups themselves. Group processes work at basically two different levels: one is a goal-oriented, task-oriented, or conscious level in which all the participants are aware of the events that are going on. The conscious level can be said to reflect the content of the material being discussed. The second level is a less obvious, often emotionally influenced level which reflects the processes of the group that are functioning at an unconscious level. The unconscious level can be said to reflect the thoughts of the group members about the material being discussed and the dynamics of the group process. It is probably influenced by biological and psychological factors of group processes that we do not completely understand yet.

A basic difference between group counseling and group

therapy is that group counseling is conducted at a conscious level. The group tries to handle the obvious events that occur within the group session, events that have been clearly delineated and of which all members are aware. Group therapy, however, is usually led by a person trained to recognize and interpret not only events that are being elicited at a conscious level but also the processes that are occurring at unconscious or less obvious level. One of the difficulties that people have had is that when they try to run a group therapy program without having been trained in techniques that allow them to technically and professionally reflect on the unconscious level of performance of the individual and the group, they are very apt to get into difficulty that they neither understand nor can handle. One of the reasons that educators have done such an excellent job with group counseling within the schools is that they orient themselves to the problems they are aware of and know a great deal about. Consequently, they become excellent group counselors. They often do not understand nor do they necessarily try to reflect on the unconscious levels of the group.

Most people, unless well trained, are not capable of working with the so-called unconscious factors in group work. The school counselor providing group counseling is usually more efficient when he works with and discusses those factors that are readily available to both him and the students involved. When the counselor works within an educational model, he is usually aware of all the events that occur. When the counselor is not successful in using an educational model, he quickly recognizes it and should know when to refer to an outside provider of services. When the educator attempts to use a psychological or psychiatric model for group work and has difficulty, he often does not know whether that difficulty should or should not be present. The educator may not be sure when to refer and when not to refer for treatment.

Although the counselor may understand the group dynamics that are occurring at an unconscious level, it does not mean that he has to interpret that performance with the student members. Many effective therapists who reflect on the unconscious level of performance often do not share this with the youngsters. Group members continue to function and develop psychologically at both levels, that is, conscious and unconscious, whether the events are interpreted or not.

Counselors should not attempt to act as trained psychiatrists. This is not the role of the school. If the youngster needs more extensive counseling, or does need psychotherapy, then this should be provided in special programs under the direction of trained mental health professionals. Although the general school and counseling programs often do alter the personalities of our students, this is the result of the educational process. The primary responsibility of the educational institution is to facilitate the process of teaching and learning. It is to this end that this book, oriented to group counseling, will direct itself.

The third reason for the apparent lack of success in some group counseling programs is that counselors often initiate group programs with students drawn from their "problem" case load. They start their "initial" groups with their most difficult youngsters instead of working with average and above-average students. The students selected often are not candidates for group work in the school setting. What is even more important is that the counselors may not be prepared to work with difficult groups. They may become frustrated and unfortunately drop the group technique prematurely. (See Page 18, "Selection Of Group Members.")

The basic difficulties that can be encountered in group counseling can be prevented by proper planning. Techniques that can be utilized will be discussed in subsequent chapters. Enough information has been obtained to be able to start group counseling programs with many different "type" groups (including disruptive students) with little technical or administrative difficulty. Although large group counseling programs have been initiated with little difficulty, it is important to note that one of the reasons for the success of the programs was the strict adherence to established precautions. Precautions reflect the seriousness by which group counseling should be undertaken. For example, all the large programs were initiated by a training seminar.

This text is written in an elementary way and may at times over-simplify a complex phenomenon. However, one of the reservations that educators have had about group work had been built out of the myth that group work is more complicated than it is. If the counselor works within the educational model, there is no reason why group work should not be initiated within the school program, provided the proper precautions and training are established.

# *SUGGESTED READINGS*

Alvarez, Ann Rosegrant. (2002). Pitfalls, pratfalls, shortfalls, and windfalls: reflections on forming and being formed by groups. Social Work With Groups. 25(1), 93-105.

ASGW: Best Practice Guidelines, Revised, Association for Specialists in Group Work (March 23, 2007)

Brigman, Greg. (2001). Group Counseling for School Counselors: A Practical Guide. J. Weston Walch. 2nd ed.

Brown, Nina W. (1998). Psychoeducational Groups. Accelerated Development: Philadelphia.

Connors, Joanie V.; Caple, Richard B. (June 2005). A Review of Group Systems Therapy. Journal for Specialists in Group Work. V30 n2 p93-110.

DeLucia-Waack, Janice L. et. al. (eds.) (2004). Handbook of Group Counseling and Psychotherapy. Sage: Thousand Oaks, CA.

DeLucia-Waack, Janice L. (Nov 1997). Measuring the Effectiveness of Group Work: A Review and Analysis of Process and Outcome Measures. Journal for Specialists in Group Work. V22 n4 p277-93

Fleming, Victoria. (June 1999). Group counseling in the schools: A case for basic training. Professional School Counseling. 2(5), 409-13.

Gazda, George, Horne, Arthur M. (Sep 2005). Rex Stockton and the Association for Specialists in Group Work: The Power of Working Together. Journal for Specialists in Group Work. V30 n3 p203-207.

Gazda, George Michael et. al. (2000). Group Counseling and Group Psychotherapy: Counseling and Application. Allyn and Bacon.

Grant, Debra, &Berkovitz, Irving. (1999). Values of long term group counseling in middle and high school. Journal of Child and Adolescent Group Therapy. 9(1), 17-35.

Horne, Arthur M,: Rosenthal, Robin. (Nov 1997). Research in Group Work; How Did We Get Where We Are? Journal for Specialists in Group Work. V22 n4 p228-40.

Jacobs, E.E. et al. (2001). Group Counseling: Strategies and Skills. Wadsworth. 4th ed. Johnson, Sharon K.; Jonson, C.D. (Jun 2005). Group Counseling: Beyond the Traditional. Professional School Counseling. V8 n5 p399.

Kist-Kline, Gail E.; Quantz, Richard A. (Jul 1998). Understanding a School-Based Mental Health Program: Creating a Caring Environment. Journal for a Just and Caring Education. V4 n3 p307-22.

Koocher, Gerald P. (Nov. 2003). Ethical issues in psychotherapy with adolescents. Journal of Clinical Psychology. 59(11), p. 1247, 10p.

Mahler, C. (1969). Group Counseling in the Schools. Houghton Mifflin: Boston.

McCarthy, Christopher; Mejia, Olga L.; Llu, Hsin-tine Tina. (Mar 2000). Cognitive Appraisal Therapy: A Psychoeducational Approach for Understanding Connections between Cognition and Emotion in Group Work. Journal for Specialists in Group Work. V25 n1 p104-21.

McCoy, Patricia C. ((Nov 1997). Group Research: A Practitioner's Perspective. Journal for Specialists in Group Work. V22 n4 p294-96.

O'Halloran, Theresa M.; McCartney, Teri J. (Mar 2004). An Evaluation of the Use of Technology as a Tool to meet Group Training Standards. Journal for Specialists in Group Work. v29 n1 p65-73.

Ohlsen, Merle M. (Ed.) Counseling Children in Groups, (1973) Holt, Rhinehart, Winston

Pope, Kenneth S. and Melba J.T. Vasquez. (1998). Ethics in Psychotherapy and Counseling: A Practical Guide. Jossey-Bass: San Francisco.

Shechtman, Zipora; Bar-El, Orit; Hadar, Efrat. (Sep 1997). Therapeutic Factors and Psychoeducational Groups for Adolescents: A Comparison. Journal for Specialists in Group Work. V22 n3 9203-13.

Sonstegard, Manford A. (Summer 1998). A rationale for group counseling. Journal of Individual Psychology. 54(2), 164-76.

Sonstegard, Manford A. and James Robert Bitter. (Summer 1998). Counseling children in groups. Journal of Individual Psychology. 54(2), 251-68.

Stroh, Heather R.; Sink, Christopher A. (Oct 2002). Applying APA's Learner-Centered Principles to School-Based Group Counseling. Professional School Counseling. v6 n1 p71-78.

Thomspson, Charles L., and Linda B. Rudolph. (1999). Counseling Children. Wadsworth. 4th ed.

Whiston, Susan C.; Sexton, Thomas L. (Fall 1998). A Review of School Counseling Outcome Research: Implications for Practice. Journal of Counseling & Development. V76 n4 p412-26.

Wilson, F. Robert; Rapin, Lynn S.; Haley-Banez, Lynn. (Mar 2004). How Teaching Group Work Can Be Guided by Foundational Documents: Best Practice Guidelines, Diversity Principles, Training Standards. Journal for Specialists in Group Work. v29 n1 p19-29.

# CHAPTER II

## *HOW TO ORGANIZE A GROUP*

Group counseling can be a valuable adjunct in the educational process. It is particularly effective when the counselor has considered the organizational needs of the group. This chapter will review the major considerations of "how to organize a group" for group counseling.

## *GROUP GOALS*

The most important consideration in organizing a group is to know why the counselor wants to form the group. What are the counselor's goals? This is an elementary point, but should be considered carefully. When counselors do not consider why they are organizing their groups, they usually do not know what they want to cover or in what way they want to help the youngsters involved. The group session that ensues is often poorly done with little feedback either to the counselor or to the students. Both counselor and children quickly become bored. When the counselor is not sure of what she wants to accomplish, the group will become restless; for if the counselor does not know, the children certainly will not. When a counselor knows what the goals are, the group is better organized, the selection of youngsters is more effective, and the counseling sessions are more successful.

Well-delineated goals help the students to determine what their roles in the group should be, stimulate interaction among the group members, and influence how the group members relate to each other.

Initially, the goals of the counselor may be only to learn how to conduct group counseling. The group members may be selected specifically with this goal in mind. When this is the case (and this is reasonable) the counselor can share this with the youngsters telling them that the purpose of the counseling sessions is to try a new technique in counseling (that is, that of group counseling), and she would like them to participate in this particular learning experience. The kids usually respond favorably, and there is generally no difficulty.

Sometimes the goals have to be vague. For example, it is not uncommon in large schools to have at least an occasional classroom in which there is difficulty in maintaining order. There may be a nucleus of troublemakers, but whether this is the source of trouble or not is hard to determine. One of the goals of the group might be to find out why there is so much difficulty in the classroom.

Sometimes the goals are clear-cut. In a vocational or college-orientation program the goals are fairly well delineated. The only technical question may be how to present the material to be covered.

One of the cardinal rules when establishing group goals is never to relate goals to a group if they are not the goals that have been formulated. Youngsters have a built-in radar system. They know the facts, whether they are related or not. If the group leader is going to retain the trust of the youngsters, then he has to be both realistic and honest with them. I was working with a group of potential dropouts and had related to them that the goal of the session was to discuss career planning. When I asked the group members if they knew what this meant, one of the youngsters looked at me and said, "Yeah, you don't want me to become a dropout." I said, "Yes, you're right, and why not?" which was the introduction for discussing some of the salient points of career planning.

Not all goals can be openly shared with the students. There are times when the primary goals can be shared but the secondary or tertiary goals may be too "threatening." The counselor may elect not to share them with the youngsters, with the realization that perhaps the topics can be shared at a more appropriate time during subsequent counseling sessions. The counselor should simply present the material that she can and say no more. As in any other setting of the school system, material may be omitted, but material that is presented should be as factual as possible. In summary, a counselor should, prior to organizing her group, know what the goals are and be prepared, when possible, to share these goals with the members of his group.

The number of goals that are picked by the counselor should be proportionate to the number of sessions that she plans on having with the youngsters. If this is a one-session meeting with no subsequent sessions planned, then the goals should be few in number, concentrating on one or (at the most) two goals to be achieved during the one session. If the sessions are to be continuous on a periodic basis (i.e., once weekly or once bi-weekly), then the number of goals can be increased with one or two primary goals and as many as reasonable secondary goals. The basic rule is not to attempt to accomplish too much over too short a period of time.

It is important not to establish goals that are unrealistic. For example, a youngster may be having a particular learning problem that she has had for four or five years. It would be unrealistic for the counselor to think that one group session would alter the behavior or study patterns of this youngster. If the counselor attempts to change a behavior pattern in one session, whether it be individual or group, she would create a situation in which the youngster would fail. If the counselor established the goal for the session as "understanding how to study better" without the realistic provision of informing the youngsters that to change study patterns takes time, then a youngster might experience the same failure that she had been experiencing in the classroom for the last four or five years. This would be unfair. The goals of the session should be oriented to what can be easily, or at least realistically, accomplished within the time limit assigned to the session or sessions.

It is often helpful to program goals. The group starts with an obtainable goal that can be easily reached by the youngsters involved. The initial goals are reflective of the level of performance at which the group is operating when the group is initiated. More sophisticated goals are added as the level of performance increases. This is a particularly effective technique because it reinforces the group's performance. The group is continually working with tasks or goals that the group members are capable of handling. The momentum is maintained by the feeling of accomplishment.

The goals the counselor establishes may or may not be the same as the goals of the students. It is important for the group leader to establish goals with which the student is comfortable. Whenever possible, the group leader should try to correlate her goals with those of the group members. When the goals of the leader and the goals of the group are conflicting, then the interest, motivation, and involvement of the group members is usually unsatisfactory. It is the counselor's responsibility to recognize the youngsters' needs as they perceive them, and then try to design a program to meet their needs and at the same time achieve the counselor's goals. In general, the goals selected by the counselor are usually accepted by the students. If the student members understand what the counselor is trying to achieve and think that they are capable of interacting at that particular level, then they are usually more enthusiastic about becoming involved. One technique that is often helpful is for the counselor to outline her goals, and then to ask the group members how they think the group might go about accomplishing these particular goals, what topics might be discussed, how frequently they should meet, etc. Depending upon the group that is involved, this technique can sometimes be helpful in correlating group interests with the goals as outlined by the group leader. The important consideration is for the counselor to recognize that the interests of the group members may or may not correlate with the goals that he has defined. There are occasionally groups in which the members are not initially enthusiastic about the goals but which develop into excellent groups. It is very unusual, however, for a group to be productive when the group leader is not enthusiastic about the goals.

Occasionally, the goals selected by the counselor are worthwhile but her manner of presenting them may be confusing to the group. Working with an underachiever group, the counselor would have to use language that could be understood by the group members. If the group leader uses more sophisticated language, then the group may reject the goals simply because they do not understand what the counselor is trying to say.

## *GROUP SIZE*

The size of the group will depend upon the topic the counselor wishes to discuss, the goals that she has established, the degree of involvement she expects from the group members, the physical space available, the frequency that she plans to meet, and the availability of the group member to attend the meetings.

A group counseling program for students can be geared to four different types of groups. The first group would be the entire school student body. This purposely would be utilized for an orientation or a superficial sensitivity of a subject. The second group would consist of all the members of a particular grade – for example, all the seventh grade classes. This would also be a superficial sensitivity to a general topic but would be much more personal and localized to the needs of the group members. The third group would be a single classroom. In this setting the counselor could direct the sessions to problems concerned with the particular classroom or present selected material she wants to cover to a group smaller than the combined classes but larger than a small group. She could also utilize the positive characteristics of the particular classroom (for example, an enriched or above-average group) and anticipate more involvement than he could expect in a school or entire grade orientation.

The last group (for which this book is written) is the small group. The small group will number anywhere from six to fifteen students, depending upon the factors mentioned above plus the number of students that the counselor feels she can handle. It is in a small group that there is the highest degree of involvement of group members. *A group of six to eight members provides the optimum degree of control by the counselor.* With six to eight students the counselor can generally perceive all the physical activity of the group members, maintain control of the group, and give all the students the individual attention that they may need. Interestingly enough, when the counselor works with groups of *ten* children, she usually finds the same degree of involvement of the student members, but the extra two students make a definite difference in the ability of the counselor to maintain his degree of involvement with the group members. For small group work, six to eight students as the ideal. Some experienced counselors concerned with particular general topics, such as career planning and vocational planning, may elect to work with a larger group, such as nine or ten students, or larger.

## *SELECTION OF GROUP MEMBERS*

WHEN A COUNSELOR FIRST STARTS DOING GROUP WORK, SHE SHOULD START WITH ABOVE-AVERAGE, OR AT LEAST AVERAGE, CHILDREN. Group interaction is more spontaneous with above-average children. The counselor does not have to handle the difficulty of the passive group. Above-average youngsters are more prone to interact with each other and the counselor. They have the creative ability to present original ideas in a spontaneous way. The selection of group members by the counselor who is a novice in group work should be geared to understanding group work and obtaining the experience of group interaction. The inexperienced group counselor will learn from an above-average group of children how a "good" group works. It is this model which the counselor will be working toward with other groups of children that do not fall within the above-average or upper average range. Once the initial above-average groups are started, it is often advantageous for a counselor within a few weeks to work with an underachiever or a low-average group of children. The contrast will be significant. The learning experience of working with two very different groups will underline and emphasize differences in group interaction, group cohesiveness, and group handling of various problems. When the medical student wants to learn how to handle abnormal physiological problems of the body, normal physiology of the body is studied first. Physical examinations are usually done initially with normal people, not the individual patient with some type of illness. When psychiatric residents first start their training, their first orientation is to normal behavior of the individual. Once the resident has a basic understanding of what this is, she then turns to a more careful study of normal and abnormal variations of behavior. When the school counselor first starts group work, she too must turn to the optimum group in order to find out what the normal variations of group activity are. It is for this reason that I advocate starting with an average or above-average group of children without any particular behavior or learning problems. Investigate and find out what normal group activity is and what it is like before initiating your "problem" groups.

Random selection of students is not generally advocated. If the counselor wants to work with an entire grade of classes, or with a particular classroom, this is all right if the goals are oriented to this type of presentation or work. On a small group basis, random selection, especially for the counselor who is doing group work for the first time, is not desirable. Random selection in general is not preferred because it often indicates a less-than-desirable amount of preparation and organization for that particular group. Once the group goals have been established, then the selection of students should be narrowed to those youngsters who both need and will be able to accept the responsibilities for group work in achieving those goals.

If a particular classroom problem is referred to a counselor and the counsel has (of necessity) to work with selected members of that particular classroom, then this is not random selection; this is a careful selection of students oriented to achieving a particular goal, both for the classroom and for those students.

When the author first started organizing groups in the school setting, he allowed counselors to randomly select students for their groups out of the school population. One of the first groups that was organized was a group of ten children, all girls. The girls were randomly selected by the counselors from four different units in a large junior high school. Of the group of ten children, five were overtly psychotic and two were borderline psychotic. This was not the type of group that should be handled in a regular junior high school setting. It was a highly specialized group that a particularly well-trained counselor or psychiatrist would have difficulty handling. This was a result of random selection without careful preparations or screening of the students to be involved.

It is the type of difficulty that the counselor may encounter if the group members are selected at random. Prior to admission, the members of the group should be screened closely, either from the counselor's knowledge of the students or with personal interviews. The counselor should note whether the youngster would benefit from group work, if the student wants to participate, if there is some contra-indication for the student becoming a member of the group, and if group work would be better than a one-to-one individual counseling.

Homogeneous grouping is recommended for the early groups. Whenever possible, children should be no more than two years apart in age, be from the same grade, and be similar in their over-all academic abilities. It is unfair for the youngsters to be placed in a group in which they are strikingly different from the majority of group members. For example, if you are working with an above-average leadership group where all the members have either above-average IQ's or above-average reading levels, and you select an under-achiever for that particular group, it may be very intimidating for that student to be a member of the group. Chances are that her performance would increase, but at a rather traumatic price. If the counselor is working with a group of adolescent pregnant girls, it would be unwise to put a non-pregnant female in this group because the counselor would be identifying that youngster with a pregnant group, which would be unfair to the child.

An outstanding physician friend once told me of an experience of his. He went to a scientific meeting and became involved in one of the sessions that was concerned primarily with physics. He stated that he felt virtually intimidated by his lack of knowledge in this meeting. The majority of members were physicists. The same is true of group members. It is more fair to the members if there is a more careful selection of participants. There are qualifications when selecting students according to age. It is not uncommon in the school setting to have a mature child at a particular age and a significantly less mature child at the same age. When children are selected, the counselor should carefully consider his choices.

Heterogeneous grouping is best when considering group skills. Some members are more vocal than others, some members are passive, and some members have leadership traits. This type of "personality" heterogeneity contributes to group stability and interaction. But there should be a homogeneity whenever possible of age, grade, and, within some reasonable scope, intellectual ability and interest.

All the members of one's group can be made up of one sex, or there can be a mixed group. In general, there is more spontaneity in mixed groups (that is, four boys and four girls, or five boys and five girls) than an all-male or all-female group. However, there is no particular reason, aside from the spontaneity that one gets, to selectively exclude or include members of the opposite sex. In general, when there is a mixed group of boys and girls from the third to the tenth grades, it is more comfortable for the group members if there is a rather equal distribution of the sexes, but there is no hard and fast rule. When talking about general topics and general subject matters, it is usually an advantage to have a mixed group. Selective groups according to sex will usually be more advantageous. In elementary school there is sometimes increased hesitation on the part of the children to sit next to members of the opposite sex. How the group handles this mixture of sexes depends upon how the counselor handles it. If the counselor becomes particularly concerned about the sex differences, then the children will become unduly concerned; if the counselor "takes it in stride," then the kids generally will "settle down." It has not been infrequent to have a counselor work with a group of boys from the same classroom because of a "classroom behavior problem," have the boys do fine in the group, and then have them return to the class only to "act up." It was only after the counselor had worked with the boys in a mixed group (boys and girls) simulating the classroom that the boys then "settled down" in the classroom itself.

The counselor should not work with a group of overtly psychotic children in the school setting. The group approach may be too "anxiety producing" for a psychotic youngster. A one-to-one classical approach is preferred until the individual has improved to the point that she can tolerate an increase in the anxiety level of her environment (that is, being able to handle the environmentally-produced (external) stimuli). In a group setting, when the youngster has improved she can be added to a more stable group of youngsters. The counselor can put an "improved" psychotic youngster into a "stable" group but should not attempt a group exclusively psychotic or so-called borderline psychotic children.

Hyperactive children (in the elementary grades) generally do not do well in a group setting. These are the youngsters who do fine on a one-to-one basis but when placed in a group or classroom setting become hyperactive. I would recommend a one-to-one approach. Both psychotic and hyperactive youngsters should be referred to a physician for diagnostic evaluation.

Occasionally the group is selected by someone other than the counselor. For example, the administrator may select a group of youngsters that she may want her counselor to work with for a particular reason, or the teacher may request the counselor to work with a group from within her class. In these particular cases the counselor has no control over selection and therefore can anticipate almost anything in the composition of the group that she has been asked to work with. With this type of group, the counselor has to coordinate her goals with the goals of the administrator or teacher as well as the goals of the youngsters involved. It usually takes patience and skill to coordinate the goals of everyone concerned. The most important factor in establishing goals for a group selected by somebody else is to maintain good communication between all parties concerned: that is, between the administrator and counselor, counselor and teacher, counselor and students. Without good communication, the counselor will have no opportunity to alter the goals or to alter the group composition as she feels may be necessary as the group progresses. When there is good communication, there is a sharing of experience so that there can be more meaningful selections of future groups that are selected by someone other than the counselor. When there is difficulty in achieving success in a group selected by someone else, it is not usually because the goals as indicated are not worthwhile, but because of poor communication between the staff members. When the communication is poor, it is not uncommon for someone, (either the counselor, administrator, or teacher,) to feel that someone else should be doing the job. If a group that is selected by someone else is to be successful, there has to be open and frank communication among all the involved staff.

## *THE NEIGHBORHOOD EFFECT*

There is one difficulty that the inexperienced counselor or group leader may encounter: the cohesiveness of a sub-unit of a group that has been established prior to the organization of the group for counseling. This is referred to in the text as the "neighborhood effect." This effect may reflect the established cohesiveness of a group or gang within a classroom, unit, or neighborhood. This is particularly striking when working with a number of children from the same family. This is essentially a cohesive or group effect that has already been established by the association of the selected members, within either the family, neighborhood, classroom, or unit of the school. Their unity and identity is not to the counseling group that has been recently formed, but rather to the group in which they have been active prior to the formation of the counseling group. The identity to the neighborhood or the gang, at least initially, is stronger than the identity to the newly formed group. This will often make the group leader's job more difficult because the members of the group have formed ties that will tend to dilute the leadership effect that the counselor would normally anticipate. The neighborhood effect can be offset if the counselor recognizes and is willing to initially accept it. With experience that counselor will learn to utilize the neighborhood effect rather than "fight it." If the counselor tries to weaken the loyalty/identity bonds already established, she will not achieve the group unity she wants for effective interaction and may weaken the cohesiveness of the group. If the counselor is starting a group for the first time, she probably should, when practical, select children from different neighborhoods, classrooms, or different parts of the school to offset the neighborhood effect.

There are many times when the cohesiveness of the neighborhood may work to the advantage of the counselor. For example, when the counselor wants to work with selected members of a particular classroom, she would want to utilize this pre-group cohesive effect in working with them. She could not for practical reasons try to disrupt it, for the youngsters have to carry the cohesive effect back into the classroom and utilize it whether the counselor wants them to or not. The priority obligation of the youngster is to be able to adapt to his usual environment. The counselor attempts to create a positive identity within the group so that this can be transferred to the setting in which the children usually participate.

## PHYSICAL SETTING

The physical setting for the group session should be in a location that is comfortable for both the group members and the group leader. The setting should be as conducive as possible to spontaneous group interaction. Small rooms with close quarters tend to reflect a constricted atmosphere. Preferably the session should be held in an area that can be exclusively used by the members of the group. This will allow for spontaneity and enhance the cohesiveness of the group. When the group session has to be held in an area or room that has to be shared by others, this will tend to distract the group members. Distraction from the environment tends to decrease the cohesiveness of the group, especially with those youngsters who are more hyperactive and have a short attention span.

The group session should be held in an area that does not dilute the leadership of the counselor. If there are other adult members of the school staff in the area, this sometimes acts as an inhibiting factor on the group session, because of the dilution effect of leadership. The counselor (and/or the other adults present) should note this by saying something to the effect that "Mrs. Jones, your counselor, will be in charge of this session." This will emphasize the group leadership of the counselor.

Whenever possible the group should be seated either around a table or in a circular fashion. This reinforces the feeling of group unity. The optimal physical setting will encourage a feeling of unity but will not be so small that the youngsters are almost sitting on top of one another. All the group members should be able to see each other. When the physical area is too small, it is better to decrease the size of the group rather than to have a larger number of students that are unmanageable. Extreme closeness in a group setting will invite physical acting out, which could develop into a control problem for the group leader. Physical closeness will also tend to increase the anxiety, especially in a mixed group and particularly in the pre-adolescent and adolescent age groups. Extreme closeness should be avoided in almost any group but particularly in those youngsters who have a tendency to be more restless, have a shorter attention span, and be more resistant to group situations.

Extremes in distance between group members should also be avoided. Just as sitting too close may invite trouble and physical acting out, sitting too far apart may be a way that an insecure leader may distance himself from the group. The students may perceive it as indicating that the leader does not want to become particularly involved in group interaction.

The group leader can utilize the physical setting to help organize the group. For example, when the group first enters the area that is going to be used, the group leader can indicate immediately to the group what her initial role is going to be. The leader may structure the group so that she tells each one where to sit, as she might do an acting-out or behavior-type group, indicating that this is going to be a "no-nonsense" group with firm limit setting. With most groups, however, the leader would usually say, "You may sit where you want," indicating to the group members that they are going to have freedom of choice and opportunity and that their actions are going to be their responsibility.

The setting can be changed from time to time. In the schools this is often necessary, especially when there is a shortage of classrooms and all available space, including parts of the hallway, may be utilized for classes. The groups, once organized and on-going, will usually adapt to those changes with little difficulty, especially if the counselor is comfortable in making the change. When the counselor is dissatisfied, then the kids may have difficulty. If the comfort of any single member has to be considered, it has to be the group leader, because the kids will adapt to the feeling of comfort or discomfort of the leader.

When the group meets in a different place, then the change should be briefly discussed with the group at the beginning of the meeting. Otherwise, the group members will be uncomfortable while they attempt to adapt to the new setting, but may not recognize why.

Youngsters do have a tendency to sit in the same place at each session, and where they sit and how they select their seating arrangements is often of some significance. There may be youngsters who repeatedly try to sit next to the leader, others who do not. Sometimes the entire group will try to sit next to the leader's chair; at other times entire groups may elect to sit apart from the leader. Where group members sit may be reflective of their dependency, their interests, their previous sub-grouping, or simply the random selection of seats. Occasionally a youngster will have been sitting in the same place and another youngster may decide at the next session that she wants to sit at that place. This may be used as a confrontation or test of the leader by the group. At this time the leader has to decide whether she thinks that each individual can have territorial rights within the group area or whether she wants to develop an overall group cohesiveness, saying in effect that it's a first-come first-served basis: "We're here to work together as a unit; it doesn't make any difference where any individual member of the group sits." Depending on the group, the leader may also elect to reinforce the concept of territorial rights for the individual and simultaneously develop group cohesiveness.

The physical setting is important, but group interaction and leadership are more significant in influencing the group. When the group is involved, the physical setting becomes secondary. It is not unusual to hear supervision tapes of group sessions in which there is a great deal of background noise that the group members have not even recognized because of their involvement in the session itself. However, careful selection of a physical setting will help in influencing the group activity.

## *LENGTH OF TIME FOR SESSIONS*

The length of time for each counseling session will depend upon what the goals of the sessions are, the number of sessions that are to be held, and the routine school obligations of both the students and the counselor. In general, sessions are about one classroom period long. The length of time may be shorter if a group meets prior to the first period or after the last class. The average classroom time has been between 40 and 50 minutes. The children seem to tolerate this well. The session time is usually decreased to between 20 and 30 minutes for the younger elementary students, especially when they are a more hyperactive group. In general, a 40- to 50-minute session has been the average time recommended for the school setting. For the older senior high school students, a 60-minute session is not inappropriate. The length of time, however, is not the key factor. It is what is done during the given time that is important. One seventh-grade above-average or leadership group met for only 25 minutes once a week and accomplished its goals within this short period of time. The kids will usually adapt to any period of time as long as the youngsters are well selected, the goals are well outlined, and the counselor knows why she is having the group. The counselor should not attempt to cover extensive or complicated material in a short (i.e., 20 minute) period of time. She would want to allot a longer period for complicated material. When the counselor does set up goals that are unreasonable to cover or accomplish in a short period, she may leave her group frustrated and discontent. Variable periods of time with the same group should be discouraged because the group members may never adapt to the time given and may be hesitant about bringing up material that they did not know whether they had time to cover. The most important factor with the length of time in a group counseling session is that the group members know when the group is to start and what time the group session is to end.

## FREQUENCY OF MEETINGS

The number of sessions that the group will have will depend upon the particular goals that the counselor establishes. It is important for any counselor who is doing group work to have the experience of having worked with different groups that had different meeting schedules: for example, a one-session group, a six-session group, a four-session group, a one-school-semester group, and a one-school-year group. Each of these various groups will present different problems and will be a different experience. The goals and what can be accomplished with different groups will usually vary. By working with groups with different time schedules, the counselor will attain a broad general experience of group activity and will enhance her group skills.

One important consideration in establishing the frequency of meetings is to share the scheduling of the meetings with the group members. It is of particular importance that at the first group session the leader relates how long the sessions are going to continue and how frequently they are going to meet. This adds stability and organization to the group, which in turn enhances the feeling of security among the group members. When a group counselor neglects to tell the students when their meetings are going to be held and how many sessions they are going to have, she inadvertently increases the workload. The youngsters will continually come to the counselor's office to ask her when the next group counseling session is going to be. In addition, the youngsters may be hesitant to become involved in some issues during the sessions because they do not know exactly when the next meeting is going to be and whether the issue can be resolved within the loose schedule that has been established. The organization of the group counseling sessions is the responsibility of the group leader. When she neglects this responsibility and fails to do certain things, such as scheduling of group counseling sessions, it may indicate the disinterest of the counselor, which is transmitted to the students. The scheduling of the group sessions and the adherence to that schedule (whenever possible) is a stabilizing factor within the group.

It is important to schedule the sessions in coordination with the over-all school program. There is occasionally a teacher who really does not know what the group counseling sessions are all about and who penalizes the students for not attending class (when there is a conflict in time between the group counseling session and the regularly-scheduled class). This, of course, is unfair to the students, and the responsibility has to be partially assumed by the counselor. There is no reason why there should not be good coordination between the teachers and the counselor so that there will be an understanding about the goals of the particular group counseling session. In general, the regular classroom schedule has to have priority, with only an occasional exception. It is the responsibility of the counselor to keep the teachers informed of their students who will participate in the group counseling sessions. It is important to inquire of the teachers whether there has been any change in the youngsters' academic and social performances in the classroom. Coordination between the counselor and the teacher increases the feeling of stability and security that the youngster has regarding the sessions themselves.

## SUGGESTED READINGS

Birnbaum, Martin and Andrew Cicchetti. (2000). The power of purposeful session endings in each group encounter. Social Work With Groups. 23(3), 37-53.

Cheng, W. David; Chase, Mark; Gunn, Robert W. (Dec 1998). Splitting and Projective Identification in Multicultural Group Counseling. Journal for Specialists in Group Work. v23 n4 p372-87.

Conyne, Robert K. (1999). Failures in Group Work: How We Can Learn From Our Mistakes. Sage: Thousand Oaks, CA.

Couch, R. D. (1995). Four steps for conducting a pregroup screening interview. Journal For Specialists in Group Work. 20(1), 18-25.

Doel, M., and Swadon, C. (1999). The Essential Groupworker: Teaching and Learning Creative Groupwork. Jessica Kingsley: London.

Gazda, George Michael et. al. (2000). Group Counseling and Group Psychotherapy: Counseling and Application. Allyn and Bacon.

Gladding, Samuel T. (1999). Groupwork: A Counseling Specialty. Merrill: Upper Saddle River, N.J.

Henderson, Donna; Poppen, William A. (Nov 1995). Student Perceptions of "Group Work: Leading in the Here and Now." Journal for Specialists in Group Work v20 n4 p207-14.

Hines, Peggy L. and Teesue Fields. (Dec. 2002). Pregroup screening issues for school counselors. Journal for Specialists in Group Work. 24(7), 358-76.

Johnson, David W. and Frank P. Johnson. (2003). Joining Together: Group Theory and Group Skills. Allyn and Bacon: Boston.

Kivlighan, Dennis M., Jr.; Goldfine, Debra C. (Apr 1991). Endorsement of Therapeutic Factors as a Function of Stage of Group Development and Participant Interpersonal Attitudes. Journal of Counseling Psychology. V38 n2 p150-58.

Price, John R. (1999). A Guide to Starting Psychotherapy Groups. Academic Press: San Diego.

Ripley, Vivian, and Gary E. Goodnough. (Oct. 2001). Planning and Implementing Group Counseling in a High School. Professional School Counseling. 5(1), 62-5.

Roberts, Sylvia M. and Eunice Z. Pruitt. (2003). Schools as Professional Learning Communities : Collaborative Activities and Strategies for Professional Development. Corwin Press: Thousand Oaks, CA.

Sonstegard, M.A. and J.R. Bitter. (1998b). Counseling children in groups. The Journal of Individual Psychology. 54(2), 251-267.

# CHAPTER III

## *THE ROLE OF THE GROUP LEADER*

The most important member of any group is its leader. In the case of group counseling sessions, the counselor or teacher is the leader of the group. It is around the leader that the activity, interaction, and spontaneity of the group will revolve. The counselor has the basic responsibility for what the group does, how it reacts, and what it accomplishes. How the group responds will be determined by the way the counselor organizes and structures the group. One of the misconceptions about group counseling has evolved from analytic techniques of group therapy in which the group members are encouraged to accept the responsibility of the group. But what is often overlooked is that in group therapy, the therapist structures it so that he still retains the responsibility of the group and at the same time establishes as part of the "working" goals that the members share this responsibility with him. This is true of group counseling also but not to the same degree. A counselor has to and must retain the basic responsibility of the group. He should share this responsibility with the youngsters when it is to the advantage of the group and when the group is ready to accept that responsibility. As the group continues to meet, this responsibility is passed on increasingly to the members. Their participation and action are a reflection of the fact that the counselor is willing to share the responsibility of leadership with them. Although the responsibility for the group interaction and spontaneity may be given to the group members, the single most important member is still the counselor.

In the school setting, this transfer of responsibility is never total. This is not unrealistic because in most adult-child relationships the children involved do not want to accept responsibilities which are not theirs. Adults should not relinquish responsibilities which children are sometimes neither ready to accept nor should accept. Spontaneity in group interaction is greatest when the kids feel that the counselor is in charge.

## THE ORGANIZATION OF GROUP LEADERSHIP

For practical reasons, a single counselor should routinely run a group. The counselor's job is too demanding to share with another counselor the same number of students during a session. However, there are exceptions to this. When a school or a department of guidance within a school is starting group work for the first time, it is sometimes helpful to work in teams. For example, one counselor could be leader of the group, a second counselor a co-leader, and a third counselor an observer. The observer would write down what is said, the physical interaction in the group, the characteristics of the group, the attitude of the group, etc. In the beginning stages of group work, which can be called the training period, it can be a significant learning experience for counselors to work together. With the team approach, counselors can share each other's experiences, give pointers to one another, criticize each other's techniques, and share information about their observations. Another time when working as a team is helpful is when the group is particularly large (i.e., a classroom, or an entire grade of classes, or a school). Team work is particularly helpful when starting to work with a specialty type of group which is difficult to handle, such as a "disruptive type." In a group that needs (and asks for) a great deal of direction, both the counselor and students often feel more comfortable with a team approach, especially when the counselor is starting groups for the first time. When a team is formed with a leader and co-leader, it is helpful (if available) to have both a male and a female counselor participate. When the children involved are having family problems that they "bring" to school and that interfere with the learning process, it is helpful to have male and female co-leaders. However, teams of all-male or all-female counselors can also be quite effective.

## COUNSELOR'S PERSONALITY

There are some counselors who seem to have a natural "art" of leading kids. They seem to be able to communicate spontaneously, with little inhibition, gain the confidence of the students they work with, and project the feeling of acceptance in the child. There are other adults who seem to be inhibiting. They do not project a feeling of acceptance within the group members. In reviewing the personalities of various counselors, educators often reach a hasty and false conclusion in believing that there are some counselors who, because of their personalities, tend to do a better job than other counselors.

The key factor in doing group work is not the personality of the counselor. The major factor in group work is the technical know-how of the leader. This can be a conscious awareness by the leader, or a "natural flair." The leader should know how groups will react and how he will react as a leader. He should be willing to handle the difficulties that may arise in the group as well as to share the confidences that the children may want to share with him. After working with many counselors with literally hundreds of various types of groups, the author has concluded that the personality of the counselor is not as important as the counselor's technical know-how.

Another important consideration is sincerity. If the counselor is sincere, respects the group, knows enough about the group, and feels comfortable in handling the group, the youngsters will adapt to whatever personality the counselor has. The author has seen rigid, conservative, "proper" types do extremely well with group work because they have the technical know-how of running a group as well as a sincere interest in the kids. Other "spontaneous" types did not do as well because they did not understand what was going on and/or did not have a sincere interest in the students with whom they were working. There have been inexperienced counselors, just starting group work but who were sincerely interested in the kids, who worked out technical difficulties with little trouble because their sincerity prevailed over everything else. The technical know-how of group work is something that any counselor can learn. Sincerity in one's job, genuine interest, and respect for the kids are things that cannot be learned from a textbook. These are things which the counselors themselves have to decide and "handle."

The major factor that the counselor has going for him is that most children want to please the adult, especially the adult counselor. Few children, with the exception of some children with emotional problems, may not want to please the adult, but these are by and large very rare or unusual children. Even those youngsters who are notoriously the "behavior problems" in the school setting usually are so because they are seeking some type of communication and help from the leadership of the school. They may not know any other way to ask for help. Every counselor should start with the premise that the child involved wants to be able to relate to him. If the counselor does start with this basic premise, half of his job will be significantly more easy.

There are difficulties in shifting from a one-to-one (classical counselor-to-student relationship) to a one-to-group or counselor-to-group relationship. In the one-to-one role the counselor often has to assume a dominant "tell-you-what-to-do" role. He is used to giving advice and does so freely in order to conserve time as well as to deliver the message that has to be delivered. This is a startling exception in group work. The group leader has to learn how to listen and how to be patient in order to stimulate group discussion. (This should be done also in the one-to-one relationship, but lack of time often decreases the counselor's opportunity for an optimum approach.)

## THE LEADER'S INFLUENCE

The counselor, in his role as teacher, adviser, counselor, parent-substitute, theologian, and social worker, has immeasurable influence on the lives of the children that he counsels. But even without these added responsibilities, the leader of any group has significant influence in that group. If the counselor is to be effective, he must not underestimate this influence. The counselor has a responsibility to utilize it to the student's advantage.

The counselor must review his own values and learn to

recognize his own bias, for his bias will influence his actions and the response of the youngsters. The organization, functioning, efficiency, interaction, achievement of goals, and rapport between group members are more significantly influenced by the leader than any other single person. This, of course, means that the group leader has a responsibility to periodically review his own actions to see what influence he is having. If things are going poorly, a good leader would first review his own position to see what he has contributed or not contributed in influencing the poor performance. At the same time, if a group is doing particularly well, the leader should review his position to see what techniques, attitudes, or understanding he has had in order to influence the group's performance. A leader with less experience often reflect first on the group members' performance and how it is affecting the group rather than reflecting on his own performance. This is a cardinal mistake and will increase the frustration of both the leader and the group members. Introspection of one's self is perhaps the most important thing that a group leader can do. It is from this point that he starts investigating the group as a unit.

There are times when the group performs poorly due to circumstances that have nothing to do with the leader. If selected group members are not performing well or are influencing the group in an untoward or negative way, it is the obligation of the leader to correct the difficulties. The group member may be antagonistic or have a negative personality that irritates the other members. He may not want to cooperate with either the leader or his peers. The leader should reflect primarily on two things: What is wrong with the youngster? How can he help the youngster? The easiest situation that can occur is when the leader detects or diagnoses a particular difficulty within a youngster that he, the leader, cannot correct. For the sake of the group, this youngster may have to be excluded and given personal counseling or referred to a physician or someone who can treat the youngster medically.

One of the most difficult problems for the leader to handle is a situation that the leader has allowed to persist for a long time. This is more difficult because the leader has to ask himself why it is that he has allowed the situation to exist for so long. The answer, of course, can be many things. It can be that the leader has denied the existence of the problem (and this is not uncommon). All of us at one time or another, as leaders, (for one reason or another) have denied the existence of a problem. The reason for denial is complicated. It may involve decisions that the leader does not want to accept or decisions that the leader knows have to be made but does not feel that he wants to handle. When this is the situation the group's anxiety will increase significantly because the leader is not giving the direction necessary. Denying the existence of a problem may reflect on the concept of oneself. Many of us, as group leaders, deny that a problem can exist in a group that we are leading. "How can I, such an understanding leader, have a problem such as this within my group?" At one time or another all leaders are guilty of this; but the leader who repeatedly denies the possibility that a difficulty could exist within his group is a leader who will eventually have trouble of monumental proportions.

Another cause for persisting difficulties is that sometimes the leader is not aware that there is any difficulty or of the proportion of the difficulty. This is not infrequent with inexperienced counselors. Long-standing difficulties may be diagnosed only in retrospect after the trouble has reached significant proportions. The experienced counselor is wary of the iceberg when he sees the tip. The less experienced leader may pass it off as another piece of ice. However, the inexperienced counselor who has encountered difficulties may think that with every piece of floating ice there is an iceberg underneath. He may think that every minor incident represents a major problem. Insight may or may not be enhanced by experience.

The experienced leader has to be sensitive to react, but not over-react, to major and minor incidents. A good leader recognizes the potential for difficulties, is able to diagnose the severity of the trouble as it is when it occurs, does not overplay a problem but yet does not underestimate the potentiality for its mushrooming. He is aware of the influence that his direction in the group has in aborting a possible difficult situation, or his lack of direction may have in stimulating the growth of a problem which may be present. In summary, a good leader is aware of his influence on the activity of the group.

## *THE COUNSELOR AND GROUP DISCUSSION*

The counselor should not dominate group sessions except for a specific reason ( for example, decreasing the anxiety of the group). He must be willing to accept ideas that may be at odds with his own. The group should be allowed to handle part of the job that in the classical one-to-one relationship the counselor felt was his. If a problem is presented by a group member that may be contrary to the principles of the counselor, the counselor may have to be tolerant. He should encourage the group members to discuss the ideas presented; he should be hesitant to rush in to contradict, to present his side, to defend the school policy or the role of the parent or adult world. The counselor in a group setting must be patient.

An adult staff member should start with the basic assumption that most kids know right from wrong. When the youngsters do present material that is contrary to the generally acceptable standards of right or wrong, it may be for one of several reasons. The group and/or group member may want to test the leader to see if the group members can present material that is unusual or contrary to the general standard. It may be that a student may want more attention or is particularly concerned about the subject material being discussed. He may have a situation in the school (or outside the school) that is troublesome. In a good group, the other student members will accept the responsibility of the topic presented, discuss it thoroughly, and help their fellow student, with or without the support of the counselor. The leader should not deprive group members of the opportunity of handling a problem presented by one of their colleagues.

Experienced counselors know that most kids have a built-in radar or ESP system that can often indicate to them exactly what the counselor thinks about a particular subject, without the counselor ever having verbally expressed his opinion. This is usually quite noticeable in a group that has been meeting for more than two or three sessions. The counselor represents the adult world, which the students want him to represent. Within this frame of reference the kids know for the most part what the counselor thinks. It is for this reason that the counselor does not have to "rush" to defend topics that may be contrary to his basic feelings. The kids usually know how he feels. It may be necessary, however, to reinforce ideas that have been presented by the student members. The counselor can do this by either summarizing what has been said, or when a student makes a point that he feels should be reinforced, by commenting, "I agree," with no further discussion. The counselor may challenge a member of the group by simply saying to the entire group, "Well, what do the rest of you think about this?" indicating to the group that perhaps he does not agree with the material that has been presented.

The counselor should never allow any subject or material to be presented in the group that he feels is morally wrong without making sure that either a member of the group has contradicted what has been said or that the counselor challenges what has been said. When working with youngsters who advocate something that is wrong, either the counselor or a group member must challenge it some time before the end of the session. (The leader does not have to challenge material immediately.) If the subject is not challenged, then the youngster and the group may think that tacit approval has been given to what the student has said. Depending upon the severity of the topic, the counselor can use many different ways of disagreeing. He can flatly state, "I don't approve of this activity." He can also present questions to the group to investigate the topic more thoroughly so that group members understand exactly why he disapproves, for what reasons, and what the alternatives could be. For example, one group of children in the inner city lived in a neighborhood in which there was a high incidence of narcotic use. The leader immediately became involved by stating emphatically, "I feel that the use of drugs is bad business. It can be harmful to your health," etc. He did not hesitate to discuss this with them and direct the interchange. None of the group members were known drug users. If the counselor was working with a group of children who were drug users, then he would have to be more tolerant and allow the group to handle this problem; for if he rejected the use of drugs in a group of known drug users, he would, at least within the frame of reference of the children, be rejecting them also. The counselor would have to emphasize that he is accepting them but not their use of drugs. If in a college- or vocational-orientation program a counselor emphatically states that he thinks that "this group of children should go to college," when in fact there are group members who do not want to go to college, he would be creating a hiatus between himself and the non-college-oriented youngsters. The counselor may make it very difficult for them to build a meaningful relationship with him. When the counselor elects to be emphatic, he has to have some background of both the topic and youngsters involved.

The inexperienced leader may become anxious, angry, or impulsive when the student member presents a question that my be morally wrong or presents an idea that is basically different from that of the leader. The leader should not feel that he has to defend his position, nor should he impulsively try. It is not uncommon for the inexperienced leader to quickly give personal examples from his own experience of why he feels the way he does. The dynamic factor that the leader should note is that the issues that are being presented by the student member may have nothing to do with the position that the leader has taken. Disagreement may be used as a "ticket of admission" for the youngster and/or the group for more important subjects that may present later. The disagreement by the student may simply be a test of the leader to see whether he can handle the disagreement of the group members. The leader can share from his personal experiences, but the key is not to be impulsive. When the leader does share personal experiences, it should be done in an anecdotal way that will emphasize general points that he is trying to emphasize, or to illustrate general discussion topics. When the leader does share personal experiences, he should not feel that this has to be part and parcel of the group counseling session. It does not have to be. He should share experiences only when he wants to and feels comfortable doing so. The leader should also feel that this not an introduction to other family data that he has to relate. It is sometimes unwise to share too much with the student members. Discretion as to when to share and when not to share should be an objective professional decision.

Invariably, youngsters in spontaneous group sessions will start talking about adults and their world. The discussion will eventually center around their parents, how their parents react to each other, and how they react to them. It is not uncommon for the youngsters to place their parents in the role of villains. Sometimes the accounts of their parents' mistreatment or overindulgence seem unbelievable. Regardless of the tale, it is important for the counselor not to ally himself with the child against the parent. It is all right for the youngster to complain about his own parents and say what he wants about them, but it is not all right for another person, particularly another adult, to side with him and agree that his parents are less than satisfactory. When the counselor does this, he makes a breach between himself and the youngster which sometimes cannot be overcome. No matter what the youngster says about his parents, he still wants to communicate, love, and feel that if not now, at least some day he will be able to have a reciprocally positive relationship with them. When the counselor allies himself in an anti-move against the parent, it is often impossible for the child to build the positive relationship that he wants with his parents and at the same time relate effectively with the counselor.

There is perhaps a more significant reason why the counselor should not ally himself against the parent. Part of the story that may be related by the youngster may be fantasy, or at least the interpretation may be only a facsimile of the truth as it actually is. Counselors should be quick to accept material as given, but not quick to pass judgment on it. The youngster at a later date, or even in the same session, may produce material that is particularly favorable, sometimes surprisingly so, about the parent. The counselor must leave the youngster room in which to maneuver. He must allow for flexibility and significant changes in mood (especially with the adolescent) within a session, a semester, or any given period of time.

Another difficulty that may present in working with youngsters is that they may present habits or customs of the neighborhood that the parents are involved in that may be contrary to acceptable middle-class standards. For example, with one group of youngsters, the entire neighborhood drank excessively. Most of the youngsters in the group were drinking alcoholic beverages and smoking since the age of eight or nine. The counselor did not challenge this and accepted it for what it was. Instead, he pursued what the alternatives could be to smoking and drinking. To challenge these concepts and customs of the neighborhood would be to challenge the relatives, neighbors, and parents of the group members. This would have been both unwise and unsuccessful. However, to offer alternatives to the habits or customs was both acceptable and reasonable to the children and was interpreted by them as part of the learning process.

The second topic that comes up, more sooner than later, is the teachers who are involved with the group members. Depending upon the type of group that the counselor is working with, the topic of teachers can be either favorable or unfavorable. It has been my experience that the inexperienced counselor is very quick to come to the aid of or defend the teachers who are being criticized, especially in a more fragile school system or school with less than favorable administrative control. The fear of repercussion or causing waves in the faculty-counselor or faculty-administrative relationship is felt. It is important that the youngsters feel free to complain about their teachers because this is often a test of whether the counselor means what he says when he states, "You can talk about anything relating to this particular topic," etc. When youngsters start complaining about their teachers, they often complain most vehemently about those teachers whom they like best. Some of the "stricter" teachers whom the kids complain about are often the teachers they respect most. One way to decrease the counselor's anxiety about this issue is to recommend at the beginning of the first session (when the ground rules are established) that group members can talk about anybody at all, but qualify this rule by stating that they can use first names only when talking about other students, and can only talk about their teachers by subject matter. For example, instead of referring to "Mrs. Jones," the youngster would refer to "my math teacher." This gives the kids freedom of discussion and gives the counselor control over the situation.

## *THE COUNSELOR CAN MAKE MISTAKES*

Most leaders (and most group members) want to give a good performance. They would like to think that their colleagues and students feel that they are at least average, perhaps above average, show a high degree of competency, and are proficient in their tasks. No one likes to feel incompetent or think that his peers think that he is not qualified. For this reason many group leaders feel that they are not allowed to make mistakes. When the counselor elects to work with groups of children, he must realize that he still has the same fallible traits that he does when he works on a one-to-one basis. Working with a group does not make one infallible. Sooner or later, as every human being does, the counselor will make a mistake. No one is consistently a good leader. The counselor will either commit himself to a course of action which he should not have, express an opinion or a fact which turns out to be wrong, or make a poor "judgment" call. The importance is not that the mistake has been made, because anybody can make mistakes and most people do; the importance is how the group leader handles a mistake when it is made. "Honesty is the best policy." There is no substitute for being straightforward with the kids and simply saying, "I am sorry; I made a mistake," or "I am sorry, but I was wrong." Kids do not expect adults to be perfect, and when they find out that adults are not perfect it is reassuring to them (and part of the growing process). When the youngsters can share with somebody that they, too, have made a mistake, it is a significant experience.

Children should learn that people do make mistakes but yet can handle them in reasonable ways. When the counselor tries to "bluff" his way out of a mistake, he loses credibility with the kids. Even when the counselor does not make a mistake, he should feel free to be able to change his mind.

Mistakes by the group leader are easiest to tolerate when there is no crisis or pressure, and less easy to tolerate when there is increased pressure on the group. Mistakes will come in both crisis situations and non-crisis situations. The important thing is to recognize when a mistake is made so it can be corrected as well as possible. The difficulty for the leader occurs when, in order to preserve his own self-image or the image of the group, he denies that a mistake has been made. This tends to perpetuate the mistake and increases the discomfort of all the members including the leader. A mistake can be shared by the leader with the student members, but does not have to be. When it is shared it reemphasizes the human qualities of the leader and is an excellent learning experience for the members. They recognize that the adult whom they respect has made an error and can observe an appropriate way of correcting that error. It offers an opportunity to see that making a mistake is not an all-or-none proposition; mistakes can be corrected in an appropriate way. It is important for the group members to recognize mistakes when they are made and allow the fact that people do make mistakes. When too many mistakes are made by the leader, he should completely reevaluate his role and his techniques. If the leader thinks it is indicated, he should discuss them with a colleague who can critique his technical approaches, methods of handling the group, decisions, and perhaps his values and attitudes.

Children, especially adolescents, have a wonderful way of getting themselves behind the 8-ball. They say that they are going to do things or make declarations for which there is no possible solution. It is up to the adult to give them a helping hand and to get them out of the "hole" they usually get themselves into. This often means "eating crow," or going back on something said previously. It is unwise for the counselor to get himself in an immovable position. The counselor should allow himself the flexibility within his own frame of reference to either change his mind, retreat, or admit perhaps that he used poor judgment. The group will function better as a result of it. There is an exception. When the group is trying to test the leader, this is sometimes the time not to be flexible and not to retreat. There is no hard-fast rule, however, and even then the leader may be willing to change his mind.

## CONTROL OF THE GROUP BY THE LEADER

Humans are social animals. They want and need to interact with both their environment and their peers. As humans have evolved into more civilized creatures who need to participate in social process, they also have shown the need for guidance and direction. Even in the higher primate kingdoms (i.e., the monkeys) there is a highly organized social structure built upon direction and guidance from the leaders of the tribe. This permeates our primitive human cultures as well. It appears that highly-sophisticated communities need leadership as much as do the higher primates.

One of the interesting phenomena of doing group work is that there are a series of reproducible events in most groups that occur some time during the group session. The counselor can anticipate certain things that will happen in his group; he can anticipate other things that may happen if he does not take the proper organizational precautions in the planning of his group.

A group is basically defined as two or more individuals interacting or interrelating in some way for a common purpose or with a common interest. The group usually has some type of planned organization such as a classroom or group counseling session, or spontaneous organization such as a crowd gathering at a sports event. Both the planned and spontaneous groups follow essentially the same basic dynamics of group behavior. Each group member has his own individual role and tries to coordinate his role with that of the other members, so that the entire group will be working toward some specific goal.

The performance of the group is usually a reflection of the leadership. In the classroom this would be the teacher. In the group counseling session this would be the counselor. When the group is operating efficiently, there is generally good leadership, which means direction and communication, either directly or through channels, between the leader and all the group members including its most junior member. There is a feeling of well-being if the group is operating in the manner in which it should. When the group is not functioning properly (i.e., poor direction, feeling of insecurity, and/or poor communication between the leader and the group members) there is usually a reaction by the members. This reaction can happen in different ways. The group can become less efficient. The motivation of the group members may decrease considerably, or there may be open antagonism to the leadership. With little or no leadership, there may be anarchy, as we may see in selected classes when the teacher loses control of the classroom.

When groups react more belligerently than usual and are more active in their criticism of the leader, they do so (in terms of group dynamics) primarily for one of two reasons. They are either very uncomfortable with and feel that they do not have the leadership that will be able to cope with their acting out, or they react more vigorously than usual because they are demanding more direction from the leadership. When there is responsible leadership, the group is comfortable to openly discuss, disagree, and sometimes challenge the leader because they feel that he is so stable he will be able to tolerate and handle any group activity that presents. The teacher may present an opinion to stimulate discussion. The kids may disagree with him but disagree in an adult manner, retaining their spontaneity and originality. When the leadership is not effective and the group continues to act out, they will usually do so until the group leader or another leader shows direction, guidance, or firm control over the activities of the group. It is not uncommon to see this in a classroom in which the kids start acting up and continue to do so until an administrator walks in and brings the situation under control.

When the leader does not have the control he should have, there also can be a second effect. Instead of acting out, the kids may withdraw and become passive. They are obviously angry but do not verbalize their angry feelings because they think that the leadership of the group or classroom is weak. The group members basically feel that any criticism might destroy the semblance of the leadership that is present.

Destruction or weakening of leadership is contrary to one of the basic laws of the group. *A group will never destroy its leader unless the leader is so intolerable that survival of the group members is at stake.* Leadership is essential to the structure of a group, regardless of how bad the leadership may be. This basic premise, that the group never destroys its leader, is very important to the understanding of how to control the spontaneity. Sometimes in a school setting leadership breaks down because the teacher, counselor, or administrator involved does not have the confidence that he can handle the situation; it is obvious that with those administrators who do have confidence and can project it, the group will tend to "settle down" much sooner than with an administrator who does not. In general, a leader who is patient and still feels comfortable with the group with which he is working projects this comfortable feeling and will not have to put unusual demands on the group in order to correct an unfavorable situation. Sooner or later, student members of the group will start to support the leader. This has been observed repeatedly in group counseling sessions. For example, student members of the group may disagree with the leader or challenge his position in some way, usually by disagreeing with the material presented. When the leader is not anxious to defend his position but is patient and tolerant with the material that is presented (although it may be in disagreement with what he said), other student members will defend the position which the leader presented, usually within a short period of time.

When a leader starts a new group, he should usually be more directive in the initial sessions. This has a tendency to make the group members more comfortable and enhances an early cohesive effect. When the group members recognize that the leader has control of all the events in which the group is participating, then the leader, if he feels it is indicated, can elect to be less directive and share part of the responsibility of "running" the group with the members. One of the difficulties that many group leaders have is that they share, prematurely, the responsibility of the group with the group members. This usually works to the disadvantage of the group, especially when the members have not had an opportunity to identify their roles and develop the cohesiveness helpful for group stability. It is for this reason that during the early stages of group formation a more directive leader usually develops better organization and cohesiveness than does a more permissive leader.

It is possible, especially for a skilled leader, to share the responsibility of direction in the early stages of group formation with the members. This can be done more easily with a sophisticated group. For example, a group leader may present the goals of the group to the members and then ask, "Where do you want to start?" The initial group discussion will be about organizing the group itself. This increases the awareness of the members that responsibility for group activity is also theirs. This should not be done, however, with a group whose members have not had experience in group counseling or other group activity. If the members are less sophisticated in group organization, they will usually refuse to accept the responsibility, either because of lack of experience of because they feel uncomfortable, or both. If the group members are more sophisticated, they, too, can be irritated that the leader is not more directive in the initial stages, and may test the leader in different ways.

Occasionally students will request permission to write their ideas on a piece of paper prior to the group session. This occasionally is an indication that they are asking the leader to more effectively organize the group. They may be requesting more stability within the group and/or more awareness of the goals. However, it may also reflect a sincere interest and enthusiasm on the part of the youngsters and may be the students' way of relating to the counselor how stimulating the sessions have been.

## TESTING THE LEADERSHIP

People experienced in group work know that within the first few sessions, or with some groups within the first few minutes of a session, the counselor's role as leader will be tested in some way by the student members. This may be in the form of one student poking another student, or presenting material that may not be applicable or appropriate, or challenging the idea of the session itself. The test may be in the form of challenging his (the student's) role in being chosen for the group. The manner in which the leader is tested can come in many different ways. The counselor should be aware of this and anticipate it. He should try to handle it as casually as possible. If there is some minor pushing, the leader should immediately tell them to stop. It is important with youngsters not to let physical interaction continue because if the leader lets one type of physical acting out go by, it may increase in severity until the group counselor may have a wrestling match to handle. The kids will continue to "act out" until some type of direction or guidance is given them. Physical acting out is not tolerable nor should it be considered appropriate for a group session. However, verbal acting out should be in the realm of being more tolerable if the language used and the topic talked about are appropriate.

A group member may disagree with the leader to see whether

the counselor is comfortable enough to tolerate disagreement. The group wants to know and receive this reassurance. If the group leader can tolerate it and remain patient, the group will usually come to the "rescue" of the leader and defend the position they think he might hold. If the leader remains calm ("or cool"), the group members will recognize that they can be spontaneous and original because the leader has the group counseling session under control. If the counselor hastens to defend his position or will not tolerate or allow disagreement with his position, then he will have failed the test of the group. The group members will be less ready to be spontaneous in a constructive way and will think that the counselor is less secure than he should be to handle the spontaneity that may present. In general, it is not a good idea for the youngsters to defeat the leader unless the leader structures it that way. Kids usually are asking for direction, not control of the group. If they did get control, it would be a frightening experience for them. They would act up until adult supervision was reinstated.

The initial test of a new leader in a group is usually part of an adaptation procedure. The group members learn to adapt to each other and to the leader. They become sensitive to his mannerisms, process of communication, likes, dislikes, skill to perceive events that are happening in the environment, and administrative ability. Testing of the leader, especially in the initial stages of group formation, is part of the normal group process. The leader should accept this and not be resentful because the youngsters have not yet adapted to his style or are not sure that he can handle the group. In a group that elects its leader, the group also tests him, but part of the adaptation period is the election procedure itself. The candidate expresses his ideas. Those who are for and against the candidate express their ideas. The group then adds up the pros and cons and adapts to the candidate as he is. In a group counseling session (in the schools) the group members are usually selected by faculty. When the group organizes, the members have to go through the normal procedure of adaptation and in doing so test the leader and his ability.

When there is significant group resistance against the leader, or a difficult group problem arises, it is not uncommon for the leader to spontaneously revert to a one-to-one conversation with one of the group members. This is usually less desirable than handling the issue as a group problem. When the group leader keeps an issue a group concern, he usually enhances the cohesiveness of the group and solidifies his position of leadership. When the group leader reverts to a one-to-one conversation, he is often establishing a style that may lead to many one-to-one conversations within the group. These one-to-one conversations will continue until some type of group interaction is established either by design or by accident.

When group members get angry, at each other, at the leader, or about something that has nothing to do with the group activity, they express this anger in different ways. Hopefully, they will express their angry thoughts in the group. If the anger is a reflection of group activity or the leader's role, it is important that the group members know that they can get angry within the group and, if necessary, at the group leader rather than having to do something else. It is better for the group leader to tolerate angry feelings against him than to have the group members act out their feelings by running down the corridors, acting up in class, etc.

Even a good group with a good leader will periodically test the leader. As noted above, when group members get together they adapt to each other and to the group leader in a definite way. They get used to handling different events and topics in a routine way. But every ongoing group will occasionally have something which influences or alters its usual behavior pattern. When this happens, the group may test the leader in some minor way to make sure that he is aware of all the events that are happening. The group can then adapt or re-adapt to handle the given situation. It is important for the counselor to recognize that when one group member starts acting up, he may be reflecting the concern of the entire group and in effect may have been elected, via group process that we do not understand yet, to play the role of the "acter-outer" in that given situation. It helps when the leader is aware of extenuating circumstances.

When the group members are not comfortable with their leader, they may pick another group member as a scapegoat and divert their concern and anger at this member (or topic of discussion) rather than the inadequacy of the leader. It has been emphasized above that every group basically needs a leader and will not weaken the leadership except in the most dire circumstances. Paradoxically, a strong leader often gets the most abuse because the group thinks that he not only can tolerate the abuse but can control the events that will occur during a given session. This is frequently seen in organizations and schools in which people may be very angry about a neighborhood school but have never reacted overtly because they felt that the principal or administration was, in fact, weak. The interesting phenomenon that sometimes occurs is that when the institution gets a strong leader, it is not uncommon for him to inherit the abuse and angry feelings of his predecessors because the neighborhood group recognizes that he can handle their complaints. This is short-lived, because a good leader utilizes the complaints and circumstances of the complaints to develop a cohesive unit.

## STUDENT EXCLUSION FROM A GROUP

Generally, the most severe penalty that can be levied against a group member is exclusion from the group. There are exceptions. Sometimes a youngster will purposely act out in order to be sent to a counselor's office or to get out of a classroom or group that the student thinks he cannot manage. But the average student wants to remain as a member of the group to which he is supposed to belong.

In doing group work, the counselor should not hesitate to exclude a member of a group if the person is not capable of handling the group experience or has been misplaced. Prior to the beginning of the initial group session, especially in a group that is to be ongoing for a long period of time, the counselor can tell the members that if he thinks at any time during the semester that a particular member would benefit more from individual counseling, he will not hesitate to withdraw the member from the group in order to work with him in individual one-to-one counseling. Usually, this will be sufficient. The group will accept this. If a group member has to be excluded, the group has been prepared and will tolerate it much better.

If a member is excluded, some mention should be made of it. For example: "I felt that John would benefit more from individual counseling." This transmits the message that the counselor is in control of the group, is willing to take the proper action to preserve the integrity of the group, but is still willing to work with the individual and give him the help he thinks the student needs.

*It is very important for the counselor to recognize that no individual student or individual group can be placed above the overall working of the school. The counselor should not hesitate to stop a group completely or to exclude a member from a group if for some reason the individual or the group is disrupting the general school program.* In the many groups that were involved in large group counseling programs that he has supervised, the author has never had to stop a group because of its acting out. This can be attributed to the careful selection of group members. However, occasionally individual members had to be excluded from a group. These have been few in number. In each of these cases the student had psychiatric problems. The youngster was counseled on an individual basis and referred to a psychiatrist for more intensive evaluation. The consideration for exclusion of an individual member or stopping a group should be part of the routine of the average counselor. The counselor should not hesitate to utilize these measures if and when he feels it necessary.

## *QUESTIONS ASKED THE COUNSELOR*

Perhaps the most important consideration in answering questions is that when the counselor answers a question, he has a tendency to cut off further discussion about the subject. The counselor also deprives himself and the group members of the opportunity of learning what the thoughts of the different group members are about that particular topic. When a direct question is asked a counselor and the counselor answers it, there is little room for maneuverability by the students. It is difficult for a student to disagree with a counselor who answers a direct question, especially if the counselor provides factual material with the answer. It is unfair for the counselor to expect otherwise. There are some questions that have to be answered immediately and matter-of-factly to reduce the anxiety of the group; but in a good group, these are few.

When a direct question is asked a counselor, he has the option to ask the question of the group. This can be done in different ways. The counselor can ask the group what they think about it. He can comment and reinforce the value of the question by saying, "That's a good question. How do the rest of you feel about it?" or the can qualify his position by saying, "I'll be glad to answer that question, but before I do, how do the rest of you feel about it?" The counselor then has an obligation to return to the original question and both summarize the statements that have been made and offer his own opinion. When possible, he should utilize the comments of the group members.

When a student asks the group leader a question, he does not always want an answer. Sometimes his question is a means of expressing his own opinion. A simple "That's a good question" from the counselor is sufficient. The group can then continue with general discussion. Sometimes a question put to the counselor is in the form of a test. The youngster presents it as an either/or, yes-or-no question. The leader should not become defensive with this type of question. He can handle it by saying, "That's a difficult type of question. It takes more than a yes or no answer." The counselor can then "throw" the question back to the group. A counselor does not have to agree or disagree with every question asked. When the counselor is able to handle a difficult question with a fair degree of comfort and facility, he often enhances his leadership position.

Sometimes a youngster may ask a question to help relieve the anxiety of the group. Usually this is done spontaneously with no special design by the student. The youngster assumes a supporting role for both the group and the leader. It gives the counselor an opportunity to be directive by interpreting the question and expanding his comments, which helps to reduce the anxiety of the group. It also gives the counselor an opportunity to terminate the discussion by answering the question.

Occasionally a question will be asked the counselor as an avoidance technique by introducing a new subject. This is usually done because the material being discussed is too uncomfortable or unpleasant for the youngster. The counselor should not be quick to point out to the student that he is avoiding the subject. The counselor must weigh a decision as to whether the group should continue talking about the current topic, or link it to the question asked which would divert the discussion to a new topic. A counselor is not obligated to pursue a topic that is being discussed. There must be flexibility. If a topic that is producing discomfort is not adequately discussed, the same basic material is usually presented later but in a more tolerable and less anxiety-producing way. In reviewing tapes, it is not uncommon to find the same topic discussed throughout a particular group counseling session. For example, if the topic being discussed is responsibility, the youngsters may talk about several different topics which superficially appear to have nothing to do with responsibility; but as one dissects the tape, one finds that the discussion is usually relevant to the general topic. Group members reflect on a topic in ways that the topic is important to them; consequently, the discussion appears to be unrelated but the connecting link is the same.

In answering questions, it is important for the counselor not to "come down to the level of the kids." If the youngsters are angry or being discourteous, or talking about behavior that the counselor does not feel is appropriate, then the counselor should handle it as a professional and as an adult. It is not helpful for the youngsters if the counselor tries to "talk their language." The youngsters will tolerate and understand that the adult does not understand their generation or their jargon, but the youngster becomes uncomfortable if the adult tries to play the role "of a kid." The group leader should handle each question in a professional, sincere way; he should try to reinforce and develop the positive aspects of a question.

When youngsters are discussing a subject, it is not uncommon for them to ask each other questions, especially when they disagree with each other. Sometimes these questions can be very angry and intimidating. It is the responsibility of the counselor to act the part of a referee (when it is indicated) and not allow any particular youngster to intimidate another group member by the questions asked. The "spirit" of the group should be one of investigation rather than intimidation.

When the group is going well and all the members feel relatively comfortable, they will want to handle the responsibility of the questions that come up themselves. Sometimes the group member may not give the counselor an opportunity to comment because they are interacting so intensely with each other. The counselor then assumes more of a chairmanship role than a directive leader type role.

The basic rule is that the leader does not have to answer all questions asked of him. If he does answer prematurely, he may "cut off" helpful discussion pertaining to the topic.

## RELATIONSHIP BETWEEN THE COUNSELOR AND THE GROUP MEMBERS

In many cases when the counselor starts to do group work, he increases his work load because the student members want to become more personal in their relationships with him. They tend to bring more problems to his office. In some cases this may be advantageous, especially with the youngster who has a tendency to isolate himself and/or needs individual counseling. (Group work for an isolated child can be an excellent technique to teach the child socialization skills.) However, this increased awareness that the counselor exists can be a handicap for the busy counselor. The counselor should set limits, be friendly with the youngsters but tell them, when it is indicated, that they should present the question to the group. When the counselor is firm but kind in handling increased demands by the youngsters, they are usually quite realistic and accept it with no difficulty.

*A major problem presents when the counselor feels guilty that he is not able to spend more time with the youngster who wants to have a closer relationship.* When the counselor is able to set limits, the youngster usually accepts it. When the counselor is not, then both the counselor and student usually have considerable difficulty. When increased demands by the group members become a significant problem and cannot be resolved, counselors have often worked with students from each other's units or grade assignments. This is less satisfactory. Whenever possible, the counselor should work with the children who are a part of his usual assignment of grade, unit, or school. This is more realistic and practical. Students usually like a kind adult who is willing to listen and accept them. However, limits have to be set because these same youngsters, especially those from emotionally deprived families, will, if given the opportunity, overwhelm the counselor so that he is not able to perform adequately. A single individual cannot be placed above a school program. If the youngster is not satisfied with the limit setting, then re-evaluation of the youngster's status should be made. The youngster can be switched to a one-to-one relationship. If the problem on re-evaluation is more significant than originally thought, the youngster can be referred for further help. The average youngster, however, will settle down and do well when the counselor sets limits.

Students generally do not want to get "too close" to the counselor. They want a counselor who is talented, kind, and firm, but they do not want a fellow student. They want the counselor to be a counselor and the teacher to be a teacher. They do not want the teacher or counselor to be one of the gang. When a counselor tries to be one of the gang, he is putting the youngsters at a disadvantage. They both respect and feel more comfortable with the teacher and counselor who is the professional and acts the part of the professional. It is not an either-or proposition. The counselor can be friendly and kind and still be professional. In any organization, the most effective groups are ones in which there is a realistic hiatus between, in this case, the student body and the professional staff. This hiatus offers both the student and the counselor a natural boundary around which they both can work, to the advantage of the counselor and the development of the youngster.

## TRANSFERENCE

Every counselor, whether working on an individual or group basis, will experience some transference: that is, a "phenomenon of the projection of feelings, thoughts, and wishes onto the counselor, who has come to represent an object in the patient's past" experience[1]. Slavson[2] points out that transference can also be involved with the identification of other members of the group. There can be an identification with the concepts and values that are projected by the group as well as individuals themselves. It is usually best if the counselor does not make an interpretation of the transference, but he should be aware of the transference in order to understand some of the reactions by the various group members.

When there is a team of male and female counselors working together as co-leaders, they will often be projected into the transference role of parents. This is certainly not unnatural on the part of the students and should be accepted at face value by the counselors as part of the natural or usual phenomena that can occur with youngsters working with adults.

1. Robert J. Campbell, *Psychiatric Dictionary.* New York, Oxford University Press, 1981, 661.
2. S. R. Slavson, *Analytic Group Psychotherapy*, Columbia University Press, 1950, 88.

## *OPTIMUM PERFORMANCE BY THE LEADER*

Most people recognize that they cannot give a top performance all the time. This is important to note. Sometimes group members expect their leader to perform one hundred percent all of the time. When he does not, they are disappointed and have a tendency to get angry. This may also be true of a counselor who expects students to perpetually perform at an optimum level. This is unrealistic and unfair, both to the students and to the counselor. Nobody, neither the leader nor the group members, can operate at one-hundred-percent efficiency *ad infinitum*, nor do they have the desire. "People just aren't built that way." If the leader gives one of his poorer performances, the group will react. They might be angry and react in a way that neither they nor the leader is accustomed to. It is important for the leader to note that perhaps this may be due to his poor performance. When he does recognize it, the leader can attempt to rectify his leadership. He can acknowledge this to the group and make some adjustments in his own performance that will reduce both the leader's frustration and the frustration of the group members.

## TASK-ORIENTED LEADER VERSUS
## RELATIONSHIP-ORIENTED LEADER

There are different reasons for a leader not performing to his usual peak performance, or at least his average performance. These reasons vary from fatigue to boredom. Fiedler has stated that group leaders can be divided into two primary groups: that is, the task-oriented leader who is particularly concerned with getting the job done and the relationship-oriented leader who is concerned with the relationships between himself and the group members and between the group members themselves. It appears from research that has been done that the so-called task-oriented leader seems to do his best work in two situations: when things are going well, and when things are difficult. When things are going well, he is able to maintain the momentum of success because of the reinforcement that he receives from his successes. In a problem situation, the task-oriented leader becomes quite directive, feels very comfortable, involved in his work, and does quite well. However, the task-oriented leader does not do as well when things are going neither very well nor very badly and seem to be at a plateau or "in-between state." The relationship type of leader does better in this in-between state than does the task-oriented leader, but does less well when the group is performing very well or at times when problems are very difficult.

Little research has been done about the leader who can be both task-oriented and relationship-oriented at the appropriate times. The leader who can be task-oriented when there is a problem and relationship-oriented when there is not is an extraordinary person and the optimum type of leader. The reason the so-called task-oriented leader is effective is that he gives direction when direction is needed. This reduces the discomfort of the group members. They perform more efficiently and are able to solidify around him because of that direction. This is also true when things are going particularly well. A good leader will use the success of the group and the efficiency of the group as rewards and reinforces for their performances, "giving them credit when credit is due." He allows the group members to share in the success of the overall performance. A good leader recognizes that group success is not due to the performance of any single person but is the coordinated activity of several people. The success of a program should be shared by the several people involved. The leader should note, however, the relationships between people. This is fundamental in a counseling group.

When the group is neither performing very well nor very poorly, many things tend to happen. Efficiency is not usually at its maximum, but is sufficient to maintain relatively efficient momentum. People are not prone to handle particular problems and have a tendency to relate more to each other than to the tasks that have to be done. The leader cannot always afford the luxury of being either a task-oriented or relationship-oriented person. The counselor, because of his psychological training and job that necessitates an understanding of human behavior, has a tendency to become more relationship-oriented than task- or goal-oriented. The successful administrator is task oriented. This may be one of the reasons why school administrators and counselors often have a different approach to particular problems. It is important for each to recognize the other's orientation and to utilize their respective strengths. It is obvious that an effective leader cannot be all task oriented or all relationship oriented. He has to be oriented to both the relationship of the group members and the goals that have to be achieved.

With few exceptions, groups have a tendency to become more relationship oriented when they are not (or do not have to be) oriented to specific tasks. Army units are an excellent example of this. When there is a crisis or a difficult job to be done, group cohesiveness becomes optimum, everybody is working together oriented towards particular goals that have to be achieved, and socializing is decreased. The group is oriented primarily towards accomplishing the goals and not relating to each other. When the goals have been achieved or nearly achieved and the crisis is over, the members of the unit start to relate to each other about things other than the tasks involved. There is a tendency for efficiency to decrease and interrelating to increase. It is at this point that boredom may become a factor. Boredom can also become significant when things are going particularly well. People have a tendency to become bored with continued success. This is analogous to the youngster who has ice cream every day. He may become bored with the monotony of the ice cream itself. This may also happen during a group counseling session.

It is important for the leader to recognize the overall perspective, including the goals and momentum of the group. When topics are particularly interesting, the attention of the group members is focused on the question being discussed. Involvement is usually at a maximum. When less thought-provoking topics are being discussed, there is a tendency for the group members to start talking with each other. A good leader has to be aware of his own involvement, the group members' involvement, and the general goals and momentum of the group. It is around these factors that the leader must judge his own performance in relationship to the group's requirements so that he can influence, when necessary, the relationship or task orientation of the group.

## *WHEN IN DOUBT*

A good leader usually has some insight into what is happening within the group. He usually understands the interaction that is taking place. He knows what the group is trying to accomplish. The leader can reflect on the performance of the individual members by what they are saying and how they are acting. He can recognize when the group is working well and when the group is not working well. There are times, however, when the group leader does not know what is happening. He may have only an impression of what is going on. Events may be happening within the group without his direction. This is a not-uncommon experience which may make the group leader uncomfortable. If the overall performance of the group has been good, if the group leader has had a reasonable semblance of group response and is heading towards goals that have been outlined, then this experience of not knowing what is happening at a particular moment is usually not of serious consequence. Things will probably proceed fairly well. If a situation is occurring within the group in which the leader does not know what is happening, the consequences of which are particularly upsetting to all the group members, then the group leader has to be cautious in what he does. Too often group leaders will over-react before they know what is going on. This sometimes leads to more difficulty than was originally present. In general, when the leader has some doubt about what is going on, it is better that he do nothing. He may listen. He may ask questions. *The leader should not impulsively make interpretations or over-react.* If the leader is patient, sooner or later some of the group members will communicate (verbally or non-verbally) what is going on. The general trend of the group interaction and group proceedings will eventually indicate what the group, as a group, is troubled about. At that time, with more insight and more information, the leader can actively direct the proceedings in the manner he thinks is indicated.

The author has never met any counselor or psychiatrist who knows what the innermost thoughts of the individual and/or the group are. It is perfectly legitimate not to know what is going on. The key is to recognize whether you do know at a particular time and proceed accordingly. If after listening to a tape of the group session the leader still does not know what the difficulty is, then there are many other things he can do. The leader can share this doubt with the group members by saying, "As I listen to the group sessions, I am really not quite sure what is going on," or "What are we trying to accomplish?" or "Why are we discussing this? How did we get onto this subject?" Depending upon the type of group session and what the goals are, any or all of these questions are legitimate. The group leader can, if the session has been taped, review the taped session. He can also bring in his colleagues to share what is going on, to see if they might be able to help. If the counselor is patient the group members will usually work the problem through to some satisfactory conclusion by handling the material directly (or indirectly).

## THE DROPOUT COUNSELOR

Occasionally it is necessary for the group leader to withdraw and prematurely terminate the group, or transfer the leadership to another counselor. Sickness, change in schedules, increased work or other obligations with higher priority for the group leader and/or for the student members may influence the decision of a counselor to drop out and relinquish his role as the group leader. Whenever possible, this should be done in a planned, systematic way so that the student members do not feel that they are suddenly being dropped or rejected. Whenever possible, they should know why this is being done. If the counselor has to drop out for personal reasons, it may be inadvisable to share these reasons with the student members. A simple statement may be sufficient: "Because of other obligations that have come up, I am not going to be able to continue with the group;" "Due to unexpected family obligations, I am not going to be able to spend as much time with extra-curricular activities this semester as I had planned." When there is a good relationship between the group leader and the student members, this is usually not a problem. Whenever possible, the group should be informed at a prior meeting rather than at the last meeting. They should have an opportunity to discuss plans for continuing the group or terminating the group in some reasonable way. If a situation arises where the group has to be informed at the session, then it is the obligation of the group leader to inform the members at the beginning of the group session rather than a few minutes before terminating the session. The group members then have an opportunity to work through any separation anxiety and/or thoughts of displeasure that they may have because of the sudden termination of the group.

There are delinquent counselors also. These are counselors who form a "dropout population" with an absentee rate. They arrange a scheduled program with a group and for one reason or another, sometimes justified, sometimes not, have to cancel or frequently change the schedule. The youngsters continuously come to the office saying, "When are we going to have our next meeting?" or "Why didn't you show up at the last meeting?" This is one of the cardinal sins of group work: The group leader does not give the group direction it needs in one of its simplest phases, that is, scheduling of meetings. If a counselor finds that he cannot schedule his meetings with some consistency, or that he cannot show up at the scheduled times even though the schedule may be irregular or planned irregularly, then it is probably better for the counselor to terminate the sessions. If the counselor knows that he is a "delinquent type," then he should plan for this in his initial session. There can be a definite irregular structuring to the sessions if it has been planned from the beginning; that is, if at the first session the counselor tells the group members that the schedule for meetings will be irregular, the group members will adapt to the *planned* irregularity of the meetings. The counselor may also schedule routine meetings with the notation at the first meeting that his schedule is very busy and there will be times when he may have to cancel. The youngsters will understand and the counselor will not be looked upon as a delinquent or rejecting leader. The students have been prepared and, within the structuring of a difficult schedule, will anticipate that the leader will show up when he can. Youngsters generally can handle anything if they have been prepared for the possibility.

There are other reasons for the dropout counselor which should be noted. Occasionally the counselor (and/or the group members) becomes bored with the group and the topics that the group is discussing. If this is so, it should be noted, shared with the group, and the group terminated or changed in a reasonable way. Occasionally the counselor is frustrated because of his inability to project ideas or to relate in a satisfactory way with the group members. He may reject the group in an angry way by becoming delinquent himself, just as a frustrated, angry student may do by becoming a high-school dropout or absentee problem. It is important for the group leader to review his own role and attitudes when he does become less effective in attending to his leadership duties. When the counselor becomes frustrated, perhaps angry, at the group members, thinks that he cannot do anything about it, has sought counsel from his colleagues, and for one reason or another does not think that he can "follow through," then it is best for him to terminate the group. He should do so in a reasonable way, leaving the door to his office open so that the group members can come in for individual counseling or help whenever they feel it is indicated. There are group situations which the group leader may not be able to resolve. There is no contra-indication to terminating the group in an organized way when the leader thinks that it is indicated.

## TRANSFER OF LEADERSHIP

When leadership has to be transferred from one person to another, it should be done (when possible) in a definite or organized way. This is particularly important when the current group leader is going to remain as a member or as a participant in the activities of the group. For example, when a counselor goes into a classroom to work with the students, the leadership of the class is retained by the teacher; but for that particular period the counselor is in the leadership role. Leadership of the classroom is temporarily transferred to the counselor. If the counselor is to be effective, the classroom teacher should tell the youngsters specifically: "Mrs. Brown, the counselor, is going to work with you during this period. She will be in charge of the class. I will be out the room." Or if the teacher prefers, "I will be in the room, but Mrs. Brown will be conducting the class." The children will have no hesitation about who is to direct the events. There will be no division of leadership; the scepter of leadership has been clearly passed from the classroom teacher to the counselor for that given period. At the end of the period the counselor should then pass the scepter back to the classroom teacher: i.e., "I enjoyed working with you today. Your teacher will be back in a few minutes. Perhaps I can meet with you again soon," etc. The idea is that the scepter is then clearly passed back. This does not have to be stated. If the counselor is going to be leaving the room, this is clearly indicated. With an adult group, it is taken for granted.

The major complication may come when somebody is invited to participate as chairman of the group while the leader of that group is present. Depending upon the type of discussion and the age of the youngsters, the leadership should be clearly defined. It can be done in a very casual way by saying, "We have invited Mr. John to come in and talk to us. He will run the group for today." The main consideration is that there should be a clear definition of where the leadership is, and where the direction is to come from. This is especially important with problem-type groups or when the group is concerned with a particular crisis or problem area. It will decrease the discomfort of the group members. They will respond quicker and more favorably when the roles of leadership are clearly delineated. Any change of leadership, either momentary or permanent, brings about some discomfort. The group members need time to adjust to the cues, attitudes, techniques, and mannerisms of people with whom they have not been working. How long it takes to adapt depends upon the style and content of the program and the leader. A new leader should not anticipate too much too soon from the group. The more familiar the student members are with the leader (and the leader with the student members), the quicker the consolidation and group effect. The main consideration is to have a clear delineation of where the leadership is and in what manner the leadership is to be shared, transferred, or retained.

## HOW TO REPROVE A GROUP

There occurs from time to time occasions when the leader is not satisfied with the performance of the group. Either the group's members have not acted as the group leader thinks they should or they have not accepted the responsibility of group activity. There are many variations of this, but suffice it to note that occasionally the group leader may feel it is indicated to discipline the group. The most common reason is that the group is asking for more direction from the leader, but this is not always the case. Sometimes even a good group will "feel its oats" and act up more than it should.

When the leader thinks that it is indicated that he comment to the group about inappropriate behavior, there are certain considerations that should be made by the group leader. It is better to comment to the group about their negative behavior in the privacy of the group session, that is, without any "outsiders" present. The group leader should not take the opportunity for correcting the group as a reinforcement of his own position outside the group setting; that is, he should not take the opportunity to reprimand the group as a sounding board to further himself with people outside the group membership. This is not fair to the student members.

It is a poor idea to use discipline of one group as an example to many different groups, although it is often done. If the leader feels that many groups need correcting, then he should address all of the groups together as a unit or address them individually, as he sees fit. When a group leader does reprove a group, he should do it in a manner in which the group members feel free to agree or disagree within the confines of the individual group session. There may be extenuating circumstances; there may be different thoughts about ideas discussed. The group leader may have inaccurate information. When a group is doing something wrong, the best teaching or learning experience for the group members is one in which the facts can be presented by the group leader and the group members can react with each other and the leader. When the incidents can be discussed within the group, the leader avoids a "you do it my way" approach. The group members can learn by reviewing the situation and, when possible, find alternatives and gain insight into the situation.

The hard-line approach – that is, immediate scolding the group as soon as they sit down – is generally not the best approach. If the group leader initially introduces subject material which is concerned about their better performances of the past (or present) and then reflects on their unsatisfactory behavior, the feedback is usually better. If the group leader reacts very angrily to a group, the group may immediately react angrily to the group leader. There is an angry-to-angry interaction which takes time to resolve, for the leader and the group members have to resolve the anger that has been precipitated by the introductory comments of the group leader before they can resolve the situation which the group leader is angry about. If the group leader introduces his comments with favorable anecdotes about the group, or at least in a less-than-harsh-manner, the group members have something upon which to build. They will be more apt to discuss the issue in a less-than-angry way.

There are occasional situations that call for an angry retort on the part of the leader, but by and large these are very selective. It may occur in a crisis situation in which the average student group would not be participating. It may be a situation in which there is a clear-cut right or wrong: for example, a student picnic during which the youngsters are hanging over cliffs or doing things that may be dangerous to them and/or to their fellow students. In this case, the leader may be justified in becoming angry. Usually this is not necessary in a well-run group. A cautionary note (i.e., "this is not indicated" or "please don't do this") is sufficient. There are group leaders who have an angry way of presenting issues, but usually the youngsters adapt to the counselor's personality. As they get to know the counselor, they usually adapt to his style whether they enjoy his style or not. The author does not advocate people trying to change their personalities, but at least recognize what they can accomplish by it and what they cannot, and alter things accordingly.

In summary, when a leader has to discipline a group, it should be done within the privacy of the group itself, should be preceded by some type of reinforcement (when indicated), and should not be done in an angry way. This allows for free discussion and interaction which lends itself to a better learning experience for the group members. It also gives the leader an opportunity to gain more insight into group activities.

## THE LEADER'S SILENCE

The individual group members and the group as a unit can be more silent at certain times than at other times. This can also occur with the group leader. When the group leader is silent, however, it is more significant. He is the most influential member of the group. The leader influences and directs the action and interaction of the group more than any other single member. His verbal participation reflects his moods, but also influences the activities of the group. Silence itself is not the sole influencing factor. A leader can be verbally silent but very active, animated, and directive in the group discussion. His involvement may be complete and his enthusiasm may be projected without saying anything.

The group leader should recognize that when he is silent, this may be reflective of as many things within himself as it is when the group members are quiet. The leader may be quiet because he is reflecting on what the group says, because he does not understand what is going on in the group, or because he is reflecting on personal matters. The leader may be silent because he is angry with the group, does not know how to express himself, and withdraws from the group. When the leader is angry and his silence reflects this anger, it will increase the anxiety of the group. When the group is working through a problem subject and the leader is silent, it may make the members extremely uncomfortable. It may be necessary for the leader to be verbally active and directive. Silence should not be allowed to persist if it is increasing feelings of discomfort of all the members including the leader. When the group members are uncomfortable, they will be looking for more direction from the leader. The technique of silence is used by some leaders as an expression of anger; it is not usually a satisfactory technique. Occasionally, silence can be used when the leader wants to make a point, but in general it is not desirable. If the leader disagrees with what is said or becomes angry about the group's performance, it is better for the leader to discuss it at a level that is reasonable than it is to internalize the feelings and not express them.

There are situations during a group session in which the leader's silence can be most effective. If the group members are interacting with each other, the leader's silence may be effective in reinforcing the interaction. The leader should not impulsively comment or become involved in a discussion that the youngsters seem to be handling well. When the group members can actively participate in the group interaction and the group leader has become essentially a moderator, or less active verbal participant, then it is usually an indication that the group is comfortable with the leadership and is willing to accept the responsibility of group activity at the group-member level.

The group leader's silence, when used effectively, can strengthen the group members' activity. For example, two group members may be arguing or disagreeing about a particular subject and reach an impasse, when one group member may refer to the group leader by saying, "Well, how do you resolve a situation like this?" The group leader may answer the question directly, or he may respond by saying, "I think you are working toward resolving this problem. You are on the right track and doing a good job." His silence and then brief comment reinforce the fact that the group members are capable of handling the discussion. They do not need more direction; the leader is not going to accept responsibility on this particular question. He is giving the responsibility back to the student members. The leader's silence in a situation like this can be an extremely useful technique. It is used to project the leader's confidence in the group members.

A group can react in many different ways to a leader's silence, but the most important consideration for the leader is why the leader himself is silent. Is it by choice, to reinforce the responsibility of the group members? Or is it because of anger, frustration, the material discussed, or not knowing what his role should be? When the leader recognizes why he is silent, he will be able to direct the group more effectively. In summary, the leader must be aware that his feelings, cues, and responses do influence the group.

## THE LEADER CAN ENJOY THE GROUP

Counselors and other group leaders usually orient themselves to the problems and/or to the technical aspects of working with groups (making them as efficient as possible). This is reasonable and usually increases the efficiency of the group. However, within the realm of work, the counselor should not over-look that the experience can be enjoyed. He is allowed to laugh. The counselor is allowed to converse with other group members and enjoy that conversation. He is allowed to look upon the experience as fun. It is unfortunate for both the group leader and the group members when the leader orients himself solely to the work or problem aspects of group counseling. Group counseling is part of counselor's responsibilities. But when the counselor can allow himself the comfort of being relaxed and enjoying the session, the positive feedback for the individual leader and for the members is usually enhanced. When the leader is relaxed, this will (from a technical point of view) also relax the group. It is unfortunate when the professional thinks that laughing and being able to say "I enjoyed that" indicates that one is not being as professional as one should. Sometimes enjoying one's self is being more professional than not.

## THE COUNSELOR'S ROLE

The roles of the counselor can be many, but in general these can be divided into two basic roles. One is an objective role – that is, the role of a professional. The second is a more subjective role, or the role of a parent. The differentiation of these two roles is important. It often determines the performance of the student in his relationship to the counselor. When the counselor assumes a more professional objective role, the youngster has a chance to bring to him problems that he may not otherwise do. A professional hiatus enables the youngster to discuss with another adult (i.e., a parent, relative, or close friend). This does not mean that the objective professional is not friendly or sincere; it simply means that he tries not to become emotionally involved in the youngster's problem so that he can help the youngster in whatever way he thinks indicated. When the counselor assumes a more subjective or parental role, it may handicap both himself and the youngster. He is less apt to make decisions which need to be made and to give guidance when it should be given. For example, a group or group member may become angry with the counselor. When the counselor acts as a professional, he will objectively try to decide why the youngster is angry at him, what appears to be the precipitating factors involved, and what has to be done. The counselor attempts to be patient and objective. He does not react angrily towards the youngster. When the counselor is less objective and assumes a parental or subjective role, he may respond impulsively or in anger, just as a parent might do. This is fine for a parent. It is a so-called "gut" reaction that a parent might have. But in a professional capacity, it is not the best technique for the counselor. When the counselor becomes angry, it should be (although it cannot always be) as objective as possible.

There are situations in which it is helpful for the counselor to become angry. There are neighborhoods in which youngsters are used to having adults get very angry at them before they will respond. When the adult talks to them in a less-than-angry voice, the youngsters consider it evidence that they do not have to pay heed to what is being said. When the adults in the neighborhood become very angry, then the youngsters know they "mean business." When a teacher or counselor starts working with a group of youngsters from a similar neighborhood, it is often necessary to start the group in a way that will stimulate the youngsters to respond, i.e. to be more directive. The counselor should then program the group to a point that the members are able to relate with each other in a manner that may be more appropriate for the school setting.

When the counselor reacts as a parent, he deprives himself of an opportunity of being objective. He deprives the student (or the group) of an opportunity to see how a responsible adult reacts in a difficult situation, and of an opportunity of ventilating his thoughts. If the counselor reacts as a parent might react, then the youngster is getting the same experience and the same reaction as he might at home. This may deprive the student of an opportunity to learn how to handle a given situation in different way.

## THE FEMALE COUNSELOR AND MALE YOUNGSTERS

One of the critical problems in staffing the schools is that there are not enough male teachers. Many of the male students do not have a chance to associate and identify with adult males. Contact and identification with adult males is often confined primarily to physical education teachers. The youngsters need to continue to grow intellectually and emotionally; they need to test themselves against male adults who are not parents or relatives. Unfortunately, male teachers are not plentiful. This means that the burden of responsibility of the female educator is greatly increased. The need is often greater in the inner-city areas where the family structure may be predominantly a matriarchy, the father often being absent.

Although the need for male teachers is great, this does not mean that the female educator cannot help to compensate for this need and help the young male identify as a male. In group counseling sessions it is obvious that there is a great opportunity for female counselors to give the youngsters an opportunity to identify as young men. One way is to accept the ideas that the youngsters present and try to evaluate and to consider them in a reasonable and adult manner. These ideas may or may not be in conflict with the female counselors. The male youngster may be confronted with a female educator who does not allow him to disagree. This may reinforce the dominant role of the adult female rather than allow the youngster to challenge and disagree in a reasonable but masculine way.

The second thing that the female counselor can do is to

reinforce the responsibilities that the young men in the group accept. For example, if they are accepting the responsibility of the group, the female counselor can reinforce this by saying, "Well, you are certainly acting like responsible young men." This will allow the youngsters to identify in a responsible way and will reinforce their own male identification and growth.

Some of the problems that occur between female counselors and male youngsters are because of the dominant attitude that the female counselor may take. It would help the youngster and at the same time make the counselor's job easier if the female counselor would reinforce the young man's positive qualities in a way that would reward his masculine role.

## COMFORT OF THE INEXPERIENCED COUNSELOR

One of the things that the inexperienced counselor doing group work should know is that virtually all counselors doing group work for the first time have feelings of discomfort about working with groups. The counselor should anticipate it. This is especially true of counselors who have been trained in or have been doing individual counseling for a number of years.

The inexperienced counselor should anticipate that he will learn considerably from the group experience itself. Group counseling is not different than good teaching. A good group counselor is observant and will listen to the cues and recommendations of the students, and then evaluate these recommendations with professional scrutiny.

One very important consideration is that the only way to really learn how to do group counseling is to do group counseling. No matter how much you review a text on group dynamics or group counseling, there is no substitute for experience itself.

## WHEN THE LEADER THREATENS TO WITHDRAW

One of the interesting reproducible phenomena in groups is the reaction of the group when the leader threatens to withdraw or resign. Group members want to feel secure enough that they can get angry at the group leader when they want. They want to feel that they can bring pressure upon him and influence his action. But, as has been pointed out previously, the group members basically do not want to destroy their leader. They want to preserve him and the integrity of his position. When the group leader threatens to withdraw himself from the position of leadership (or the task outlined), the group members usually rally to his support. For example, the group members start to react negatively towards this task. If the leader responds by saying, "Well, perhaps we should drop this project, or perhaps I should withdraw from the leadership of the group," the initial reaction of the group members usually is to rally to the immediate support of the group leader. If the need for change is evident, they will establish procedures to bring about a change of leadership in a less precipitous way. This usually does not occur in group counseling sessions with students. The counselor does not absent himself because of pressure from the student members in most normal school settings, nor can he readily drop a given task that is part and parcel of the school curriculum.

Sometimes the task that the group has been assigned is more sophisticated or complicated than the group can handle, and their recommendations and comments may be very appropriate. If this is the case, then the leader's recommendation to withdraw or change the task is reasonable and would probably be supported by the group members.

## CO-LEADERSHIP OF A GROUP

The luxury of a co-leader in a group counseling session (in the schools) should be reserved primarily for training purposes. A great deal can be learned by using co-leaders. Co-leadership emphasizes attitudinal differences of the leaders and the ability of some youngsters to relate better to one leader than the other. Student members can learn from the interaction between the co-leaders as well as with their interaction with the group. For example, the two adults may disagree on a particular point and share their differences in a friendly, reasonable way. When there is co-leadership, it generally works better if one co-leader plays the more dominant role. Co-leadership in the school setting is excellent for training purposes. The school counselor often has a reservation, even during the training period, for having co-leadership of the group. The inexperienced counselor is often hesitant to expose his skills or lack of skills with another person. This hesitation is generally short-lived when the value of co-leaders in the training period is realized.

Co-leadership of a group makes it easier for the inexperienced counselor. When the inexperienced counselor does not know what to do, he has the support of a co-leader. When the counselor is less spontaneous or feels uncomfortable, he can talk to his co-leader during the group session. There are advantages for the student members also. If they have trouble relating, for example, to males, they may relate to the female co-leader, and vice versa. It is also excellent for handling particular types of behavior or problem groups in which more direction is necessary. However, co-leadership is a luxury which few schools can afford, except for selected instances (see Chapter III).

## *WHEN THE LEADER COMES LATE*

When the leader comes late to a group session, he should immediately note this with the group members so that they have an opportunity to react. The late leader should not immediately introduce new or important material because the initial reaction may be negative. The negative reaction may be a reflection of the leader's coming late rather than reflective of the material. When the counselor has many duties and may anticipate coming late frequently, he should share this with the group members so that they understand that he will be there "as soon as possible," but that other obligations may make this difficult. This will put the starting time in the proper perspective. What generally happens if the leader is a chronic late-comer is that the members also start coming late and a cycle is established that is difficult to break.

## SUGGESTED READINGS

Arachtingi, Barrie M. and James W. Lichtenberg. (April 1998). The relationship between clients perceptions of therapist-parent similarity with respect to Journal of Counseling Psychology. 45(2), p.143-50.

Carter, Emily F., Sharon L. Mitchell, and Mark D. Krautheim. (Mar. 2001). Understanding and addressing clients' resistance to group counseling. Journal For Specialists in Group Work. 26(1), 66-80.

Clark, Arthur J. (Mar 1995). Modification: A Leader Skill in Group Work. Journal for Specialists in Group Work. v20 n1 p14-17.

Conyne, Robert K.; And Others. (Mar 1990). Effective Group Leadership: Continuing the Search for Greater Clarity and Understanding. Journal for Specialists in Group Work. v15 n1 p30-30.

Corey, Gerald; And Others. (May 1990). Role of Group Leader's Values in Group Counseling. Journal for Specialists in Group Work. v15 n2 p68-74.

Couch, R. David. (Mar 1995). Four Steps for Conducting a Pregroup Screening Interview. Journal for Specialists in Group Work. v20 n1 p18-25.

Dies, Kathryn. (June 2000). Adolescent development and a model of group psychotherapy: effective leadership in the new millenium. Journal of Child and Adolescent Group Therapy. 10(2), 97-111.

Fiedler, Fred (1965) Engineer the Job to Fit the Engineer. Harvard Business Review 43:5, 115 (September – October, 1965).

Gitterman, Alex. (2002). Reflections on dealing with group members' testing of my authority: oy vey. Social Work With Groups. 25(1), 185-92.

Glass, J.Scott; Benshoff, James M. (Mar 1999). PARS: A Processing Model for Beginning Group Leaders. Journal for Specialists in Group Work. v24 n1 p15-26.

Haley-Banez, Lynn; Walden, Susan L. (Dec 1999). Diversity in Group Work: Using Optimal Theory to Understand Group Process and Dynamics. Journal for Specialists in Group Work. v24 n4 p405-22.

Kane, Thomas D., et.al. (Feb. 2002). An examination of the leader's regulation of groups. Small Group Research. 33(1), 65-121.

Kivlighan, Dennis M., Jr.; And Others. (Jan 1994). Projection in Group Counseling: The Relationship between Members' Interpersonal Problems and Their Perception of the Group Leader. Journal of Counseling Psychology. V41 n1 p99-104.

Kline, William B. (Nov 1990). Responding to "Problem" Members. Journal for Specialists in Group Work. v15 n4 p195-200.

Korda, Louis J.; Pancrazlo, James J. (May 1989). Limiting Negative Outcome in Group Practice. Journal for Specialists in Group Work. v14 n2 p112-20.

Kottler, Jeffrey. (2000). Learning Group Leadership: An Experiential Approach. Allyn and Bacon.

Kraus, Kurt L., Jesse B. DeEsch, Anne M. Geroski. (Mar. 2001). Stop avoiding challenging situations in group counseling. Journal for Specialists in Group Work. 26(1), 31-47.

Muller, Lynne E. (Sep. 2002). Group counseling for African-American males: when all you have are European-American counselors. Journal for Specialists in Group Work. 27(3), 299-313.

Polkin, Douglas L. (Mar 1991). Prescriptive Group Leadership. Journal for Specialists in Group Work. v16 n1 p8-15.

Posthuma, Barbara W. (1999). Small Groups in Counseling and Therapy: Process and Leadership. Allyn and Bacon: Needham Heights, MA.

Sklare, Gerald; And Others. (Nov 1996). Ethics and an Experiential "Here and Now" Group: A Blend That Works. Journal for Specialists in Group Work.

Soo, Edward S. (Dec. 1998). Is training and supervision of children and adolescents group therapy necessary? Journal of Child and Adolescent Group Therapy. 8(4), 181-196.

Trotzer, J.P. (1999). The Counselor and the Group: Integrating Theory, Training, and Practice. 3rd ed. Accelerated Development: Muncie.

# CHAPTER IV

## THE MECHANICS OF GROUP COUNSELING

This chapter will review many of the routine situations that the counselor will commonly encounter during his experience with group counseling.

## GROUP SPONTANEITY

One of the goals that the leader hopes to achieve in a group that is designed for group interaction is some type of constructive spontaneity. Group spontaneity can be defined as a high degree of involvement by the group members whereby everyone is attentive to the topic being discussed (whether they are verbalizing or not), and whereby everyone is enthusiastic and unconstrained enough to participate in some way. Hopefully, this high degree of involvement on the part of the members (who would be able to interact with each other) would enhance the spontaneity of original and creative thought on the part of the students. A constructive type of group spontaneity is desirable in most counseling sessions unless it is a didactic type of group (i.e., for orientation purposes).

The big question is, how does one develop group spontaneity? This varies according to the population of the group. The above-average leadership group has already developed many skills necessary for spontaneity and makes the group counselor's job easy. The counselor presents a topic; they accept the responsibility and start discussing it. An under-achiever or drop-out population, has the tendency to be much less spontaneous, and sometimes passive. The group counselor may feel that encouraging youngsters to interact is "like pulling teeth." In working with an under-achiever or less spontaneous population, the group counselor has to recognize that her job may be difficult and arduous. She should not expect under-achievers to be spontaneous. Usually they have neither been given the opportunity nor taught how to be spontaneous in the classroom. These youngsters respond in the group as they do in the classroom.

The counselor has to be patient. At the same time she has to build the foundation on which group spontaneity can be developed. The best way to work with a more passive group is to start with topics that they are familiar with, topics that they all have knowledge about. It does not make any difference whether the topic selected to initiate the discussion has anything to do with the ultimate topic that the counselor wants the group to discuss or whether it reflects the goals of the group. *The basic consideration should be teaching the youngsters how to interact with one another.* This is done by starting with topics that the students will feel both comfortable and familiar with. All youngsters, regardless of their backgrounds, can share ideas about family, neighborhood, playground, what they would like to be when they grow up, current standings of the home town sports teams, overall school program (i.e., the subjects they study, the teachers they have, how often they should go to school, etc.). As the group begins to interact the counselor then builds or introduces more sophisticated material, but does so only as the group learns how to interact and handle the material already presented. The counselor does, in a very real sense, "teach" the youngsters how to participate and how to be spontaneous. Hopefully, the overall performance of the youngster will then improve. This is, in fact, what has been observed with the under-achiever groups that have been initiated (Chapter X).

Starting with topics that the youngsters are familiar with is the first step in developing spontaneous interaction within the group. Group Counseling is very similar to good classroom teaching in that both should attempt to develop spontaneous interaction among the youngsters participating. The significant difference is that in group counseling the number of youngsters is usually less and the interaction can be more intense. The counselor should first prepare the group members with topics which they can easily talk about and feel comfortable discussing. After the students are ready to interact and know how to interact, the counselor can then introduce didactic or academic material to discuss. She will find the students' reception significantly better. There are a small number of youngsters who are withdrawn and do not participate because of significant emotional problems. They may need to be evaluated and referred for more intensive counseling and/or treatment.

When there is interaction the counselor should be willing to accept all appropriate material. She should utilize the material presented to keep the momentum going. For example, if a youngster comments, "My math teacher is a neat teacher" and does not go on, the counselor can ask, "Well, what makes your math teacher a neat teacher?" When the child relates more specifics about his teacher, the counselor can then generalize with the group and ask, "What do you feel makes a good teacher?" When the youngsters present a list of different things, the counselor should pick the appropriate topics and then ask leading questions so that the group can expand the discussion from that point. As the youngsters develop the ability to interact, they will probably start disagreeing with each other about material and ideas presented. At this point there is usually significant spontaneity and interaction within the group.

One thing to avoid is yes-and-no questions. A yes or no answer will cut off any feedback. When you ask a question like, "Do you like TV?" the youngster, especially the less spontaneous youngster, will answer "Yes" or "No" and drop the subject at that point. A question like, "What is there about baseball that you like?" or "What is there about soccer that you do not like?" will give the youngster more of an opportunity to express herself. However, a general question may not get much of a response at all, or only a shrug of the shoulders from a more passive youngster. The general question may be more difficult for a passive youngster, whereas a yes-or-no question gives her an opportunity to answer succinctly without a great deal of effort. The passive child has often never been taught how to handle questions and interact positively in a group situation. She feels awkward. A simple yes-or-no question may be indicated for her. A mere yes or no answer on the part of a passive youngster may be comparable to a verbal outpouring on the part of an extrovert.

Whenever possible, it is best to avoid the use of the word "Why?" in group discussions because it often puts the youngsters on the defensive. A question like "Why did you do that?" may give the impression that the youngster should feel guilty about something she has done. It may make her uncomfortable because of an idea that she has presented to the group. Most leaders use the word "Why?" in their discussion, but whenever possible they should try to avoid it. When it is used, the connotation of guilt should not be attached.

It is particularly important that the counselor establishes rapport with each youngster during the group discussion. The counselor should call upon each group member at least one time, preferably by his first name. If the counselor does not know the group members by name, then she should feel free to ask them what their names are and write them down on a piece of paper in sequential order according to the seating assignment. It is better for the counselor to make an overt admission of not knowing the youngster's name than trying to "bluff it" by just nodding to the youngster who raises her hand or not mentioning her name when she asks a question. If the counselor does not know a youngster's name, she should go out of his way to find out what it is and then address that youngster by her first name. The youngster will feel that she has been accepted, that the counselor wants to accept her both on an individual and group basis. The student will feel much more comfortable than she might otherwise. The counselor who is able to relate on a first-name basis when appropriate is able to establish quicker and closer rapport with the participants. If humans are social animals, then recognition is part of the socialization process. The author has never met a child who did not appreciate being recognized, either during a group session or afterward.

## SPONTANEITY ACCENTUATED BY ANGER

It is not uncommon, when working with a group of under-achievers, behavior problems, adolescent pregnant girls, or any group that feels inadequate or frustrated about a particular problem, to have them initiate group interaction (once they feel comfortable) by a negative expression of thought. It is important that the counselor anticipate this, whether the group gets angry or not. If she anticipates it, she will feel more comfortable in handling the group anger when and if it comes. The counselor should tolerate the angry thoughts and may establish ground rules during this time to keep the anxiety of the group to a tolerable level. Once the youngsters have had a chance to express themselves, the counselor can then start developing the constructive goals of the group. There are many people who have so much anger within them that if they do not release it they will never be able to constructively build for themselves or participate with others in a group project.

It is not absolutely necessary for participants in a group to have to express anger before they can start working constructively. Many groups whose members were under-achievers or had particular problems (i.e. behavior problems, learning problems, social problems, or physical deformities) were able to start developing in a constructive way without any overt expression of anger. Perhaps they expressed their anger in more acceptable indirect ways. Counselors often observe that group members may talk about angry topics instead of expressing overt anger itself. For example, the group members may be talking about murder, rape, fire, robbery, instead of getting angry at the leader or getting angry at each other. In other groups there is neither a direct nor indirect expression of angry feelings, but simply a sincere desire to work constructively on the goals that have been presented.

## THE ISOLATED MEMBER

One of the explicit obligations of the counselor is to make sure that every member feels that she is part of the group, whether she is a vocal participant or not. Selected group members may be passive or withdrawn individuals. They may have been selected for group participation because they were withdrawn.

One of the "traps" that the counselor may fall into is thinking that if a youngster is not a vocal candidate (that is, will not guarantee a high degree of involvement and participation in a group), she is not a candidate for group counseling. This is not so. The counselor can include a more passive youngster within an average group of children. Over a period of time the other group members may be very helpful in helping the withdrawn youngster to be more spontaneous and outgoing. But the counselor has to be patient. She cannot expect that the child will spontaneously become an extrovert. It will be difficult for that youngster; she will need support, first from the counselor and then from her colleagues within the group. As with other things, the counselor has to program that youngster's participation. At every group session the youngster must be recognized by the counselor in a vocal way. She should be asked at least one question. This is one of the exceptions when the leader can ask a yes-or-no question of a particular youngster. It may be difficult for the withdrawn youngster to expand on a question like, "What do you like about math?" for she may say nothing. The student may not know how to comfortably participate. It may be easier if the counselor asks the withdrawn youngster a specific question like "Do you like math?" She can more comfortably, or at least somewhat comfortably, answer "Yes" or "No". The counselor can then utilize the yes or no answer in the group discussion, giving the withdrawn youngster a feeling of contributing something and being part of the group. (See Chapter III.)

When the withdrawn youngster does participate in some way, especially when it is a spontaneous comment, this should be immediately recognized and reinforced by the group counselor. Occasionally a withdrawn youngster may blurt out something, or try to be facetious in some way. This may be the only comfortable way she has of participating. This attempt should not be rejected by the counselor. Whenever possible the counselor should try to find something positive within the action, or comment and reinforce the positive part of it, so that she can start "shaping" the youngster to participate in a constructive way.

When the counselor does ask the withdrawn youngster a question and she is unable to reply, it is usually helpful to ask the same question of the rest of the group and enlist their support. For example: "Let's help Johnny on that question. Jimmy, how do you feel about the question of ...?" In this way, the counselor recognizes the youngster. She does not leave the student stranded and uncomfortable; the counselor still accepts her. The youngster is not rejected for not participating. She is incorporated rather than isolated form the group by throwing her question out to the group. The counselor also enhances the group feeling that everyone is part of the group. No one is going to be isolated. When each member of the group has a particular problem, it is up to the rest of the group to help that member.

A member of the group who is withdrawn or passive in her participation is still a very active participant in that group. A verbally passive role does not mean that the child is not absorbing information that is being disseminated. It also does not indicate that the other group members do not recognize her presence. When a group member is absent, whether she is a vocal member of the group or not, the absence is usually noted in some way by the group members.

It is a mistake for the experienced group counselor to continue to work only with above-average groups. Although initially working with above-average youngsters has been advocated as one of the best ways to learn how to do group work, eventually the counselor will have to expand her selection of group members to include the isolated, or withdrawn, passive youngster.

## STUDENT MEMBERS WHO ARE ABSENT

The counselor should expect that periodically student members of the group will be absent. She should anticipate this in his planning. When there is going to be a particular session (for example, a guidance session, where didactic material is to be discussed), it is probably best for the counselor to share this with the student members. For example, "Next week the session is going to be about preparation for college." The student members can plan on being at that particular session. They will have time to rearrange school schedules, home commitments, etc.

It is very unusual for a student member who is absent not to inquire what went on at the group from one of her peers. This is the responsibility of the student and she generally accepts it.

It is particularly important for the counselor to recognize everyone who is absent, note the absence with the rest of the group, and comment on that person's absence when she returns the following session. This does many things. It emphasizes the counselor's interest in the individual members of the group, and it enhances the group feeling that everybody is working together as a unit. It also reflects the counselor's pleasure when all the group members can participate together.

Whenever there is an absence, the group either consciously or unconsciously senses that absence. They have learned to work together as a cohesive unit. When one part of that unit is missing, it creates a feeling of uneasiness in the remaining parts. By recognizing someone's absence, the counselor is able to eliminate some of the discomfort. The group can then proceed with its business and its orientation to its goals. When there is an absence, it is better to recognize it and talk about it briefly so that the members will not have to "work it through" at an indirect or non-verbalized level.

Whenever there is any change there is some degree of turbulence or anxiety. Change can be loosely interpreted as synonymous with the feeling of turbulence or anxiety. People get used to doing things in certain ways. When this equilibrium (or way of doing things) is upset, there is an uneasy turbulent or anxious feeling. When a group member, whether she is a vocal or non-vocal member, is absent, this upsets the equilibrium of the group. It is better to talk about the individual's absence than to allow this feeling to persist. For example, when a new substitute teacher comes into a class, she often finds considerable restlessness among her youngsters. If she talks about the absence of the regular teacher, she is more apt to settle the class within the first few minutes of the day. If the substitute teacher does not talk about the absence of the regular teacher, the class may remain restless for the entire day, or first few days that the regular teacher is absent. A similar situation exists when the regular teacher returns. If she talks about her absence and the substitute teacher for the first few minutes of the class, the class is much more apt to "settle down" and return to the normal routine. It is particularly helpful for the leader to recognize any absences that occur within a group.

The problem of *withdrawal* of group members is significantly less in the school setting than in the non-school setting. The curriculum and program leave little opportunity for either volunteering or withdrawing. There are reasons for absences and withdrawals within the school setting that should be noted. There usually is significant decrease in attendance before major holidays such as Thanksgiving, Christmas, and Easter. As enthusiastic as the youngsters may be about their group participation, it appears that the group counseling session itself and/or the group leader cannot compete with holidays. The youngsters get excited; they sometimes "play hooky" from school, or genuinely forget about the group session. They may leave for a vacation prematurely with their parents. Whatever the reason, the counselor should note that when handling groups, she should not plan to schedule group counseling sessions one to two days prior to a vacation except when the session is in the spirit of the holiday.

The author has the impression (although he has not tested it) that the withdrawal rate of students and student absences decrease as the group leaders have more experience. The inexperienced counselor should not take this personally. As she gains more experience with group work, becomes more relaxed, and learns practical tips on running groups, she will be able to retain a significantly larger percentage of students than she did during her earlier group experience. The counselor will have more general experience and consequently will be able to select her group members more judiciously, per the goals that she has outlined.

There are other reasons why youngsters have a tendency to not show up for group counseling sessions. Many of the reasons are reflective of the logistical problems of the school; others reflect emotional problems of the youngster. Occasionally a teacher will not allow or will discourage a youngster from participating because she feels the student should be in her class. Sometimes the youngster does not know why she has been selected to participate in the group counseling session. Other youngsters have never had group experience. They have been allowed to isolate themselves within the classroom and might have significant feelings of discomfort being placed in a small group setting where they will be group participants. It is not uncommon for youngsters who have not had an opportunity to participate in groups to be hesitant about joining group counseling sessions. They do not know how to handle themselves in groups and think that because they do not know how to handle themselves, they will be rejected by the other group members.

When a youngster becomes a dropout in the group, it is the responsibility of the counselor to call that youngster into her office. She should attempt to give the youngster the necessary support and the direction she is often asking for. If the counselor feels that participation is not indicated, then she should offer the student help on a one-on-one basis. Problems such as fear of being rejected by the group or fear of exposure are problems which could be discussed with the student on a one-on-one basis. The youngster, after the experience of individual counseling, could then be referred back to a group. She would probably be more ready to utilize the group experience and be a more productive group member.

## INCREASED GROUP ANXIETY

Group anxiety is that situation in which the group is infused with or overwhelmed by events in the environment (i.e., topics of discussion) that are, or the group members think are, too difficult to be handled or discussed. The group members may be extremely uncomfortable. When this happens, the group may become silent and reflective and/or extremely restless and talkative.

There are a number of topics, especially with secondary school students, that may make the group members anxious: i.e., death, sex, and suicide. Topics that often do produce anxiety should be handled by an indirect method unless the material is presented in an organized, educational way. When the subject matter is presented in a seminar or class, such as sex education, the lesson plan should be well prepared in advance. The counselor should be familiar with the material and feel comfortable in handling it. She should be prepared to be directive when it is necessary. When the material is presented in an organized fashion and the group leader is comfortable and knowledgeable, the group's anxiety will significantly decrease. The students will usually handle the subject as well as any other body of knowledge. They may become more interested because of the particular fascination of the topic. In a group in which anything can be discussed, the group may not have been organized to work with a topic such as sex, death, or suicide. When the information does come up, it often has some connotation which makes the group anxious. *When this occurs, the leader should become directive, handle the question immediately, and not leave the question to the responsibility of the group.* The question that was presented should not be ignored, because ignoring an anxiety-producing question or topic may leave the group more anxious and uncomfortable. It is at this time that the leader should become directive, influence the discussion in appropriate ways, and if necessary make a summation using the summary as an introduction to another topic that is less anxiety producing. The leader should not switch topics without concluding and being directive in her approach, nor should she suddenly change style. When the leader becomes impulsive, then it is usually a reflection of her anxiety. Adults in general can handle anxiety-producing topics better then youngsters. The student may not be capable or mature enough to handle a topic or may not have enough information about a topic to feel comfortable discussing it. It is therefore the responsibility of the leader to become directive and informative.

If the group is left anxious at the end of a session, without some satisfactory conclusion by the leader, then the children may "act up" in the school or home setting. When an anxiety-producing topic is presented towards the end of a session, the group leader has to become directive and conclude the discussion. However, this is one of the few times that the counselor should be allowed to spend an extra five or eight minutes in working through and settling down the group before it ends. After the group has "settled down" and is less anxious it is often helpful for the leader to give the group an "out." For example, she can say: "If you want to pursue this topic, or feel you have any other questions, we can discuss it, if you want, at the next session." The students will not have to handle the anxiety of the topic all week long because they know they will have an opportunity, if they want, to bring it up again. The question should be left to them, however, to present. Most kids during the interim will resolve their own anxiety. There may be one or two youngsters who for some reason want to pursue it. They should feel that they have this opportunity. Most of the youngsters who want to pursue potentially anxiety-producing material will not present the material again in an anxiety producing way. They will present the material indirectly and work through the same problem in an indirect, less anxious way. It is usually better for the leader not to convert the topic into a frank discussion, but rather continue to work through it indirectly, unless it is obvious that the anxiety of the group will not be lowered unless there is a frank discussion of the material.

One indication of anxiety may be silence or quiet reflection on the part of the group. Another manifestation of anxiety is that of laughing or giggling, usually to an extreme. This should not be confused, however, with the genuine laughing or giggling at a humorous anecdote. In general, when the group becomes anxious, it is the responsibility of the group leader to become directive and/ or conclude in a satisfactory manner the topic presented with the notation that if necessary it can be brought up at a later date.

## HOW TO HANDLE SILENT PERIODS

What plagues every group leader who is trying to manage a group efficiently and wishes to obtain the spontaneity and interaction desired is the problem of silence. Nothing bothers the group leader more than group silence, nor does anything increase the anxiety of a group more than prolonged unplanned silence. It is necessary for the leader to reflect on what the causes of silence are in order to effectively handle the group during these particular periods. The reasons of group silence are many.

(1) *Introductory Silence.* In many cases the youngsters may not know what is expected of them. This is especially significant during the early part of the group session. They do not know how to interact in the way the leader expects nor how to conduct themselves in the group meeting. This is initial or introductory silence. In order to offset this, the

leader should be specific in her instructions about how groups work and what is expected of the group members. She should indicate how material is to be presented and the type of interaction desired. The group members should have some idea of what the group goals are.

(2) *Lack of Understanding.* Although the students may understand the mechanics of group interaction and may participate spontaneously, topics may be presented by group members or the group leader which the student members do not understand. When vocal members are suddenly silent, it may indicate that they do not understand the material that has been presented, or are listening to absorb information as part of the learning process, and/or hesitate to speak because they do not want to reveal their own ignorance. When group members do not understand the material, it is the obligation of the group leader to "drop back" to a level of understanding that the greatest number of group members will comprehend. The counselor should then program the material from that point of mutual understanding.

(3) *Reflection.* Some group members, and occasionally the entire group, may be silent because they are reflecting on information being presented. They understand the information, are interested, and want to absorb and utilize the material. This type of silence is easily overcome. The group leader becomes more directive and asks particular members what their opinions on the subject are. If youngsters are thinking about the topic, they will usually be interested enough to participate and interact.

(4) *Anger.* It is not uncommon for a group or an individual, when angry, to be relatively withdrawn, rigid, and silent. When the group is angry, then the leader has to become directive as well as supportive of the group. She should give the group the leadership that the group members are requesting. When the leader becomes more directive, the group members may verbalize their angry feelings towards the leader. If the leader is able to tolerate and accept a

verbalization of these feelings about a particular matter, the group will generally settle down. It is not always necessary for the group leader to challenge the group about being angry. Generally when a counselor does accuse student members of being angry, they do not understand what she is talking about. The leader should present material on which the group members can disagree. If the group leader is aware of what the group is angry about, she should present the material in a way that they can take issue and discuss it reasonably. If given the opportunity, the group will work this out, either directly or indirectly.

(5) *Adaptation.* Many groups and individual youngsters are silent because this is the way they have been taught to act. They have learned at home, in the neighborhood, and/ or in the classroom to be passive, or to be "seen and not heard." The typical classroom is not one that encourages spontaneity and group interaction. In many of our larger cities, there are entire neighborhoods that reinforce a passive role for the youngster in the family. It may be difficult for youngsters to interact spontaneously in another group setting although the leader encourages verbal spontaneity and interaction. This is also true in the potential dropout and under-achiever population. These youngsters often consider themselves school failures. They think they are not able to produce in a constructive, worthwhile way. They therefore withdraw, become passive, and do not participate in the classroom or group session.

Regardless of the cause of silence, it is necessary for the group leader to attempt to recognize the difficulty. She should program in a step-wise fashion a lesson plan for teaching these youngsters how to be spontaneous. A leader cannot tell a group to be spontaneous. The leader teaches them how to be spontaneous. Initially, the group leader is very directive with the youngsters. She asks them questions that they understand and feel comfortable in answering. She reinforces their answers quickly in a positive way. The leader tries to build a good relationship with the group members. The group members usually start to interact initially with the group leader and then later with each other. It is necessary during the initial sessions to present familiar topics that they can handle and to encourage them to interact, with continual direction and support. As the group learns how to interact, the group leader decreases the frequency of the direct questions and encourages questions and comments to emanate from the group members themselves. However, direction should not be prematurely withdrawn.

   *(6) Testing the Leader.* From time to time, even in the best group, there may be topics presented that may be anxiety-producing for the group, that may anger the group, or that the youngsters feel they are not knowledgeable enough about. When this occurs, the group members may test the leadership to see if the counselor can handle further discussion on the particular topic. One way of testing group leadership is to make the leader particularly uncomfortable by being silent.

   It is not uncommon for youngsters who have been in an ongoing group and have established a positive relationship with the group leader to "tease" her by getting together before a group meeting and agreeing that nobody is going to say anything. When this is the case, or the group leader suspects that this might be the case, then the best thing for her to do is to take it in stride, handle the situation in a general way by talking to the group members about anything at all, and handle the frustration that she feels as group leader in responsible way. One thing the group leader should not do is to get angry. This would be both surprising and upsetting to the group members and would decrease their productivity.

   *(7) Intimidation by the Leader.* Occasionally there is an educator who intimidates the group by her style. The students may be literally afraid to respond. They think they cannot make mistakes; and when they do, they receive an unpleasant response from the educator. This can usually be detected by the group. This can be resolved by frank discussion with

the group leader of what effect she is having on the group members or students, or handling a "typical" problem in group supervision.

Occasionally there is an educator who does not intimidate the group but, by her demand for adherence to rules that she has established, inhibits spontaneity.

When the group leader intimidates the members, it is probably best for her not to suddenly change her style. If she does, the youngsters may over-react. Change in style should also be programmed. The leader should gradually change styles so the youngsters will learn to adapt to the new style in a non-traumatic way.

In general, the best way for the group leader to handle silence is to try to recognize the cause. It is not particularly wise for the leader to allow silence to continue. Prolonged silence may be upsetting and anxiety-producing for the group members and serves no useful purpose. In general, silence should never be allowed to last longer than a minute, and often this is too long. If the group has a co-leader, the leader and co-leader can talk to each other about the topic being discussed or anything they want. When the group leader is working alone, she can comment about the topic being discussed. She can discuss why she thinks youngsters do not participate in groups or can discuss silence in the classroom. The leader can ask what the youngster does or should do when she does not know an answer. The leader can encourage the youngsters to talk about the difficulty of participating in a group (or the classroom). She can ask the youngsters why it is sometimes easy to participate in a class and sometimes not. The students will usually answer, either directly or indirectly, depending upon the group session and how long it has been running. If the group has been together for a long time, the counselor can directly ask the youngsters why it is that "everybody is so quiet today."

When the counselor is having difficulty with many or all of her groups, she should review her techniques, the method she uses for selecting group members, and goals that she has established. If the group continues to be passive, she should also consider the use of any techniques or machines that she think may stimulate group interaction, i.e., slides, movies, paintings, and books. She can consider special projects such as the construction of models, or special programs including trips to specific place in the community that may have particular interest or may be an introduction to a particular topic. The counselor should use whatever means she has within the educational process and school organization to stimulate spontaneity and interaction. Frequently school programs are so routine that they actually bore the students. When this is the case, then a novelty approach is not only necessary but good educational practice.

Earlier in the book (Chapter IV) it is noted that whenever a group member is absent, the absence may stimulate uncomfortable feelings in the members that they may not recognize. They may be more reflective than usual. When this is the case, recognition of the absence usually relaxes the group.

In summary, silence means that the group leader should be more directive than usual.

## GROUP DROPOUTS

When you organize an ongoing group, you can anticipate that you may have some dropouts. Experienced counselors account for this possibility and plan their program accordingly. Some counselors use more students during the initial phase. This ensures a minimum number of members until after the dropout phase is past. This is usually not recommended. When the group leader anticipates that a number of the group will drop out and plans accordingly, this puts unnecessary pressure on both the group leader and the students. If the members of the group do not drop out, then the group counselor has to redesign the program. The group members may start to feel pressure because of the uneasiness and the anticipation of the group counselor. With a few exceptions (see Chapter II), the group should be organized and the number of the group members selected according to the group goals.

The reasons students drop out of a group prematurely are many and varied:

(1) Perhaps the most common reason for group dropouts is that youngsters become bored and lose interest. Students are anxious to join a group when it is first organized because it is something new, it is something novel. Unless this initial interest and novelty effect is perpetuated by the group activity and/or the originality of the counselor, the group may become bored.

Another reason for boredom is that the group goals may have been achieved. The group may be continued on the pretense of the original goals when in fact those goals have already been accomplished. When the goals have been achieved, the leader should either terminate the group or establish new goals.

(2) The counselor and/or the group members may be expecting too much of a particular group member. A group goal or project may be designed that in itself may be very exciting. However, if the group counselor has not selected the group members carefully, it may be that the project is too sophisticated (or too boring) for a particular group member. Although goals are important in organizing a group, selection of group members as related to the goals is also important. The leader must not expect too much of a youngster who is not capable of performing a particular task or too little from a youngster who is more capable than the task assigned. For example, the questions asked an above-average group may be more sophisticated and demand more knowledge of general concepts than do the questions asked of potential dropouts. Although a counselor may discuss the same topic with both groups, the questions and expectations that she has for each group may be significantly different. Both groups may be spontaneous and operate very well at their respective levels of capability.

(3) A group counselor may establish definite goals with the group and then ignore them to concentrate on goals that are completely different. The group members may think that

they have been misled, lose confidence in the counselor, and drop out.

(4) People reproduce their usual behavior patterns. When the counselor works with a problem population, she should anticipate that when she organizes the group she will be confronted with the same problems that these youngsters have displayed in the past. This is particularly true of potential dropouts or absentee students. These youngsters have a history of being absent from school. There is no reason for the counselor to anticipate that these youngsters will not also have an attendance problem in the group. If the counselor thinks otherwise, she is being unrealistic. When the counselor anticipates this problem and tries to find some subject or topic that will stimulate and retain the students' interest, she will decrease the dropout problem of his group.

(5) The youngster who is most apt to leave the group first is usually the student who is a potential leader. She is a youngster who has a very strong desire to be leader of almost any group in which she participates in. When the counselor retains the leadership of the group (which she should), this youngster may become frustrated, angry, or uncomfortable because she has not been able to direct the group in the way in which she would have liked. If the child does not leave the group, she will usually show signs of discontent. The counselor should be aware that this youngster has significant leadership potential. If she is going to succeed in helping this youngster to develop into an effective leader, then she has to give the child an opportunity to lead and also to follow.

The counselor may become uncomfortable with the youngster's challenge for leadership. An inexperienced counselor may encourage her to drop out of the group or may establish a situation in which the youngster will voluntarily have to drop out. This is unfortunate. Youngsters may go through many phases in the development of leadership ability. They have to learn how to participate in a group, how to be a leader, and how to follow another leader. The counselor, however, should retain the leadership. She may have to set limits on the potential or would-be student leader. But the counselor should also recognize what is happening and the difficulty that the youngster may be having. The counselor should reinforce the positive qualities and contributions of that youngster. If the counselor is able to reinforce the youngster's good performance and is willing to set limits on his negative behavior, the youngster will be less apt to drop out. What is more important, the student will have a valuable learning experience in group participation.

(6) Some youngsters will drop out of a group because they think this is the only reasonable way they have to send up danger signals that something is wrong. When the counselor calls them into an individual session they can then relate, in a group-free atmosphere and in the privacy of the counselor's office, particular things that may be bothering them. If a counselor does not follow up (on the student's dropping out of a group) the student may have to do something more drastic or upsetting to the school program in order to obtain the help that she needs.

If a youngster does become a group dropout, it is the responsibility of the counselor to seek out that youngster, call her to the office (or whatever is appropriate), and make a determined effort to find out why. This is important to the student. If the counselor does not talk to her, the student will feel guilty about being a group dropout because she did not go through the proper channels. It is the responsibility of the counselor to give the student an opportunity to make a "clean break." This is part of the teaching experience that the child should have and the counselor should offer. It will emphasize to the student that dropping out of a group is not that serious and will give her an opportunity to review the advantages and disadvantages. It will maintain a positive relationship with the counselor so that if a problem presents, she will not hesitate to walk into the counselor's office for help. It will indicate to the other members that the counselor is genuinely interested in all group members.

Too often in counseling we concentrate on what is of benefit to the students and give little heed to the techniques that may enhance the learning of the counselor. One technique that will augment the counselor's group experience is to "follow up" on the dropouts to find out why they did leave the group. When the counselor does "follow up," she obtains a better understanding of what effect her own personality and personal techniques have on the group, in what subject matter the youngster is interested (and not interested), and what difficulties the youngsters of that school have in relating to one another and handling new ideas and concepts. "Follow-up" is as important for the counselor's education and experience as it is for the student.

## THE MEMBER WHO REVEALS TOO MUCH

One of the goals a counselor has in doing group work is to organize and structure the group so that each student feels that she can relate material that is pertinent to the topics and goals of the group. It is hoped that the atmosphere of the group will be one that will stimulate the members to discuss material that is of importance to them. The discussion material may vary. When the counselor has achieved an atmosphere in which spontaneous and comfortable interaction can occur, the student members contribute freely and relate material that is appropriate. All the student members feel comfortable to participate. Spontaneity and effective interaction is usually indicative of a good group session.

The counselor, however, should be concerned about the group member who reveals too much of herself and her activities too soon. Counselors sometimes mistake a student member's spontaneous revelation about her own activities and thought as reflective of a good counseling session. This is often the case. However, with certain students, the fact that they are able to relate personal, sometimes upsetting information, both to the counselor and to the other student members, is indicative of youngsters who may be emotionally ill, or at least particularly troubled. Usually when this happens the other student members become quiet, passive, and reflective. Sometimes they tease each other in a nervous way. The group is uncomfortable.

The average youngster, especially the adolescent, does not reveal too much of herself too fast. When she does, the counselor should note that it may not be because her talents as a group counselor are so outstanding but rather because the youngster may have an emotional problem. The average youngster when troubled will usually be hesitant about revealing a "serious" problem. When she does, she usually "leads up to it" in an indirect way. The group member who reveals too much of herself too soon should be considered a candidate for referral to a physician, or for referral for more intensive individual counseling, or both. There are exceptions. The counselor who knows the student members and has worked with them individually in the past may acquire material that is troublesome to the students sooner than another counselor.

There are selected group counselors who can project an immediate feeling of well-being among the student members. They immediately bring the group "under control" and are able to give them the direction necessary to be able to discuss problem areas. This is usually a more experienced counselor. But even with experienced counselors the students will present material in as non-threatening a way as possible. During the course of the group session they will repeatedly make sure that the counselor is in complete control of the group and any subject matter that is presented.

## WHEN STUDENT MEMBERS ARGUE WITH EACH OTHER

Student members of an ongoing group will occasionally disagree with each other. The nature of the disagreements may vary and may mean different things. In a good group the members are comfortable enough to disagree with each other in a mature manner. Hopefully, disagreements will reflect the individual thoughts and concepts of the student and add another dimension to the group discussion. Disagreements may reflect a clash in personalities or reflect adjustment problems that a particular member or members may have during group participation. The counselor's reaction should be reflective of both the subject matter and the group interaction.

Whenever possible, the leader should remain neutral and allow the group members to resolve disagreements as they present. The youngster who has a tendency to dominate other children and suddenly is being verbally confronted by one of her peers may be learning a valuable lesson. A passive member who presents material for the first time may need the counselor's help (via some type of reinforcement). For example, a passive youngster may make a comment and the counselor may say, "That's a good point."

The counselor's job is to make sure that all members feel that they can agree or disagree and still be members of the group. In one group a youngster verbally attacked a boy who had just given a positive suggestion. The leader interjected, "Sometimes we can learn from the ideas of others." The positive suggestion given by the first youngster was reinforced and at the same time the concept that members work together, help and learn from each other was reinforced.

When group members say something that is contrary to the general attitude of the group, it is the group member herself who suffers most, not necessarily the group. The group may reject the member who presents a conflicting idea that may upset the equilibrium of the group, but the group will never reject itself. The leader of a group should recognize that the regenerative and reparative power of a group is extraordinary. It usually takes more than a group member to disrupt a group. The adaptation prowess and the ability to reorganize is significant. The counselor should note that the more difficult the crisis or severe the interaction (i.e., a disagreement), the more involvement there is. When the counselor can skillfully utilize this involvement, it will enhance the group cohesiveness. Disagreement for the sake of disagreement should not be encouraged; however, it should not be avoided when it is done in a constructive way.

When students disagree with each other, or when they disagree with the group leader, it may be an indication that they are not only questioning the decision or subject matter presented; but, more important, they may be asking for more direction from the counselor. When this is the case, there may be more than one disagreement: that is, there may be a series of disagreements between group members.

In summary, when students disagree with each other it may reflect healthy discussion about a particular subject. It may also reflect a personality clash between student members that has nothing to do with subject matter and/or a request from student members for more direction from the leader.

## PHYSICAL THREAT TO ONE OF THE STUDENT MEMBERS OF THE GROUP

Occasionally the counselor encounters group members who have been confronted with physical threats by other student members. When this occurs, the counselor should immediately take charge and give significant direction. One of the best ways to handle a physical threat during a group session is to stop the discussion regardless of subject matter and to discuss the incident with all the group members. This unifies the group. The counselor asks the group what each of them thinks about a physical threat being made, what should be done, etc. If the counselor thinks the problem still has not been resolved, then she should request to see both group members individually after the session.

One student member may physically threaten another student member before or after a group session. When this occurs there may be a drop in attendance. It may be only after a subsequent session or sessions that the complete story is related. When this does occur, it often means that the person who does the threatening is actually asking for more guidance or direction from the counselor and the school authorities. Rather than react negatively to the situation, the counselor must react very positively and orient herself to giving that youngster help. At the same time the counselor should make it known to the other group members, as well as to the youngster, that this type of activity will not be tolerated. The counselor should not ignore the incident. She should follow through in whatever manner she thinks appropriate. She should always consider offering help to the involved youngsters.

When a threat is made to student members by youngsters who are not members of the group, it is usually a reflection that the students who are not group members "want in." One way of handling this is to talk with the youngsters and invite them into a group. The counselor can utilize structured group experience to change a negative group image into a positive one. It is often difficult to work with a group that is organized because of negative behavior. One of the difficulties is trying to offset the so-called "neighborhood effect" (Chapter II). If there is a continued threat of violence, then the youngsters are probably not capable of handling a group counseling session at that time. Either the group size can be reduced or selected students can be excluded or transferred to individual counseling. If necessary, the group can be disbanded. Under no circumstances should a group be continued in a school setting that will make the youngsters so anxious or antagonistic that they will return to the classroom and disrupt the school program.

The group leader must note the physical interaction of the group and must reflect on the probable cause of the physical interaction. But the group counselor should not observe physical interaction and activity of a group to the exclusion of the content of the subject matter being discussed and the goals that the group is trying to achieve.

## THE LATE QUESTION

It is frequent for group members to ask questions towards the end of the session or when the session is breaking up. There may be many reasons for the late question.

(1) The most common reason for the late question is that the counselor has not made something clear and the member wants clarification. If the question is being raised because the counselor has not made something clear, then it is her responsibility to make sure she does clarify it in short, concise sentences prior to the termination of the meeting. Questions of this type are reasonable and should be entertained and handled by the counselor. This is part of

the counselor's responsibility.

(2) A student may not feel comfortable in asking her question during the session. Questions that emanate from hesitance on the part of the youngster to speak during the session should be weighed carefully by the counselor. Even if the youngster is passive and has difficulty talking in a group, she should not (usually) be allowed to stretch the rules of the group any more than other group members. When a more passive youngster does present a question as a late question, the counselor should recognize it but then put it in perspective. For example: "Johnny, that is a good question, but the session is ending now. We'll take it up next time." The leader recognizes the efforts of the passive youngster but at the same time points out to him that if she is going to "make it," she has to make it within the rules of the society in which she is operating.

(3) A youngster may ask a late question as an attention-getting device. This youngster must also be recognized, but it is important that she learn that his attention-getting must be done in a way that is within the rules of the group.

(4) A youngster may ask a late question to test the leader to see if she is going to terminate the session at the time she said she would or whether the leader can be made to sway even a little within the time schedule that she established. For the average group, this is of no particular concern. When working with a delinquent-type population, it may be important. When time of the session (that is, when it is going to start and when it is going to end) is used as a limit-setting device, it is important that the schedule be maintained.

There are some practical considerations when entertaining a late question. The counselor should not discuss material presented by a new question unless she has time to follow it through to a logical conclusion. If it is a question that will "fire" the imaginations and emotions of the group members, it is important for the counselor not to entertain it at that time but say, "We really don't have time to consider the question now because time is running short; however, if you would like, you may bring it up at the beginning of the next session." The counselor should feel free to reject or to entertain any question that she wants any time during the session; but at the end of a session, the counselor should field the questions as she sees fit and has time to handle.

## QUESTIONS ASKED AFTER THE GROUP TERMINATES

When a youngster asks a question after the group session has ended, the counselor has to decide why the youngster may be asking the question. Next, she has to decide whether she has time to listen to the question. She may have other commitments that take precedence. If the counselor does have time, then she has to decide whether the question asked is a group question or an individual question – that is, whether it is a question that should be brought up before the group or whether it is a question that should be investigated and answered on a one-to-one basis in the counselor's office. If the question is a group question, then the counselor should suggest to the youngster that she bring it up at the next group meeting. If it is an individual or personal question, then the counselor has to decide whether she wants to become involved in answering the question and handling the implications that the question may have. If the counselor is willing to become involved, then she can handle it in various ways. One is to listen to the youngster and let her ventilate whatever it is she has on her mind. This gives the youngster a chance to organize her own thoughts and perhaps arrive at a decision of what to do. Secondly, the counselor can ask the youngster what she thinks is the best way to handle the question. The youngster may not know, or she may give a suggestion. She may suggest bringing it up as an example or in an indirect way (i.e., projected story) and letting the group handle it. For example, the youngster may say to the group, "What would you do if you were ever caught in a situation like this?" etc. Another possibility is that the youngster may not receive enough help from either the counselor or the group, and referral to a clergyman, family physician, or specialist, within the school or without, may be of some help.

## A QUESTION THE GROUP EXPECTS TO DISCUSS

Group members occasionally come to a group session concerned about something that has happened within the school, classroom, or international scene that has affected them either emotionally, physically, or both. It may be a situation that affects them only indirectly but directly affects their parents, their teachers in their school, or other segments of the general community. Although the issue may have nothing to do with the group goals, the counselor should be aware, if possible, of the situation and try to stimulate some discussion about the particular concern of the student members. It may be sufficient to acknowledge the situation, comment on it, and then proceed to the goal-oriented discussions of the group. This may not be sufficient. If it is not, it will influence the remainder of the group discussion. The counselor has to decide how to handle the influencing material. She can do this directly in an open discussion. This is usually the best technique unless the topic is too anxiety-producing. She may elect to handle it indirectly, utilizing the goal-directed discussion but recognizing that much of the discussion has been influenced by material the students were concerned with prior to coming to the group.

If the counselor does not consider, either directly or indirectly, material that is bothering the student members, it will increase their discomfort. The counselor will see signs of discontent. The group may become angry, quiet, restless, or passive. If the counselor is aware of a question that is bothering the student members and avoids entertaining that question, it will increase the anxiety of the group, reinforcing their concern for that topic. Complete avoidance of a topic by a group leader indicates to the student member that the counselor does not feel capable of and/or comfortable with handling the issue. As a result, the student members may act up even more, testing the leader until she gives some type of direction, either with that particular issue or another. If the counselor does not think it is an appropriate topic to be discussed in the school setting, then she should say so; but she should recognize it, give an explanation as to why it is not being discussed, and then proceed. This usually will satisfy the group.

The counselor should try to avoid an incomplete discussion of an important topic. If the topic is considered, there should be some kind of resolution. The counselor can give a definitive answer, with the notation that it can be continued next session if the group feels it is indicated. The major consideration is not to leave the group members so uncomfortable or anxious that they will then begin to be hyperactive in other settings of the school.

## THE TAPE RECORDER

Many counselors are becoming quite expert in the use of the tape recorder. They use it for demonstration purposes with other counselors, teachers, and students, as well as a teaching device for themselves. They can review group counseling sessions via the tape, replaying important discussions. It is an excellent way to gain insight into the dynamics of the group. The counselor can review the tape and interpret the interaction that has taken place, what it means, what could have been done to alter a particular pattern, what her role in influencing the group was, and the various roles that the individual student members have played. It has proven to be a helpful technique in facilitating the learning of group counseling techniques, and it can enrich the counselor's experience.

The counselor who has not had experience with tape recorders is often reluctant to use the tape recorder during a group counseling session. One reason for the hesitation is wondering how the youngsters will react to it. In general, the student members of the group have only minor reservations about the tape recorder. If this a new experience, they will usually be interested in the tape recorder, look at it, maybe comment about it, and perhaps feel slightly uncomfortable. If the counselor recognizes the tape recorder and comments, "All our sessions will be taped," this will usually be sufficient for the student members. Occasionally a member will ask "Who is going to hear the tape?" at which point the counselor should relate how the tape is to be used. If it is going to be used for training purposes for other counselors, or students, or teachers, then this should be related to the group members. If there is little objection, the subject of the tape recorders is then dropped and the youngsters can proceed with a routine goal-oriented session.

If the counselor has some reservations about the use of the

tape recorder, then the students may become more concerned and reflect the counselor's feeling of discomfort. They will question more thoroughly the utilization of the tape. In general, the youngsters are intrigued by the use of the tape recorder and often ask to hear it. This should be encouraged when requested. Some counselors have used the playback of the tape recorder to stimulate group interest; others have utilized it as a teaching device, allowing the group members to hear themselves and to discuss their reactions. Usually the enjoyment of hearing themselves on a tape is sufficient. The counselor's hesitation about using a tape recorder commonly occurs with more inexperienced counselors who may be hesitant to have other teachers or counselors review the group counseling session. The possibility of teachers hearing youngsters discussing them or the feeling of discomfort of having another counselor review her work are some of the main reasons why the inexperienced counselor hesitates about using the recorder. Once the counselor takes the precaution of setting up guidelines for the use of the tape recorder and gains more experience in working with groups, she usually does not hesitate to use it. This enables the counselor to add the tape recorder as another mechanical aid in the counseling and learning process.

## *WHAT CONSTITUTES A POOR SESSION*

Counselors are often amazed that youngsters come back, session after session, when they themselves think that the sessions have been less than satisfactory. They are surprised at the "staying power" of the group members. Their comment often is, "I feel I am having a poor session, but the kids must be getting something out of it. They keep coming back."

What does constitute a poor session?

There are several things that may constitute a poor session. These are factors that cannot always be shared with the students. The counselor should be aware of some the causes so that if she thinks the group counseling session is not adequate, she can initiate steps to improve it.

*(1) A lack of awareness of group goals.* A lack of awareness of group goals can be frustrating to both the counselor and the student members. Nothing can be quite as devastating as getting together for a group session without anybody knowing why they are there. If part of the goals of the group sessions are just to get together and verbally interact with each other, then this is sufficient; but if there is no awareness of what the goals are, then the group members will become uncomfortable, frustrated, and have a tendency to drop out, or be reluctant to participate.

*(2) Leaving the group anxious.* The second factor to consider when one has a poor group session is whether the group session has been ending with the group anxious or uncomfortable, with no opportunity to resolve the anxiety. Every group will periodically become uncomfortable or anxious about something. When the counselor is aware of this, she should handle it accordingly. Whenever possible, a group in the school setting should not be left anxious (Chapter IV).

*(3) Anarchy in the group.* The third consideration is whether there was anarchy in the group. This is usually a session in which the events that took place, both verbal and perhaps physical, are events that the group leader had no control over. Anarchy, perhaps more than anything else, is the cardinal sin of a group counseling session. Without direction the group will usually perform poorly.

*(4) Decreased verbal interaction.* The fourth major element to be considered is the verbal interaction between group members, and group members and the counselor. Decreased verbal interaction, especially when there has been a history of spontaneous discussion, is indicative of a poor session. However, the counselor should not equate decreased discussion with a poor performance and an increased interaction with a successful performance. This is not always what happens. When the topic is unusually interesting, there may be decreased verbal interaction with increased reflection. It may have been an excellent session

for the youngsters. Verbal interaction is not the *sine qua non* of a good session. Groups (i.e., with above-average youngsters) may have increased verbal interaction but the youngsters may think that the sessions are a "bore" because the subject material is dull and unimaginative.

(5) *A bored counselor.* When a group leader is literally tired of her job, or does not enjoy the work she is doing, it is very difficult for the leader to stimulate enthusiasm and motivate the students. These are necessary ingredients for a good group performance, whether it is in the classroom or in group counseling sessions. An enthusiastic and sincere counselor may make many technical errors and still maintain the enthusiasm of the group because her conviction and enthusiasm influence the performance of the youngsters. The counselor should not overlook the value of her own sincerity and interest in the children. When the counselor is so overworked, or is less enthusiastic about her job than she thinks she should be, this usually has a dampening effect on the group.

## PHASES IN GROUP WORK

It has been recognized for many years (Bales and Strodtbeck, 1951) that task oriented groups go through phases or stages of group development. These phases can be divided essentially into four parts: the introductory phase, the resistance and testing phase, the productive phase, and the terminal phase. Every group will essentially go through these four stages. The length of time that it takes to transcend from one phase to another is determined by multiple factors, including the goals of the group, the experience of the group members, the skill of the leader, the content of the material, and whether or not the group members have worked together before. A one-session group, as well as a long-term, multiple-session group, may go through similar phases.

The **INTRODUCTORY** phase can essentially be described as an orientation for the group members of what the group goals are, what the organization or structure of the group will be, and the familiarization of the leader and group members for each other.

This is usually a positively oriented phase often referred to as the honeymoon phase.

The **RESISTANCE** and testing phase can be significant or minor, depending upon what is to be accomplished. For example, in working with educational administrators the author has found that if the goal is to encourage them to work together as a unit, the resistance phase may be longer and the group members will often test the leader throughout this phase. This usually reflects their previous isolation and independence from one another. *Testing should be recognized as being reflective of the fundamental group process of a task oriented group: that is, is the leader going to be capable of handling all the events that will occur as the group members change their pattern of behavior and their conceptual framework in which they are going to work.* Group members that have had problems or have been doing things in a traditional or set pattern for a prolonged period of time will demand of the leader significant direction and will test her ability to handle the difficulties that may arise. Testing may be significant and the leader should be well informed and patient. She should not take disagreements and challenges as a personal affront.

When the session is a one-session meeting, the resistance phase is usually minimal and testing is not as great unless the goals of the group are more than can be accomplished within the time limit. It is important for the leader to recognize the intensity of resistance that she may encounter. If the leader attempts to accomplish significant change (in both concept and behavior) in a few sessions, she may never be able to reach the productive phase because the group members have not been able to work through their resistance (to change). It is not uncommon for a new group with a difficult problem to take two to four sessions to overcome the resistance phase. (See Third Meeting, Chapter IV).

There is a natural resistance to change. The author has always allowed his college students to take their own seats in class. He has found that 90% of the students (except those coming late) take the same seats in subsequent classes. There is a natural resistance to changing seats. An above average leadership group may work through the resistance-testing phase in 5-10 minutes. A behavior problem group may take 5-10 hours.

Just prior to the productive phase, there may be increased testing to see if the group leader is ready for the group to move into the productive phase.

The **PRODUCTIVE** phase is usually characterized by minimal or diminished resistance during which the group members are more cooperative and test less. The attitude is positive and the orientation is to the content of the material that has to be pursued. The group members are usually ready to become involved and their conceptual framework is one of change. They are willing to be more flexible, and at this time the group is willing to be more creative and to change where necessary. There will be periodic testing but not to the degree nor the intensity that may be observed in the resistance and testing phase. Disagreement during this phase is usually reflective of intellectual disagreement on a content level rather than resistance (due to a hesitancy to change) reflective of a process level. The most meaningful learning takes place in the productive phase.

The **TERMINATION** phase, or ending phase, is important in that it can reinforce or negate the work accomplished by the group. If the group has been productive and "worthwhile," the group members will often have a "let-down." If the group has never progressed to the productive phase, but remained in the resistance phase, the group may be relieved that the group is ending or frustrated that the goals were never accomplished. It is common for the group members to reflect on past events in their lives, community, school or family during the termination phase.

## THE THIRD MEETING

Many groups do not consolidate or become cohesive as a unit until the second or third meeting. This is important for the counselor to recognize. The counselor may anticipate that she can accomplish more than the time (process) allows. Group members have to get used to each other. They play various roles within the group at different times. They have to learn what these roles are, when they are to play them, and when they are not. Every group member considers the group in her own way, reflecting her own interests, needs, and personality. They learn how to communicate, both verbally and non-verbally, and how to interact and react.

The ability of the group members to adapt to a new group is reflective of their experience in previous groups. The youngster with the least experience will have the most difficulty; the youngster with the most imagination and the most experience will have the least difficulty. The adaptation procedure for group members is sometimes a lengthy process. If the group is not cohesive, the counselor should be hesitant to "push" the youngsters to perform at a more sophisticated level. At the second session the group members are often more verbal; at the third meeting they seem to be responding to each other as a unified, cohesive group. Their interaction increases. A unified feeling has usually been established which seems to be unique to the group.

It is not good practice for the counselor, under usual conditions, to challenge directly what a student member says. It may be particularly important that the counselor not challenge the student at a first session, especially if the student is starting to work with the group for the first time. It is better, if it has to be done, to wait until the second or third meeting, when the cohesive feeling of the group has been established. If the counselor waits until the third meeting to challenge a student member, then the student is less apt to leave the group, either temporarily or permanently. The student has usually established a concept of himself as a group member (group identity) that may offset or allow him to withstand a direct challenge or confrontation by the leader. If the direct challenge is given too early (that is, at a first or second session) the youngster would be prone to prematurely leave the group. This is another reason for early group dropouts.

Some activities that are more sophisticated and complex may need cohesive group unity and/or group interaction. It may be more effective to wait until a third or fourth session, until initiating the more complicated tasks. If a complicated task is given to a group prematurely (i.e., before the group members learn how to interact with each other), the group members may become frustrated. A negative group image may be established. This, of course, is not desirable. It should be avoided if possible.

Premature assignment of sophisticated topics frequently occurs in the public schools. For example, teachers may give class assignments during the first few days of the school year, before the class is cohesive as a unit. Occasionally, because of acting out or because of not understanding what they are supposed to do, or for other reasons, the group members develop a negative self image. This is sometimes difficult to offset, and the teacher is often in competition with this negative group identity throughout the school year. It is usually better for the teacher to initially discuss relevant material in general terms. The teacher should develop a cohesive group identity by general group discussion. After a positive group image is established and the group is working together as a unit, then the youngsters will be more ready to handle more complicated assignments, and generally will be more productive.

Occasionally, in a sophisticated group, a group leader may elect to unify a group with a complicated task. This technique can be used, but should be done by an experienced counselor with an experienced group.

In summary, the counselor should note that a new group may take two to three meetings to consolidate and become cohesive as an integral unit. If she does, she will have less difficulty starting the group.

## HOW A GROUP COMPLAINS

Every group, whether it is a large organization such as the army, or a small group such as group counseling session, develops its own unique way of complaining. It is the way the group utilizes to "let off steam," get angry, or just "grump" when the members tire or ready for a vacation. In group counseling sessions, this may be the location of the room, the hardness of the chairs, or the fact that they meet only once a week. They often complain about the teachers, or the kids in another school. In the army, it's the food. In the navy, it's the lack of girls. In medicine, it's the late hours. In the post office, it's flat feet. In the family, it may be the youngsters who do not do their chores, or the parents who give too many chores. Every group, like every family, has its own unique grumping device.

Occasionally, the group members will single out another group member to complain about. When this occurs, the group leader should become more directive. She should not tolerate or allow the members to pick one of their peers as a scapegoat or complaining device. The group members (even in a so-called perfect group) will eventually find a way to express feelings of discontent. This is not an abnormal procedure. This is a normal phenomenon that every group has, large or small.

What the counselor has to recognize is the degree of "discontent" that occurs and what it means. The group members may be getting bored; they may be ready for their vacations; the group counselor may not have gotten a good night's sleep; or there may be a legitimate complaint. When the counselor should worry is when she never receives any complaints at all. The counselor should *beware of the group that does not complain.*

## VISITORS TO THE GROUP

A visitor will influence the spontaneity and interaction of the group because she is incorporated as part of the group unit, although she may be an "outsider." The leader, no matter how experienced, is usually affected. The members will be affected by both the visitor and the leader's attitude. Because a visitor might affect the group's performance is not sufficient reason to exclude her. Visitors can be extremely useful. Invited guests (i.e., guest lecturers) can share information. They can be used as an indication of group unity to see how well the group can adapt to a new situation. Introducing visitors can be a learning experience for the students. It gives them an opportunity to share their ideas with new adults and/or peers.

There are ways to minimize the freezing effect that a visitor may have. The counselor should decide the role the visitor will have. If the visitor is to be an administrator, then the roles of leadership have to be determined. Is the administrator going to take over the group or is the counselor going to retain leadership while the administrator is there? The counselor should resolve this question by talking to the administrator prior to the meeting and/or by the introduction she makes to the group.

The leader can utilize his introduction to relax the group. The casualness and comfort of the leader is reflected in the comfort of the members. When a counselor is "up tight" the group members will also be tense. Whenever possible, the leader should tell the students at a previous meeting that they will have a visitor. She should explain why the visitor is coming, what the visitor is going to do, whether she is going to participate in the group (or just observe), and how often the visitor or visitors will attend. At the session the visitor should then be introduced and recognized. If the visitor is not recognized by a brief introduction, or invited to participate in the discussion itself, this will affect the group performance. The leader will not have handled the new event in the environment. Even when the group has been properly prepared and the guest introduced, spontaneity will usually be stifled during the early minutes of the session. In a good group, the members will revert to their usual behavior within five to ten minutes. How quickly they revert depends upon the comfort of the leader. If a guest tries to usurp the group leadership, the group members will usually be antagonistic. There may be angry retorts or passive-aggressive behavior: that is instead of responding, they will not say anything. This can be avoided with the proper preparation and introduction by the counselor.

## HOW TO EVALUATE GROUP COUNSELING

Whenever a new technique is utilized in the schools, or any other institution, one of the first questions that is asked is "Yes, but what are you accomplishing?" This is a worthwhile question that has to be considered. It is very difficult to measure some types of behavior. When a counselor or school official advocates a particular technique and indicates that she does not have any idea how to evaluate it, the author is usually suspicious as to the value of the technique. If group counseling is a useful technique, then the individual using it should know enough about group counseling to be able to evaluate what she does.

A group counseling session is evaluated primarily by the goals that have been established. If the counselor selects group counseling to transform under-achievers into college professors, and fails, then group counseling is probably a poor technique to bring about this miraculous transformation. But this does not mean that group counseling is not good for other things.

The value of group counseling and what it does or does not do should be judged primarily on the basis of the goals that have been outlined by the counselor. If the goals of the group are to handle a behavior problem occurring in a given class, and it works, then in that particular instance, with that counselor and that group of students, the group counseling technique was of some significance. However, group counseling may not be the only technique that might work. It would also be inaccurate to write that this is the sole use of group counseling. If the goals of the group are to improve the academic work of the youngsters, and in fact they do improve, then some effect was probably elicited by this technique.

One phenomenon that has been observed is that with the potential dropout and/or under-achiever population, there is usually not an immediate improvement in student performance. For example, with groups that were conducted in the spring, in one project, there was no change during that particular semester; but after return in the fall, significant increase in the youngster's academic and social performance was noted. This was not universal. It was frequent enough, however, to recognize that the results of group counseling are not always immediate. Whether group counseling was the sole affect, whether group counseling coupled with summer activity was the affect, or whether this was just a coincidence is something which is still a moot question. It does appear that in many cases the youngster has to assimilate the experience that she has had in group counseling before she can benefit by it.

## THE ADMISSION OF NEW MEMBERS

One of the basic principles of group work is that any change brings about some turbulence. The turbulence may be minimal or major. The introduction of a new member brings about some change in the group. The new member, as well as the old members, have to adapt to a new situation. The introduction of a new member, especially in a small group, may influence significantly the personality of the group.

There is a phenomenon that appears to be reproducible in many groups, and that is the concept of initiation of a new member. It is not uncommon for a new member to have to go through a ritual, whether major or minor, before she can be accepted as an integral part of the group. In formal organizations this may be a ritual. In small groups, this may be asking questions, sometimes personal. It is the responsibility of the leader to make sure that this initiation process is as minimal and non-traumatic as possible.

In general, the "open-end" group is not advocated in the school setting: that is, as one member drops out, a new one is added. In the open-end group there may be a difference between the level of performance and sophistication of the members already in the group and the members added. The older, experienced members are usually more ready for traumatic or anxiety producing issues, i.e. talking about themselves in the first person. They know the routine and can adapt to changes faster than the new members. It is the responsibility of the group leader to make the transition as comfortable as possible, for the old members as well as the new. Open-end groups are usually more beneficial when the goal is information sharing and is more didactic in style.

The "closed group" is easier to work with. It does not generally admit new members (except in an early session). It begins with a set number of people and continues until termination of the group, regardless of the number of students left in the group. The students do not have to adapt to new group members and can be oriented primarily to the goals that have been elicited. In the open-end group new members are constantly being added and old member are dropping out. The youngsters usually have more difficulty orienting themselves to the goals of the group because they are continuously adapting to the changes in the group.

The admission of new members is probably easiest in a volunteer group. A volunteer group is usually more spontaneous. In the school setting, a non-volunteer group, especially when it is organized because of a particular problem, may make the initiation of a new member difficult.

## *SUGGESTED READINGS*

Berg, Robert C., Garry L. Landreth, and Kevin A. Fall. (1998). Group Counseling: Concepts and Procedures. 3rd ed. Accelerated Development (Taylor and Francis), Philadelphia.

Carrell, Susan. (2000). Group Exercises for Adolescents. 2nd ed. Sage: London.

Carroll, Marguerite R. and James Wiggins. (2001). Elements of Group Counseling: Back to Basics. 3rd ed. Love: Denver, Colorado.

Carter, Emily F.; Mitchell, Sharon L.; Krautheim, Mark D. (Mar 2001). Understanding and Addressing Clients' Resistance to Group Counseling. Journal for Specialists in Group Work. v26 n1 p66-80.

Clark, Arthur J. (Summer 2002). Scapegoating: Dynamics and Interventions in Group Counseling. Journal of Counseling and Development. v80 n3 p 271-76.

Coyne, R.K. (1999). Failures in Group Work: How We Can Learn From Our Mistakes. Sage: Thousand Oaks, CA.

Johnson, Sharon K.; Johnson, C.D., (Jun 2005). Group Counseling: Beyond the Traditional. Professional School Counseling. v8 n5 p399.

MacNair-Semands, Rebecca R. (Sep. 2002). Predicting attendance and expectations for group therapy. Group Dynamics. 6(3), 219-28.

Perrone, Kristin M.; Sedlacek, William E. (Sep 2000). A Comparision of Group Cohesiveness and Client Satisfaction in Homogeneous and Heterogeneous Groups. Journal for Specialists in Group Work. v25 n3 p243-51.

Phelps, Rosemary E.: Luke, Equilla (Mar 1995). A Structured Group Approach for Dealing with Self-Criticism. Journal for Specialists in Group Work. v20 n1 p48-58.

Picard, Cheryl A. (2002). Mediating Interpersonal and Small Group Conflict.

Pistole, M. Carole (Mar 1997). Attachment Theory: Contributions to Group Work. Journal for Specialists in Group Work. v22 n1 p7-21.

Ripley, Vivian V. and Gary E. Goodnough. (Oct. 2001). Planning and Implementing Group Counseling in a High School. Professional School Counseling. 5(1), 62-6.

Rose, Sheldon D. (1998). Group Therapy with Troubled Youth: A Cognitive-Behavioral Interactive Approach. Sage: Thousand Oaks, CA.

Schreiber, Daniel (ed.) 1967 Profile of the School Dropout. Vintage/ Random House, New York

Shechtman, Zipora; Hiradin, Aya; Zina, Samahar. (Spring 2003). The Impact of Culture on Group Behavior: A Comparison of Three Ethnic Groups. Journal of Counseling & Development. v81 n2 p208-16.

Tuckman, B.W. and M.A. Jensen. (1977). Stages of small group development revisited. Group Organizational Studies. 2, 419-427.

Wheeler, Jan L.; Kivlighan, Dennis M., Jr. (Aug 1995). Things Unsaid in Group Counseling: An Empirical Taxonomy. Journal of Counseling & Development. v73 n6 p586-91.

Zimpfer, David G. (Nov 1986). Group Work in the Treatment of Text Anxiety. Journal for Specialists in Group Work. v11 n4 p233-39.

# CHAPTER V

## *TECHNIQUES TO STIMULATE GROUP INTERACTION*

It has been emphasized throughout the text that the group leader is the most significant member of the group. He is the most influential factor in influencing both group interaction and group events. Techniques that counselors use to stimulate group member interaction vary considerably but are probably more influenced by the experience of the counselor. The techniques are not the same. There is no hard, fast rule that says one technique is better than another. What is important is that the technique used is reflective of the counselor's comfort. If the counselor is relaxed and comfortable in using a particular technique, then the students will adapt accordingly and will reflect the feeling or relaxation and comfort that the counselor has. If the counselor tries to adapt to another technique, and does not feel comfortable in using it, then his discomfort will influence the group more than a "superior" technique that he does not feel comfortable in using. Unorthodox techniques can get good results but are not encouraged. Standard techniques may get poor results, depending on the counselor. The important consideration is that the counselor is comfortable using the technique selected.

The experienced counselor does not use the same techniques for all groups. Groups are different. Their population is different. Their personalities are different. Groups, like individuals, have selected needs. It is up to the counselor to decide what those needs are and at what level of performance the groups are operating. He can then more judiciously select the techniques that he wants to use.

## REINFORCEMENT OR REWARD TECHNIQUE

One of the best methods for stimulating spontaneity and interaction among the group members is to reward the student members for participation and verbal response. This can be done in many different ways. The most common way is when the student makes a statement for the group counselor to comment, "That's a good point," or "That's an interesting idea." The leader can accept what the student says, comment on it, and "throw" it back to the group. For example: "Johnny brought up an interesting idea. I'd like to hear what the rest of you think about it."

The reinforcement technique is particularly helpful when you are starting a new group. The student members do not know how the counselor is going to react; they do not know whether what they say will be acceptable or not. When the leader uses a reinforcement technique, the group members quickly recognize that anything appropriate can be said. The counselor will not only accept it, but will reward them for participating.

Video-tape and audio-tape demonstrations illustrate how the reward technique works. It becomes obvious that when a group counselor reinforces a youngster for talking, the youngster has a tendency to want to respond again to receive the acceptance of the leader. This is probably a "socialization effect" (Chapter VIII).

When the group begins to interact, the counselor can respond and reinforce them in different ways. A nod of the head may be sufficient. Utilizing what the student member says in asking another question is particularly helpful. A smile may be a reinforcement cue. It is important to reward the youngster for participation, especially in the early sessions. After the group has met for a number of times, or after the first thirty minutes of a group that has been well-prepared by the counselor, the discussion and verbal interaction itself will be sufficient reinforcement to continue the momentum of the session and to stimulate the motivation of the participants.

The counselor who uses a reinforcement technique usually gets a good response. He should recognize (as does a good classroom teacher) that too much praise can outlive its usefulness and have little or no effect. This is comparable to the child who eats ice cream two times per day. By the end of the summer the youngster is no longer asking for ice cream. After the group is well primed, an interrupted schedule (variable reinforcement) is indicated: that is, periodically giving praise, a nod, or verbal indication of a good job rather than every time a student participates.

How the counselor phrases his questions is particularly important. He can ask a question one way that reinforces the student. The counselor can ask a similar question in another way that puts the same student on the defensive.

The leader can reinforce the group as well as the single individual. At the end of a session he can tell the group members that they accepted the responsibility of the group sessions well. He thought that they did a good job. This reinforces their participation and response. It also reinforces the cohesive effect; they are told that they are working together well as a group.

There are times when the group has done a particularly spectacular job and the group leader is quite proud. Being overly complimentary, however, may negate some of the student's feelings of accomplishment. A proud look on the part of the counselor may be sufficient to project his thoughts to all the group members. The job may be reward enough to reinforce the students for their performance.

The best reinforcement is when the students are working together, give a good performance, and feel pride in the job that has been accomplished.

## SUMMARIZATION TECHNIQUE

After the youngsters have discussed a topic, the counselor may summarize what has been said. This can be a helpful technique when used with definite goals in mind. For example, if a question has been thoroughly discussed and interest in that particular question is starting to wane, it is often helpful to summarize what has been said and then conclude the discussion on that particular topic. Summarization can be very helpful in preparing the group for another topic that the counselor wants the group to discuss. For example:

Counselor: "Most of you feel that the most important member of a group is its leader? If this is true, what do you think is the most difficult job that a leader has to do?"

The counselor summarizes the previous discussion and then utilizes the summary as an introduction to the next phase of the counseling session. He reinforces the discussion that has taken place and can, by both inflection and attitude, confirm what has gone on. *The summarization technique has a tendency to stop further discussion on a particular topic.* It therefore should not be used prematurely; otherwise, the group will be frustrated because they have not had the opportunity to investigate, discuss, and digest the material that was being presented. When the summarization technique is used by the counselor, he should know what he is going to do next, because there will be a brief pause in the discussion after the summary has been made.

## PICK-UP TECHNIQUE

An effective technique, especially when the counselor has outlined his goals well, is the "pick-up technique." With this technique, the counselor takes what is said by a student member and uses the statement (or question) of that member as the introductory statement to a new question. For example:

Johnny: I went to the circus on Saturday. I thought it was great.

Counselor: How many others of the group have gone to the circus this year? Show of hands.

The counselor can then discuss the circus. He stimulates discussion by asking questions. No matter what his goal-oriented topic is, he can utilize the basic structure of the circus as the introduction. For example, if it is career planning, the counselor could talk about the careers of circus people and then branch out into many different types of careers, using the same base. If the goal of the session is to discuss study habits, he could use the study habits of the performers as the core of his discussion. The counselor could correlate the study habits of the performers with the study habits of mechanics, professionals, etc. If the topic is about concentration, he could discuss the concentration necessary to be a performer. He could then expand the discussion to concentration in school work. The counselor could compare the activities of a professional person with the activities of a circus professional. The opportunities are endless.

The key is to "pick up" some topic that is presented by a student member and then utilize it as a tag for the next idea. This will help to maintain the continuity of the discussion. The youngsters will usually understand the subject material better because of the thin tie between the original ideas discussed (i.e., circus) and the goal-directed topics.

## COMPARISON TECHNIQUE

The comparison technique is closely related to the pick-up technique. The counselor selects a subject with which all the students are universally familiar, such as school organization, teachers, homework, grades, etc. He then asks a question such as, "What is the similarity between the grades that you get in school and the pay check your mother or father gets for working at his job?" This makes a realistic comparison between work in general and school work. How some types of reward are easier to accomplish and are more desirable than others could be possible topics for comparison.

Comparison between two subjects or two ideas can be particularly helpful. It tends to stimulate many different ideas. Although an idea may be presented by one student, another student may have a completely different concept, interpretation, or idea to discuss. This continues to stimulate group inter-action. It is a technique which is easy for the members to use. They feel comfortable because they understand what they are talking about.

## PROBING TECHNIQUE

This technique is often used by inexperienced counselors, although everyone uses it at times. The counselor continuously asks questions until he gets the answer that he wants. It is something like a twenty-question approach. At selected times this may be indicated, especially if the group is joking about a particular topic and is in a particularly jocular mood.

The probing technique can also be used as an introductory technique to stimulate the youngsters' interest in subject matter the counselor is going to present.

There are some hazards of which the counselor must be cautious. When the counselor seeks one particular answer he may be imposing his values on his students. If the members do not agree with the counselor and he has made a dogmatic stand (utilizing a probing technique to obtain what he thinks is the correct answer), the counselor may decrease group interaction. Youngsters generally interact more if they think that what they have to say is being accepted. When the counselor becomes selective and wants only one answer, youngsters tend to become quiet. They do not want to be rejected or wrong. They are also probing their own thoughts for the answer that they think the counselor may want. This probing technique usually does not allow partial credit for an answer. It becomes an all-or-none affair, which is a poor stimulus to group interaction.

The probing technique can be utilized for a fun session in which the probing technique is used, such as the twenty questions game. It offers a novelty effect which may stimulate the interest of the group. It should be done, however, in a non-serious, "light," or humorous mood. If the youngster does not have the right answer, the counselor should feel free to "kid" with him about it, or tell him he is partially right, or "You're getting warm," "You're getting close," Who's got it?" etc. When the probing technique is used in this way, it can be quite effective. It will have a tendency to stimulate rather than inhibit the discussion.

## DIRECT QUESTION TECHNIQUE

The technique used most frequently by the counselor is the direct question technique. For example: "John, what did you think of the assembly that we had this morning?" This technique is an outgrowth of classical teacher training. The teacher often relates on a teacher-to-student basis rather than a teacher-to-class basis.

Group members respond to this technique; they feel comfortable because this is the style their teachers use. The counselor, usually being an ex-teacher, also feels comfortable in using this technique.

The direct question technique can be particularly helpful in working with an under-achiever population, when organizing the group in a definite way is important. When the counselor persists in using this technique to the exclusion of others, it establishes a one-to-one or counselor-to-student behavior pattern. This technique tends to cut off or decrease the group's opportunity for interaction between members. The lines of communication are established in a conventional teacher-to-student model, leaving little room for student-to-student interaction.

If one of the counselor's goals is to increase student-to-student participation, then he must modify the counselor-to-student approach. He can do this by utilizing the answer of a student for his next question to the group (as a group). This encourages a spontaneous reply from a group member which is the beginning of group interaction. For example:

Counselor: Johnny, how did you like the assembly this morning?

Johnny: I thought it was all right, but it was too long and I got restless towards the end.

Counselor: What do the rest of you think? Did you get restless as Johnny did?

This second question by the counselor then "opens up" the group discussion.

The direct question technique should not be reserved only for a counselor-to-student question, but also for a counselor-to-group question. This technique can encourage the spontaneous interaction of group members. It may also help to illustrate that it is tolerable for one group member to disagree, agree, and comment upon another's statement.

## *DIDACTIC TECHNIQUE*

This technique is usually used for a one- or two-session group in which the delivery of information is what is most important. The emphasis is generally not on discussion. The counselor lectures to the group in a didactic way just as the teacher might in the classroom. If the technique is over-used the kids become bored, restless, and inattentive to what is being said. It decreases the opportunity to develop an atmosphere of original thought and interaction among the youngsters.

Sometimes didactic material is necessary to prepare youngsters for group discussion and/or to accomplish the goals of a particular session. When it is necessary to lecture to a group of youngsters, it is important to organize the material so that the information is given in the shortest time and simplest form. When possible, there should be time allotted for questions and discussion.

## *INTERPRETATION TECHNIQUE*

When the counselor utilizes the interpretation technique, he makes an interpretation of what is being said by the group members. He has to be cautious. The most precarious part of using this technique is that the interpretation given by the counselor may be wrong.

The counselor should not be anxious or expect the student members of the group to accept one hundred percent of his interpretation. The group members may not completely understand what he is trying to "get across." They may have different backgrounds with different interpretations. Their needs, both social and personal, may be different. Family-neighborhood environments may be such that they cannot completely accept the idea that is being professed.

The interpretation technique may be used by the counselor who is trying to "convey" an idea to the group. For example, the idea may be that it is acceptable to disagree with the leader. Regardless of the reason, it is often easier for the group members if the counselor states directly what he is trying to convey rather than to use an interpretation.

Counselors may make interpretations that are purposely wrong, hoping that it will stimulate more discussion and reinforce the individual's ability to disagree with the counselor. *This is not recommended.* Occasionally it can be helpful, but the counselor has to be careful and skillful. If he is working with a youngster who is passive or comes from a family in which the youngsters are not given permission to disagree with the parent, he is placing that youngster in a very difficult position. If the counselor makes an interpretation, either knowingly or unknowingly, that is wrong, this youngster may say, "Yes, you are right." The youngster may then feel guilty, angry, or frustrated that he has not been able to express himself and has consented to an interpretation that is not his.

When the counselor does use the interpretation technique, he should be aware that his interpretation may be wrong. If he senses that it is in spite of the consent of the group or the individual, he should not hesitate to investigate the point with the group. If the counselor was mistaken, he should explore with the group why the consent was given. The counselor can then share the fact that the members can disagree with him.

The interpretation technique is a good technique but has to be used with caution.

## *CONFRONTATION TECHNIQUE*

The confrontation technique is used less in group counseling than in other types of group work (i.e., group therapy). In the confrontation technique, the student member of the group is confronted directly by the group leader. For example, the group leader may comment, "It sounds like you're angry," or "Do you feel that way?" Usually, the student member does not understand what the counselor is talking about. For example, the youngster may truly be angry, and may be expressing this anger in an indirect way such as talking about violent things, e.g. war, or violent incidents that he read about in the newspaper. When the counselor confronts him with the fact that he thinks the student is angry, the student may not understand the unconscious level of interpretation that the counselor has made. If the counselor follows this up with, "It sounds like you feel that way," the student may look at him in wonderment, really not knowing what the counselor is talking about.

There are experienced counselors who use a modified confrontation technique quite well. Instead of confronting the youngster directly with a statement like "I don't believe you would do that," the counselor might make a statement like "Oh, come on, now, Joe, do you really believe this? With your ability in athletics, do you really think you'd back away from a job like that?" In this way, the counselor has confronted the youngster with a challenging question, but does it in a way that simultaneously reinforces some of the positive qualities of the youngster, and refers to the student in a "buddy" or friend type of approach. The counselor sets the stage for confrontation with a question, but in a light or humorous vein. It gives the other group members an opportunity to also joke, and relieves any anxiety that they may feel about one of their peers being confronted by the group leader. It also gives the youngster a face-saving way out. When a confrontation technique is used in this fashion, it is often very helpful.

Another type of confrontation may occur when a youngster is projecting his own feelings but doing it in a way that is not uncommon among students: that is, referring to "a friend of mine who did this." It usually is unwise for the group counselor to confront the student with the fact that "It sounds to me like you are describing yourself rather than somebody else." When a counselor does this, he (1) confronts the youngster with the fact that he is "lying," which puts the youngster in a defensive, perhaps guilty, position; and (2) deprives the youngster of a common technique used in children and adolescents, that of projecting their own feelings onto an imagined, fantasized, or make-believe but usable character that they can relate. They can avoid embarrassing themselves but still recount incidents that have happened to them. They have an opportunity to "work it through" in an indirect, less embarrassing, but very real and acceptable way. When the counselor confronts the youngster with the fact that it may be himself and not a friend, it also places the student in the uncomfortable position of having to face all issues, no matter how difficult or emotional they may be, in an open, direct way. Most youngsters are not able or willing to do this. The average counselor is usually not trained to handle the tremendous anxiety that may come with a direct revelation in a group setting.

When the counselor confronts the student member in a direct challenge or direct way, it also makes the other student members very uncomfortable. They identify with their peers.

Confrontation with one of their fellow students tends to make them feel uncomfortable. It may inhibit them from wanting to produce relevant material or ideas of their own for fear of being confronted or challenged in a direct way. Unless the counselor is extremely skilled with this technique and has been working with the youngsters for a prolonged period of time, this is not the technique of choice in a group counseling session. It may increase the anxiety level and feelings of discomfort of the members so that they may start "acting out" to such a degree that the counselor will have to divert his attention from the topic and handle the acting out. (This will tend to give the youngsters the direction they need.)

## *PROBLEM ORIENTED TECHNIQUE*

Many of the counselors, when organizing their groups and planning their goals, center their groups around a problem orientation. They orient the group towards negative goals, that is, trying to rectify or correct something that is presented as wrong (i.e., poor study habits, poor concentration). It seems that both the counselors and student members feel more comfortable when the orientation is to correct something. This may be a reflection of our American culture whereby Americans seem to be able to relate to each other more comfortably in negative rather than positive terms. It seems Americans are often able to relate to each other more comfortably in aloof, withdrawn, isolated ways rather than warm, affectionate ways.

It seems unfortunate that our groups should be oriented mostly to a negative rather than a positive orientation. What is important is that the counselor must note how his group is oriented. If the group is problem oriented, that means that the student members of the group often have to present problems in order to gain admission to the group and to continue to present problems in order to remain an effective group member. The greatest reward comes for the student member who says, "I've a problem I'd like to discuss today." The counselor and student members then start "licking their chops," knowing that they can get into something "real" with an obvious pay-off for both them and the group member presenting the problem.

The counselor may be working with a potential dropout population. The goals of the counselor are to improve study habits. He can present the goals in two ways: the counselor can say, "We are going to discuss your poor performance and how to improve it," or "We are going to share with each other experiences that we have all had in helping us to study better." The difference is very great. In the first example the counselor has oriented the discussion towards the negative aspects of the person's performance. In the second example the counselor reinforces the good work that has already been done (minimal as it may be) and is ready to build on that positively-oriented base. This is a significant difference.

The counselor should be careful when working with a group that is oriented primarily to successful performance. If the youngster does have a problem, and the entire orientation of the group is to optimum performance only, then this youngster, who may sorely want to discuss a particular problem that he is having, may feel intimidated by the fact that he is not performing well. The counselor should attempt to establish an atmosphere within the group that is positively oriented but that will welcome any problem-oriented questions.

Counselors and teachers have a tendency to fail to reward anything except optimum performance. For example, an under-achiever who had failed three years, achieved a "D." The teacher's comment was, "With a little more work you'll be able to bring it up to a reasonable grade." In a situation like this, the teacher or counselor is almost inviting disaster. A much better comment would have been, "I can see that you are improving. You seem to be getting a better grasp of your work. Now that you recognize that you are a solid 'D' student, you can start working on the next level which is a 'C.' But I think what is important for you to recognize is that your hard work has paid off and you have brought yourself up to a 'D' level from a failing grade." This reinforces the work that the youngster has done. It reinforces the youngster's feeling that at least he can perform at some level, although a low level, and that with a little effort he might be able to bring it up. With no reinforcement of any kind, the youngster feels completely overwhelmed that he is not able to perform acceptably at all. The author has seen "C" students come up to a "B" with the same result: no reward for the "B" work that he has done, but rather a comment, "Well, with a little more work you can get an 'A.'" If the counselor wants good behavior to persist, then he has to offer some type of reinforcement or reward that will tend to perpetuate that performance. Frequently the most significant reward the youngster can obtain is recognition by the counselor.

## *SUMMARY*

The counselor should not become so inflexible that he is comfortable in using only one technique. He must be aware that there are many techniques, many more than have been presented in this short discussion. The counselor should adapt the technique to fit his personality, the student members with whom he works, and the goals of the group.

One technique should not be used to the exclusion of others. This is important when teaching other counselors. The utilization of one technique may or may not be indicated, depending upon the group, the goals, and the counselor. One counselor can use one technique with a group and another counselor, with the same group, oriented to the same goals, may use completely different techniques, getting equally good results. It is apparent that it is not the technique that is used, but how the counselor uses the technique, that is the most important factor.

## *SUGGESTED READINGS*

Ang, Rebecca P.; Hughes, Jan N. (2002). Differential Benefits of Skills Training with Antisocial Youth Based on Group Composition: A Meta-Analytic Investigation. School Psychology Review. v31 n2 p164-85.

Appleton, Valerie and Cass Dykeman. (1996). Using art in group counseling with Native American youth. Journal for Specialists in Group Work. 21(4), 224-31.

Beck, Kirk A. (Apr 2005). Ethnographic Decision Tree Modeling: A Research Method for Counseling Psychology. Journal of Counseling Psychology. v 52 n2 p243-249.

Bensley, Kate R. (Dec 1999). Anger Management: Immediate Intervention by Counselor Coach. Professional School Counseling. v3 n2 p81-90.

Berman, Dene S.; Davis-Berman, Jennifer; Gillen, Mark. (Sep-Oct 1998). Behavioral and Emotional Crisis Management in Adventure Education. Journal of Experiential Education. v21 n2 p96-101.

Bloomgarden, Joan, Kaplan, Frances F. (1993). Using Visualization and Art to Promote Ego Development: An Evolving Technique for Groups. Art Therapy: Journal of the American Art Therapy Association. v10 n4 p201-07.

Bowman, R.P. (Feb. 1995). Using metaphors as tools for counseling children. Elementary School Guidance and Counseling. 29, 206-16.

Bowman, Vicki E.; Boone, Rebecca K. (Dec 1998). Enhancing the Experience of Community: Creativity in Group Work. Journal for Specialists in Group Work. v23 n4 p388-410.

Butler, Scott F.; Fontenelle, Scuddy F., III. (May 1995). Cognitive-Behavioral Group Therapy: Applications with Adolescents Who Are Cognitively Impaired and Sexually Acting Out. v20 n2 p121-27.

Campbell, David P. (Oct 1996). The Use of Interest Surveys with Groups: A Useful Team-Building Technique. Measurement and Evaluation in Counseling and Development. v29 n3 p153-62.

Capuzzi, David ed. (2003). Approaches to Group Work: A Handbook for Practitioners. Prentice Hall.

Clark, Arthur J. (Mar 1998). Reframing: A Therapeutic Technique in Group Counseling. Journal for Specialists in Group Work. v23 n1 p66-73.

Cormier, Sherry, and Harold Hackney. (2004). Counseling Strategies and Interventions. 6th ed. Allyn and Bacon.

Drewes, Athena A., Lois J. Carey, and Charles E. Schaefer, Eds. (2001). School Based Play Therapy. Wiley: New York.

Fletcher, Teresa B.; Hinkle, J. Scott. (Summer 2002) Adventure Based Counseling: An Innovation in Counseling. Journal of Counseling & Development. v80 n3 p277-85.

Garrett, Michael Tianusta; Garrett, J.T.; Brotherton, Dale. (Mar 2001). Inner Circle/Outer Circle: A Group Technique Based on Native American Healing Circles. Journal for Specialists in Group Work. v26 n1 p17-30.

Hall, Jewell; Hawley, Lisa. (June 2004). Interactive Process Notes: An Innovative Tool in Counseling Groups. Journal for Specialists in Group Work. v29 n2 p193-205.

Hogg, Michael A. and R. Scott Tindale. (2001). Group Processes. Blackwell: Malden, Mass.

Jones, Karyn Dayle; Robinson, E.H. "Mike", III. (Dec 2000). Psychoeducational Groups: A Model for Choosing Topics and Exercises Appropriate to Group Stage. Journal for Specialists in Group Work. v25 n4 p356-65.

Kees, Nathalie L.; Jacobs, Edward. (Mar 1990). Conducting More Effective Groups: How to Select and Process Group Exercises. Journal for Specialists in Group Work. v15 n1 p21-29.

LaFountain, Rebecca M.; And Others. (Mar 1996). Solution-Focused Counseling Groups: A Key for School Counselors. School Counselor. v43 n4 p256-67.

MacDevitt, John. (Spring 2001). Authoring Fiction as a Form of Group Work. Journal of Poetry Therapy. v14 n3 p135-44.

Miller, Mark J. (May 1993). The Lifeline: A Qualitative Method to Promote Group Dynamics. Journal for Specialists in Group Work. v18 n2 p51-54

Nims, Donald R. (Jun 1998). Searching for Self: A Theoretical Model for Applying Family Systems to Adolescent Group Work. Journal for Specialists in Group Work. v23 n2 p133-44.

Rosenberg, Rhonda (Apr 1992). Islands of Healing: A Guide to Adventure Based Counseling, by Jim Schoel, Dick Prouty, Paul Radcliffe [Review]. Pathways. v4 n3 p24-26.

Rybak, Christopher J.; Brown, Beverly M. (Mar 1997). Group Conflict: Communication Patterns and Group Development. Journal for Specialists in Group Work. v22 n1 p31-42.

Stanley, Paula Helen. ( Mar 2006). Using the 5P Relay in Task Groups. Journal for Specialists in Group Work. v31 n1 p25-35.

Timberlake, Elizabeth M. and Marika Moore Cutler. (2000). Developmental Play Therapy in Clinical Social Work. Allyn and Bacon.

Tubman, Jonathan G.; Montgomery, Marilyn J.; Wagner, Eric F. (Oct 2001). Letter Writing as a Tool To Increase Client Motivation To Change: Application to an Inpatient Crisis Unit. Journal of Mental Health Counseling. v23 n4 p295-311.

Utay, Joseph M.; Lampe, Richard E. (May 1995). Use of a Group Counseling Game to Enhance Social Skills of Children with Learning Disabilities. Journal for Specialists in Group Work. v20 n2 p114-20.

Wenz, Kathie; McWhirter, J. Jeffries. (Mar1990). Enhancing the Group Experience: Creative Writing Exercises. Journal for Specialists in Group Work. v15 n1 p37-42.

Webb, Linda D.; Bridgman, Greg A.; Campbell, Chari (June 2005). Linking School Counselors and Student Success: A Replication of the Student Success Skills Approach Targeting the Academic and Social Competence of Students. Professional School Counseling. v8 n5 p407.

Wessler, Richard, Sheenah Hankin, and Jonathan Stern. (2001). Succeeding With Difficult Clients: Applications of Cognitive Appraisal Therapy. Academic Press: San Diego.

Winter, Travis; Haines-Burnham, James. (Spring 2005). "Just Because" Interventions: Engaging Hard-to-Reach Students. Reclaiming Children and Youth: The Journal of Strength-based Interventions. v14 n1 p37.

Zins, Joseph E.; Elias, Maurice J. (1993). Promoting Student Competence through School-Based Group Interventions: An Introduction. <u>Special Services in the Schools</u>. v8 n1 p1-7.

# CHAPTER VI

## *THE IMPORTANT GROUP SESSIONS*

Experienced counselors recognize that there are certain sessions that are more important than others. These sessions are often highlighted by the discussion of dramatic events that have occurred in the school or the nation. The students may share with each other their thoughts about major problems that concern them and/or the community: i.e., poverty, racial discrimination, concern about their future, etc. The sessions are often memorable events for both the students and the counselor.

The group counselor has to be concerned with two major sessions that she will have with every ongoing group: the first session and the last. How the counselor initiates the first group session will influence subsequent meetings. How the counselor handles the termination of the group may influence how the youngsters utilize the material that they have assimilated, their relationship with other groups, and their willingness to relate to the leader for further counseling. Both the first and the last sessions have certain characteristics which the counselor should note.

## *THE FIRST SESSION*

The first group counseling session may be the group's most important meeting. It is during the first session that the counselor presents what her expectations are, what the goals of the group are, and what the rules of the meeting will be. She indicates to the students (both directly and implied) what will and will not be tolerated, and how well she will be able to handle the group.

## CONFIDENTIALITY

The counselor should be realistic when she establishes the goals and rules for the group. She should not make commitments that she cannot keep. The inexperienced counselor probably gets into the most difficulty when she makes a commitment of confidentiality. The school counselor who makes a commitment of confidentiality (that is, that all the material presented in the group will be considered confidential by both the counselor and the group members) is being unrealistic and unfair to both the school and the students.

The counselor has neither the professional nor the moral obligation to make a commitment of confidentiality. The school program has to be run, without exception, above the needs of any single individual or group of youngsters committed to a group counseling session. When either the group or the individual interferes or might interfere in any way with the school program and/or welfare of the community, it is the counselor's obligation to make this known to the proper authorities. If she has made a contract of confidentiality with a single student or members of a group, then this is difficult for both the counselor and the students. It is difficult for the counselor because she cannot meet her community and school obligations. It is difficult for the student because in relating information she may be asking for help. *When the counselor makes a commitment of confidentiality, she often cannot help the youngster to obtain the help for which the student may be asking.*

The author has never worked with a group or supervised a counselor (working with a group in a school setting) who has been handicapped because a commitment of confidentiality was not made. In a significantly high percentage of cases it makes no difference to the student whether there is any overt commitment to confidentiality or not. A lack of a commitment of confidentiality may, however, bother a more labile or emotionally troubled student. The author has seen three psychotic children who were obviously paranoid and quite upset over the lack of such confidentiality. These children were referred to the proper medical facility for treatment.

Another group incident which frequently occurs is with the youngster who relates an event in which she was involved and then says to the group counselor, "Please don't say anything about this to my mother." Usually the youngster knows (prior to the revelation of the story) that her parent is going to talk with the counselor. In a situation like this, the counselor should not commit herself to confidentiality. Frequently the youngster reveals the incident because she wants the counselor to relate it to her parents. This is an objective professional decision which should be made solely on the merits of the incident. The counselor should recognize that children neither expect nor necessarily want a verbal commitment of confidentiality. They expect the counselor to do her job regardless of what they (the students) feel that job is.

Although it is wise for the counselor not to make a commitment of confidentiality during the session, the counselor should be aware of her professional responsibility. If information is related in a group about a particular person or family, it is the counselor's obligation not to utilize this information as a source of dinner conversation with her fellow counselors and teachers. The counselor should, however, be free to utilize whatever information she thinks might help to facilitate the process of teaching and learning in the classroom and school setting. If she thinks it is indicated, she should share the information with her professional colleagues. But it is important for the counselor to utilize information in a way that is not detrimental to the group members.

Sooner or later, the students will start talking about their teachers. This is inevitable. Frequently, they will start by making negative comments. It is unfair to both the teachers and the youngsters for the counselor to remark to her colleagues about these comments. It places the youngster, the teacher, and the counselor in a defensive position. The counselor in subsequent group sessions might not have the students' confidence, nor would she have the same cooperation or confidence of the faculty members. Students want to be able to talk about their teachers, but they also like to think that their teachers are secure from repercussion. They want their teachers to be able to do whatever is indicated in their professional role without the fear or reservation that another faculty member is going to chastise them. This enhances the feeling of security that the student wants and needs to be a productive youngster.

A decision of confidentiality should not be made on an emotional basis. The question of confidentiality should be made in an objective professional manner. While confidentiality is not committed to the students, there is a tacit professional commitment which the counselor should note.

## THE ESTABLISHMENT OF RULES

It is important that the counselor, during the first meeting, establish rules that the students can follow during subsequent sessions. This should include when the group counseling session is going to start, how long it is to last, when it is going to end, where it is going to meet, with whom it is going to meet, and who the group members will be.

The counselor should define basic general rules. The youngsters should be able to talk about whatever they want as long as it is related to the topic and appropriate for the school setting. If they want to talk about their friends, teachers, and parents during the discussions, this is reasonable; but they should be told that with friends they only use first names (if they use any names at all) and with teachers they designate them per subject, such as math teacher, science teacher, and so forth.

When the counselor designates the rules by which the group is going to govern itself and the goals to which they are going to be working, then the kids will have a reasonable way of testing the leader and testing each other. If the youngster becomes angry, she can reasonably come late or miss a meeting instead of hitting her colleague or smashing windows. If the youngster wants to test the leader's control, she can use a last name to see if the leader is going to recognize what she is doing. It is for this reason that the counselor must be aware of what the rules are that she is establishing so that when they are broken, she can immediately recognize them and bring it to the group's and the student's attention, either directly or indirectly. For example, if a group member uses a last name, she can immediately be "called on it" by the counselor, who may say, "One of the basic rules that we have for the group is that fellow students be called by first names only when referring to them." Or the leader can simply say, "When referring to other students, simply use the first name."

When the members challenge or test the leader, it may be for many different reasons. The individual student may want more attention. The leadership of the group may be lacking and the students may want some reassurance that the leader is in touch with the group members. The leader may be giving the group too much responsibility too fast and the members want to be reassured that the leader is still in charge and accepting the responsibility that is hers. The youngster may simply forget one of the rules and break it, or may not know the rules. It is up to the counselor to decide for what reason the rule has been broken and what her response should be in order to meet the needs of the individual and/or the needs of the group.

## SETTING LIMITS

Limits on verbal and physical activities should be set during the first session. For example, while one youngster is talking, a second youngster may be tapping her pencil, making a distracting noise. It is usually the responsibility of the leader to tell the youngster to stop. If the leader hesitates, then that youngster may continue to act up, perhaps in another way, until the leader does respond. Another phenomenon that often occurs is that a second group member may mimic the first student who is tapping her pencil, so that within a short time two or three students may be tapping pencils, combs, etc.

A member may be talking, when another youngster interrupts before the first youngster is through. The counselor at this point should make a recommendation to the group that "we spontaneously discuss but we wait until everybody is through expressing themselves first." This is particularly important if you have group members who have a tendency to withdraw, isolate, or be more passive. They may feel intimidated by the more aggressive youngsters who continue to interrupt. It will also stabilize the group so that the members recognize that everyone will be given a chance to participate.

During the first session the counselor starts to develop the group cooperation and cohesiveness by setting limits. However, the counselor should not establish rules or give limit-setting instructions that will subsequently give her a difficult time supervising the group. For example, in the army the first thing that an officer is told is never to give an order that she cannot carry out. The counselor should never establish a rule that she is going to have difficulty enforcing. She should be aware that limit setting is important but should specify the minimum number of rules necessary to be effective. In a good group the counselor may not make any rules except outlining the necessary information: i.e., when the group starts, when it ends, how long it is going to run, etc.

A counselor should feel free to be flexible. She can change established rules, but she should do this in definite way. For example, she can say to the group, "I have changed my mind." The counselor should be able to set limits when she wants, withdraw limits that have been established, and react to the needs of the group as they are noted, and as the group progresses. But the counselor should verbally state these changes. She should not allow the changes to "just happen." If she does not structure the changes, the youngsters will not know which rules to follow.

Setting limits can be done in different ways with different students. Too many rules with some groups will increase their dependency and not give them the proper freedom to develop. Few limits with other groups would increase the members' anxiety. The counselor should be flexible enough to meet the needs of the group with which she is working.

## GROUP IDENTITY

One of the things the counselor has to consider in formulating goals is that she does not establish the structure and identity of the group in a way that will encourage a poor performance by the group members. When a group is organized, for whatever reason, the group members soon identify themselves according to the goals of the group and the criteria for selection: i.e., above average, potential dropouts, randomly selected, etc.

There are group identity difficulties of which the counselor should be aware. If the youngsters are identified as a potential dropout population, the members of that group may have to perform as potential dropouts in order to retain their group membership. The counselor should attempt to offset this by making sure that the identity group is gradually transferred from a dropout population to that of a new identity: i.e., being retained in school, or performing well at their level. In order to remain a group member the youngster can no longer identify as an under-achiever but has to start producing, or at least making an effort to produce, at the level at which she is capable of working. This is one of the difficulties that counselors sometimes do not foresee when they organize a group of "behavior problems." In order to maintain the relationship with the counselor, the youngsters may continue to misbehave. Inadvertently the counselor may be reinforcing the poor behavior of the child, especially if she is identified as a behavior problem. The only way the student can retain membership in the group is to misbehave.

The identity of the group can be used to increase the member's performance. In one group of above-average children, the group was identified as a potential leadership group. In order to identify with the group the youngsters had to increase their performance, and they did.

In summary, the counselor should establish her goals with a positive orientation with which the group members can identify.

## HOW TO START THE FIRST SESSION

Every group counselor has her own style. The way she introduces her first session is reflective of her own personality and the techniques that she uses. (However, the introduction should reflect the goals of the group.) The way the author starts a group may be different than the way other experienced group leaders may start their groups. The style is effective only if the counselor using that style is comfortable with it.

When the youngsters start arriving at the assigned place, the leader should generally greet them. If she knows who they are, she can greet them by name; if not, she usually greets them with a "Hello" or "Hi." She may indicate where they are to be seated and start talking with them until all the members are present, at which time she makes a formal introduction. The counselor introduces herself if she is not known to the students. She asks all the members what their names are, and the names of their units if they are from different sections of the school. The counselor tells them in the introduction why the group has been formed, or reviews the reasons why it has been formed if they have already been told. She occasionally asks the group members if they know why they are present and may ask one of the group members to explain to the group the purpose. This indicates to the students that part of the responsibility for the session is theirs and that she anticipates that they will be participating. She then outlines the goals and briefly establishes the rules. The counselor then starts the discussion.

The following are introductions by four different *inexperienced* group counselors taken verbatim from tapes:

(1) Counselor: "Today, girls, we've come together with the purpose of talking about how we can help new girls coming into a class find places for themselves in the school and in the class. Three of you are new seventh graders, three of you are old seventh graders, and two of you are sixth graders. Those of you in the seventh grade have gone through this process; those of you in the sixth grade have this process facing you when about twelve new girls will come into your class next fall. Let's hear what your reactions are. Feel perfectly free to talk. There are only going to be a few ground rules. First of all, of course, we cannot have two people talking at the same time. You do not have to raise your hand and be called upon, but you can speak when you have something to say, and say it clearly. Another ground rule, we are not going to be talking about individuals by name, either pupils or teachers. Suppose you are a new girl. How does the new girl feel about coming into a situation where some of the other girls have been around for a couple of years? Sally, you are a

new girl this year. How does it feel?"

(2) Counselor: "As Mrs. C has told you, my name is Mr. W. Actually, I am taking a course with Dr. Glass at Johns Hopkins University and we are studying how to work effectively with small groups of school pupils, school children. I am, of course, one of your neighbors next door to here and decided to come over and work with Mr. C and use some sixth graders. Now we are going to talk. The things we want to talk about mostly – or have you talk about with each other - are your thoughts and questions and ideas about leaving elementary school and going on to junior high school. You may want to talk about things you have heard, or questions you may have, in reference to the junior high school and the junior high school program. You've talked to your older brothers and sisters and other friends, so I am sure you have some ideas. You know how you feel about leaving elementary school. I know, from speaking with Mr. B before I came up the steps, that she does plan to have a program involving the junior high school. Mrs. C already knows about that, too. Will the program be here or will you be visiting the junior high school?"

(3) Counselor: "Today I want you to help me out. I am asking you because you've been in the program for a good while and most of you will be leaving soon for one reason or another. I thought for that reason that you would be the best ones to ask for assistance. I have been asked to make an evaluation of the MDTA-NYC programs, school portion only. I have already written this report, which includes my views of the program, both pro and con. I have made some recommendations. I thought, however, and my superior agrees, that it might be helpful and more meaningful if I had some indication of student response to the program. For example, nine out of ten students . . . . Since you've been around a long time and know what it's all about, I want to know if there are any particular things that you were looking forward to getting when you came into the program. Had you been told any specific things? Had you established any

special ambitions as far as your participation in the program is concerned? If you had, did you get it here? I wanted to know also if you feel that the work that you have had has been of any help at all, even if it was not exactly what you had expected. If you were going to do anything at all about the school, what would you change? What would you keep? We're not talking about the teachers. What would you add and what would you delete? It might be easier if we began with the things that you didn't like first. These things will probably come to your mind more quickly. I know that this is cold and you haven't been thinking about it, so take a few minutes to get your thoughts together and then just start talking."

(4) Counselor: "First of all, let me mention the purpose of this group discussion: (1) To exchange experiences with one another with the idea of perhaps improving your inner-city work. (2) To discuss things in the inner-city tutoring work that you have found helpful, perhaps to mention any things that you found did not help you in your work. (3) To evaluate your work with inner-city pupils."

These examples illustrate that different counselors have different styles. Each of these introductions was taken from tapes of group counseling sessions that were above average in caliber for inexperienced counselors. Each reflected the personality of the respective group leader.

## THE LAST SESSION

When a leader has been working with an ongoing group, she should give some consideration to how she is going to terminate the sessions. The termination of a group can be an effective way of reinforcing work that has already been done. In short-term groups it can be used to restate and clarify questions, problems, and lessons previously presented.

There are preliminary considerations which should be made by the group leader. Whenever possible, the termination date should be made known to the group members during the first sessions.

The group leader will be able to set limits (if necessary). The group members will have an opportunity to handle the sessions according to a definite schedule. It is the obligation of the leader to inform the members that the group will be terminated on a given date. Technically, it is better for the group leader, especially when a group has been running for a prolonged time (i.e., a half semester or full academic year), to inform the group at the third or fourth session prior to the termination date. For example: "As you all know, the third session from today will be our last session." This will re-orient the group to finish the business at hand and in so doing, give the group members an opportunity to "tie things up."

In a one- or two-session group, it is important that the leader briefly summarize what has happened in the group in the last session. This usually can be done with a few selected sentences. This will tend to reinforce the group's activity.

"You've learned a great deal of material in a short time." This will tend to reinforce the group's activity.

If the group is meeting for a single one-hour session, it is usually not indicated to stress the time the meeting is going to end. The group members know. They automatically orient themselves to what they want or do not want to accomplish in that given hour.

However, it is not technically beneficial to prematurely remind the group when the session is going to end. For example, it would be to the student's disadvantage to remind them that the group will be terminated four months prior to the termination date unless the leader has specific reasons for doing so. For example, when assignments are not coming in on schedule, or the leader or the classroom teacher has given a particularly difficult assignment that will be due at a given time, it is reasonable for the leader to remind the group that "The assignment is difficult. It will be due on March 16. It will take at least that much time to accomplish, and it would be to your advantage to start working on the project now."

When the counselor hesitates to set a termination date for the sessions and/or hesitates to announce the termination date, it is usually reflective of the leader's difficulty in separating from the group. It may be reflective of the leader's concern that the group members will not be able to separate without undue difficulty. This is similar to the situation where the child has difficulty separating from the mother because the mother has difficulty in separating from the child. Group members generally handle separation as well as the leader is capable of handling it. If the leader is willing to separate and give the group members the recognition due them (that is, recognize that they will be able to separate without difficulty), then the leader will reinforce the capability of the members to handle the responsibility of separation.

Many experienced physicians who have worked with adolescents for long periods of time often remark how the adolescent, after termination, says, "Thank you very much. Good-bye," and the physician may never hear from that youngster again. This is indicative of a healthy youngster who is capable of separating and, depending upon the goals of the group, may not want to remember certain experiences or material that may have been covered. She terminates and separates the relationship with no difficulty, or at least a minimal amount.

There are situations when the leader hesitates to set a termination date, with good reason. She may not know how long the group should continue. She should set a termination date when she does decide. When possible, this date should be established prior to the last meeting.

An interesting event that often occurs during a last session is that group members talk about experiences that happened to them at an earlier age. The leader should allow this to happen because this is one way that the group members have of "working through" their separation. Why the group members revert to recall of past or earlier experiences is a moot question. One can speculate that perhaps looking to experiences of the past is reflective of the security that the individual feels in reviewing a past experience in which she knew what to do. This also may be an indirect way to share the past experiences of the group meeting, or group sessions that were held.

If an ongoing group has to be terminated suddenly because of some unexpected event, such as illness, obligations that have a higher priority, or transfer of position, the counselor should so inform the group members at the *beginning* of the last session.

Under no circumstances should she wait until the last few minutes of a session to say, "We have to terminate our sessions unexpectedly; this is the last session." This will frustrate the group members. They will not be able to "work through" feelings of frustration, rejection, anger, etc., that may be precipitated by a sudden termination of the group. It may negate much of the constructive work that has gone on in previous sessions.

In general, it is more important for the leader to let the group members work through their feelings of separation than to try to finish a scheduled program. There are exceptions. The last session can be oriented to how the individual members or the group as a unit can finish the scheduled program. This is more satisfactory than dropping the schedule as unfinished. The group can make definite plans, or at least have a more structured orientation to the future. When possible the group members should be able to finish ideas, programs, and concepts that they wanted to accomplish as a group. The group members should have the opportunity to review what has been done as well as what has not been done. The counselor should reinforce the constructive work that the group members have accomplished.

## *SUGGESTED READINGS*

Brigman, Greg and Barbara Early. (2001). Group Counseling for School Counselors: A Practical Guide. 2nd ed. J. Weston Welch.

Daniels, Debbie and Peter Jenkins. (1999). Therapy With Children: Children's Rights, Confidentiality, and the Law. Sage: London.

Kivlighan, Dennis M., Jr.; And Others. (Apr 1993). Training Group Members to Set Session Agendas: Effects on In-Session Behavior and Member Outcome. Journal of Counseling Psychology. v40 n2 p182-87.

Lizzio, Alf and Keithia Wilson. (2001). Facilitating group beginnings part I: A practice model. Groupwork. 13(1), 6-30.

# CHAPTER VII

## *GROUP COUNSELING IN THE ELEMENTARY AND SECONDARY SCHOOLS*

The basic principles that influence group counseling are essentially universal; that is, they apply to group counseling in the elementary school as well as group counseling in the secondary school. The differences that do exist reflect primarily the different maturation levels, the unique growth and development patterns, and the varied interests of the children. A child in kindergarten has not developed the concept learning and socialization and communication skills of the average secondary school youngster.

The experienced counselor understands that in order to be effective in group work he has to recognize the youngster's level of performance program his goals and techniques accordingly. The secondary school counselor may utilize sophisticated ideas, subject matter, and/or equipment in his group counseling sessions. The elementary counselor may use projective techniques utilizing toys, puppets, play sessions, and elementary stories.

It is helpful to reflect on the different maturation levels of group ability. For example, the elementary school group counselor may observe youngsters who are actually working at a much more sophisticated performance level: that is, performing at the level of a secondary school student; whereas the secondary school group counselor may have youngsters in his group who, in fact, are still performing at an elementary level.

## THE ELEMENTARY SCHOOL

Educators are learning more about group counseling in the elementary school. As they increase their knowledge, they are beginning to recognize that the basic techniques for group counseling in the elementary school are the same as they are for the secondary school. Certain aspects are modified. Kindergarten children are not expected to understand complicated games, abstract ideas or concepts (as would a child in the seventh grade). The group is well organized but more flexible.

Smaller groups are used which number (in kindergarten) two to four children ( five at the most). The child is quite individualistic. It has only been within the last twelve to twenty-four months that the kindergartener has learned how to participate with another child. Many youngsters entering kindergarten still feel that two is okay, three is a crowd. The average kindergarten child is not ready to verbally participate in larger groups for a prolonged period of time. The youngsters may gather in groups, but their play is mostly individualistic. Their reference is usually to one other child. The object is to encourage the children to be involved and aware of the events in their environment. Puppets, play equipment, dolls, gym bars, singing, and dancing are used. The counselor and/or teacher helps the children develop the skills necessary to interact with other people and their environment.

What the counselor anticipates and what he discusses with kindergarten children are significantly different than with adolescents. In the elementary school the counseling sessions are often organized around a particular activity, such as structured play. Although the child is encouraged to verbalize as much as possible, the session does not depend upon verbal interaction. The counselor's questions are not as direct or as complicated. Children are allowed to "work things through" in an indirect fashion. For example, if they are afraid of school, or of the teachers, or are having difficulties of some type at home, they are allowed to "play it out" in a play situation (i.e., with dolls rather than have to answer direct questions about their troubles), although an experienced counselor can and does discuss obvious events with them.

The counselor has to be more patient. He should be willing

to take his time, because it is usually impossible to suddenly increase the verbal performance of children who are not capable of performing more complicated social skills. The socialization skills of kindergarten children are not well developed. However, their ability to socialize and their capability to perform in small groups (i.e., two to four) is much more sophisticated than was formerly thought.

The sessions have to be well organized. The counselor should design a general plan of what he is going to allow the children to do within a given time, but should be flexible enough to change his plan if indicated. He should have available the materials that are to be used for the group counseling session: i.e., paints, play toys, rubber balls, puppets representative of teachers, children, parents, policeman, firemen, cowboys, soldiers, etc. The goals that the counselor establishes should be reflective of the capability of the children involved.

Younger children cannot "sit still" as long as older children. Children need room to expand and to work. When a kindergarten or first-grade child draws, he needs room for maneuverability. The student anticipates that he will paint a mural, not a constricted design. The physical setting should be large enough to accommodate the physical activity of the children.

The inexperienced elementary school counselor generally does not start his group counseling experience with kindergarten or first-grade students (especially if he has never taught kindergarten). However, it is important that the counselor familiarize himself with group work with kindergarten and first grade children as soon as possible. Group work with students in the early grades does not have to be with problem children. It is better for the inexperienced counselor to initiate group counseling with children who are socially and academically average or above average. After the counselor develops the style that he wants to use, and after he feels comfortable working with average or above-average groups, then the counselor should start working with problem-oriented groups.

When the counselor starts working with children when they are in kindergarten or first grade, it is much easier for him to continue working with these children throughout their elementary school careers. The children recognize that the counselor is part of the general routine. They are more apt to walk into his office as an individual and/or in groups to discuss important or "chit-chat" topics. It also serves as a ticket of admission to subsequently approach the upper grade teachers because it will be simply an extension of work that he started when the children were in kindergarten; that is, if the counselor works with the youngsters in kindergarten and first grade, then it becomes part of the routine that he will work with the youngsters when they are in the second and third grades.

The length of time for sessions usually is no more than twenty minutes for any kindergarten-first grade child; thirty minutes would be considered a long session. Kindergarten teachers know that their youngsters as a group can only sit still for short periods of time. Fifteen to twenty minutes for many groups is maximum, after which the teachers know they have to change the physical setting and/or switch to another activity.

Meetings with children at this particular age should be more frequent than with older groups. For example, an elementary school counselor may elect to see a fifth or sixth grader once a week or once every two weeks with very effective results. However, in the kindergarten-first grade he may elect to see the children at least twice a week. The more frequent the meetings, the better the result with younger children.

It is generally unwise to utilize a "completely" permissive approach with kindergarten-first grade youngsters. The children at this age have minimal controls that they put on themselves. They look to the adult environment for direction and limit setting. Firm, kind, and sincere teachers seem to do particularly well in the early years. This is not a coincidence; youngsters need closeness with adults, and they have to think that the adults in their environment have things under control. The best thing the counselor can do to relax the group is to set limits, both in the classroom and in the counselor's office. Permissiveness is allowed but only within a structured, well-organized setting. Established rules for limit setting gives the children a feeling of security. Spontaneity (and perhaps creativity) with this particular age group is increased when the counseling is more organized. When there is no limit setting and general permissiveness without limits is encouraged, then there is, of course, not spontaneity but anarchy. Permissiveness without limit setting has a tendency to retard the development of the usual socialization and communication skills that children naturally develop. Without some type of firm, but kind, limit setting these skills may develop but in a less-than-favorable way.

Third-grade students are usually capable of performing in a more classical counseling group. Their socialization skills are better developed and they can interact in a more sophisticated way. The children generally are eight and nine years of age. They have developed group socialization skills and the ability to communicate. They are able to participate in a group learning experience with verbal interaction and communication in a classical group counseling style. A group of six to eight youngsters is advocated. Member selection has to be careful to ensure that the youngsters are mature enough to handle a group counseling experience. The same general rules of group counseling as set forth in the early part of the book should be considered for this age group.

Performance of youngsters in the third and fourth grades often depends on the expectation of the counselor. This was illustrated to the author by an audiotape of a group of third-grade students that the author reviewed. At the beginning of the tape the youngsters sounded very immature. However, the counselor insisted on treating the youngsters as young people who were capable of performing at a more mature level. As a result, their performance within the session changed dramatically from immature to significantly more mature children. They handled their responsibility in the group with sophistication, originality, and more mature abstract reasoning. The key to this session was the counselor's capability. She did not infantilize the children.

If the counselor, especially with this particular age (eight to nine years), insists on treating the group members as if they were in the first grade, then the children will in fact perform as if they were in the first or second grade. However, if the counselor treats them with the expectation that they are going to perform at their age level or better, the children will in fact perform significantly better. Children usually adapt to the counselor's expectation.

Another phenomenon that experienced teachers recognize when working with children at kindergarten-first grade level is the transference that occurs (Chapter III). The counselor or teacher is often placed in the role of a parent substitute. It is not infrequent for the youngster to inadvertently call his teacher "mother" or "mama," or "father" or "daddy" or call to the parent when injured or "upset." This sometimes makes the inexperienced teachers or counselor extremely uncomfortable. The more experienced teachers or counselors will usually ignore it, or will say something positive about the parents, for example, "Wouldn't it be nice if your mother did see you playing so nicely?"

One of the main considerations in working with groups of children in the elementary school setting is to recognize that developmental levels of children vary. The teacher or counselor should program the overall lesson plan. He should start with that level of performance at which the children are already functioning. If this means organizing a more permissive, less structured atmosphere initially, then this is what should be done. The counselor should then gradually structure the group sessions as the children develop. Children at this age are particularly self-conscious. They are vying for the attention of the counselor or teacher, but they are also extremely curious and, in most cases, ready to participate. They gain self-confidence and a feeling of importance from group participation. The counselor can enhance the individual identity as well as the group identity of the youngster by a well-organized group plan that is reflective of the level at which the group is ready to perform.

There are changes within the developmental patterns of children that seem to express themselves as a group or grade effect. For example, many elementary school teachers and counselors have indicated to me that the kindergarten-first grade level is the first school development plateau. The children present with definite characteristics reflective of their immaturity, lack of experience working with groups, significantly dependency, and development of their sexual identity. There is another elementary school plateau that is discussed less. This plateau occurs at about the fourth grade. Teachers comment that there seems to be a "change-over period" between the second and fourth grades when the children's behavior changes. The children begin to be more confident, start to recognize their own capabilities, and initiate joint ventures with significant social effect. They may "feel their oats." They are more rambunctious, more confident, and more rebellious. This is a particularly significant time. The counselor and the teacher should coordinate their activities to utilize this new burst of enthusiasm and restlessness that the children exhibit in a way that can be meaningful in the learning experience. If this energy is channeled into the learning process by the development of special projects, special reports, and special interaction programs, the overall learning experience for the entire grade will be enhanced.

The next plateau in the elementary school is the fifth and sixth grades. The youngsters anticipate the change to junior high school. They are starting to have physical changes reflective of the beginning of adolescent growth. Group counseling can be particularly effective with these youngsters in preparing them to enter junior high school with new responsibilities and increased opportunity for independent work.

Sixth and seventh grade teachers often complain about the extreme dependency that the students from elementary school appear to have. Part of this can be alleviated by student preparation. Fifth and sixth grade students can start to assume more and more responsibility within group counseling sessions and the classroom. This can be programmed so that the students are more ready to accept the responsibilities of junior high school.

## THE IMMATURE CHILD

The primary goals in working with the early grades are generally oriented to the needs of the teacher as he observes the youngsters. Immaturity is one of the most common problems that the primary teacher observes. He often refers children who are not performing at the developmental level that he thinks they should for their chronological age.

When the counselor works with immature children, he should attempt to organize the session in a way that will allow the children to accept some responsibility. It is not uncommon for an immature child to ask what he is supposed to do. The counselor can initiate the counseling program by saying, "Well, you can play with whatever you want on the table" or "in the toy box." The youngster may ask, "What am I supposed to do with it?" The counselor can suggest that the child may play with the toy in whatever way he would like. Initially, the immature child may have to be guided. If the youngster is immature and has not been given responsibility at home, he might be frightened by sudden responsibility in the counselor's office. Once the youngster is able to initiate play on his own, the counselor organizes the play sessions so that the child participates with another youngster. The counselor introduces a limited number of toys or a game that two can participate in at the same time. He discusses the concept of sharing (i.e., toys, responsibility, etc.). When the child learns more mature techniques and socialization skills necessary to participate with another child (and/or an adult), the activity can then be structured at a more sophisticated level. For example, the child can be required to share toys and ideas, accept responsibility for small group activity, and interact with the counselor.

The counselor may relate an incomplete story that the children may be required to finish. The counselor can start out by saying: "One day Johnny went to the store," and stop the story at that point. The counselor then proceeds to say to the group members, "What do you think Johnny did at the store?" The immature child has an opportunity to share his ideas with the other group members. He learns how to allow others to participate, how to raise his hand, and how to participate in a group discussion at the developmental level that is expected of him. The educator helps the child to develop socialization skills in a planned stepwise fashion, continuously reinforcing those skills that the child develops. He should be patient and set limits in a kind but firm way. The counselor has to be cautious, for the immature child at this age has a tendency to be angry about things that are irritating. This is what the immature youngster is used to. If the counselor is frustrated by the immature and negative things the child may do, then the counselor may be reinforcing the child's usual behavior pattern. The key is to reinforce those positive events that the counselor allows to occur and that do occur. It is occasionally difficult to distinguish immaturity from decreased cognitive ability. Group work does help to make this differentiation.

## THE PASSIVE CHILD

The second most common problem in this particular age group (kindergarten) is the passive child. The passive child is often withdrawn, usually does not participate freely in classroom activities, and frequently appears to be immature. The teacher is usually concerned that the child's behavior is more than a reflection of immaturity. "The child just doesn't participate." This is the type of child that the counselor often has to start working with in a one-to-one or one-to-two relationship. The counseling session should be organized so that there can be constant interaction. The counselor should allow himself time to reinforce and/or recognize all positive activity in which the child engages.

One of the major goals is to stimulate verbalization; however, active verbalization may be too ambitious an initial goal for some passive children. The initial goal should be to reinforce those activities that seem to be interpersonal, that is, between the child and the counselor. Perhaps the first goal might be to encourage the child to look toward the counselor (not necessarily *at* the counselor) when he is talking, or to look at the play objects that are being used in the session. If the child does look at the play objects, which he usually does, then the counselor may reinforce this activity with either verbal praise, closer attention, or physical contact. (Experimental psychologists have used candy as a reinforcement, i.e., M&M's or some of the sugared cereals.)

The next goal may be to stimulate some type of animation within the child. After the child is able to spontaneously communicate with the counselor in a non-verbal way, then the counselor is ready to start a reinforcement program for verbalization. This may take a long period of time. The counselor has to be patient when working with children who are passive and non-verbal. The counseling sessions should be directed towards reinforcing those things that the child is most capable of doing (that is, a type of non-verbal communication). Once this is established and is reinforced, then the counselor can start developing a program geared towards verbal interaction. The program is based upon the significant non-verbal communication that has already been established.

It is often helpful with non-verbal children to have an older sibling in the play session with that child. (This is one exception to the neighborhood effect.) The passive child may feel more free to participate and to interact when his sibling is in the room than when there is only a counselor, or counselor and another child. The child has already established inter-personal communication with his sibling. He will often respond in animated ways towards the sibling. Frequently the sibling acts as a co-leader with the counselor and does not hesitate to give his brother or sister "the business" for not participating. The author observed one session in which a sibling was used. The counselor asked the passive child a question. He did not answer, either verbally or non-verbally. His older brother looked at him and said, "What's the matter with you? Why don't you answer the teacher?" The youngster turned to his brother and said, "I don't want to. Leave me alone," which was the first words the child had said in the school for four weeks. Older siblings in the early years are particularly helpful. However, in the upper grades, it can be a disadvantage to use a sibling. Sibling rivalry, independence, and the feeling of not wanting to share the adult counselor with one's sibling may be conflicting factors.

Younger children in general respond well to older students. When the counselor recognizes that he is having difficulty working with a withdrawn child on a one-to-one basis, it is often helpful to bring in one or two other children to form a group. The counselor can interact with the children and, by actual demonstration, show the passive non-verbal youngster what is expected. The counselor utilizes the other children as co-leaders or tutors in either a direct or indirect way. Sometimes passive, withdrawn youngsters simply do not understand what is expected of them because their communication skills have not been developed to the point where they readily understand what the counselor is talking about. When the counselor is not making progress on a one-to-one basis, he can utilize either siblings or other children to help.

## THE HYPERACTIVE CHILD

The third type of youngster that is frequently seen in the younger elementary age group is the "hyperactive" child secondary to emotional problems. The children of this age group who are hyperactive secondary to emotional problems may be helped only minimally by medication. They may be helped, however, by small group (two to three members) sessions. The counselor should attempt to be patient with hyperactive children, and should prepare his office so that the children have an opportunity to be active but at the same time not destroy the office (which hyperactive children are capable of doing). It is unwise for the counselor to keep his favorite porcelain jar on his desk during the initial sessions with a hyperactive child.

Hyperactive children need limit setting. But during the initial sessions they usually are not capable of responding to complicated limits. One of the first goals is to (gradually) start setting "limits." This usually involves one or two things that the youngster knows he can or cannot do. Once the initial rules are established, the counselor can generalize the limit setting both in scope and context over a period of time. The counselor should not generalize limit setting to everything during the initial stages. It is particularly important to keep the group small and not to have an all-hyperactive group which neither the children nor the counselor can tolerate. It is better that the office setting for hyperactive children be in a place where there are not many people, traffic, increased noises, or other distracting environmental factors. It is helpful to have available play-type objects, such as puppets, clay, drawing paper and pencils. Paints are all right if the counselor wants to be courageous but are generally discouraged for the sake of the counselor's office. There is one exception: that is, the child who is hyperactive secondary to emotional problems from a so-called perfectionist parent who does not allow the child to "dirty" his clothes, muss his bed, play with toys outside the room, etc. This child may need to get in something "messy" and learn how to handle the responsibility.

The hyperactive child secondary to emotional problems should not have any special "pressure" as to when his behavior must be improved. The relaxed counselor who does not feel that he is under any pressure will do a much more effective job with the hyperactive child. Socialization and kind reinforcement are generally the best antidotes for this child, plus an opportunity to "play out" his particular problems. The counselor should make an effort to avoid increasing the anxiety and hyperactivity. It is helpful if the counselor has his sessions with the so-called hyperactive child either at the end of the day when the child is about ready to go home or at a time when the counselor can spend some time with the child, walking or chatting, before the child goes back to the classroom. This is one time that the counselor would do well to "take a break" before working with the child. He should be as relaxed as possible before entertaining the hyperactive youngster in his office. The counselor should attempt to maximize a relaxed atmosphere, for the hyperactive child is often "anxious and tense."

The second type of hyperactive child is one whose clinical or genetic background predisposes to his hyperactivity. These children do well with medication specific for the hyperactive child. The medication does help the child to be more stable, less active with increased attention and increased focusing in the classroom. The hyperactive youngster who is a candidate for medicine may not initially be a candidate for group counseling. It is recommended that all hyperactive children in the younger elementary grades be referred to a physician for evaluation to help in the differentiation as to the etiology of their hyperactivity.

The goal of group counseling for the hyperactive child should be to help develop a more positive group identity. (The children usually have a very negative concept of themselves as a group member.) The second area of emphasis should be helping the child to "handle" himself when he is not on medication, i.e. techniques that will help him be less hyperactive. Reading, computers, going to one's room or study cubicle in class (to decrease stimulation), increased physical activity when possible all can be helpful. The child himself can often relate things that can be helpful. But it is the realization of his behavior off medication that makes the greatest influence on his behavior.

## *THE SECONDARY SCHOOL*

Adolescents do relatively better in group work than either their older or younger counterparts. The need for a positive group identity and the seeking of socialization with one's peers seems to have its strongest tendencies and bonds during adolescence. The cohesive effect of group interaction is most dramatic. The concept of oneself as a member of a group and the reinforcement that the group member derives from group activity are both rewarding to the individual and important to his emotional maturation. One of the current weaknesses of our entire educational system is the lack of emphasis and utilization of the group effect on adolescents.

The adolescent, during his growth and development, is concerned primarily with three things: body image, independence, and identity.

Body image can be defined as a concept of one's physical self. It is important to the adolescent, whose physique is changing rapidly both internally and externally. The most notable change is the maturation of the sex organs. But of only slightly less importance is the rapid growth in size and composition of every organ of the body. There is an increase in the activity of the sweat and oil glands of the skin with resultant blackheads and acne. Stomach size and appetite increase. The heart doubles in weight, the normal blood pressure increases, and there is a sudden increase in size and growth of skeletal-muscular system, inflicting an awkwardness on many adolescents. If the youngster is too tall or too short, or is sexually precocious, it may affect the student's classroom performance and interaction with his peers. One junior high school adolescent was referred to a group because he was non-verbal in class. After three sessions it was noted that his front upper teeth were missing. He had purposely kept his hand over his mouth to conceal what he felt was a gross physical defect.

The next consideration is the adolescent's desire for independence. He is going through an emotional maturation process which is preparing him to be an independent person. The adolescent wants to become independent but is hesitant to assume this responsibility too soon. He has significant mood swings which are characteristic of the adolescent years. These mood swings are observed most frequently in the family. It is common for an adolescent youngster to be very affectionate and close to his parents one day, and that same day be very angry and indifferent. Adolescents want to be independent, but yet when their parents become angry they feel that their independence may come sooner than they want and they swing back to being cooperative and affectionate. This is only occasionally seen in its most extreme form in the school. However, variations of this can occur in group work and account for some of the moodiness of the group members during the sessions, especially when parental transference occurs with the group leader.

The next consideration is the concept of identity: who am I? Identity is concerned with two parts, individual identity and group identity. Individual identity of the adolescent is concerned with both sexual maturation (that is, the development of an adolescent into an adult) and emotional maturation (that is, the concept of responsibilities, as well as the sexual identity between male and female). Group identity is the development of oneself as a member of a group, and the concept of oneself as a group member. The adolescent wants to be accepted by his peers, both as an individual group member and representative of his or her gender.

The psychological considerations will often be reflected in the general discussions that the adolescent has in the group sessions. He may not talk about these considerations directly, but he may try to prove his masculinity, or she her femininity, in the topics that he or she discusses. Adolescents often reflect their concerns when they talk about the career that they are planning, or the activities that they engage in. The group session reflects the adolescent's concept of themselves (both physically and emotionally) and their stature and independence as an individual, a family member, and a member of the school. For example:

Leader: "What are the goals that you have set for yourself?"

Student Member: "I'd like to become a nurse, secretary, and be my own boss, and learn basic facts in learning to operate and help other people operate."

In this brief interaction within a group session, this thirteen-year-old student in the eighth grade reflected her independence, her identity as a female, her anticipation to be an adult, and her idealized socialization concept of communicating, interacting, and helping others. The counselor should recognize that adolescents are working through important considerations. The group counseling sessions should be organized so that members are given as much leeway as is appropriate within the school to create, share, and test their ideas.

Topics of concern to the adolescent do not have to be discussed directly, but usually are worked through indirectly. When special topics, such as sex education, are to be considered, they should be well planned by the counselor or involved staff: i.e., school nurse, school psychologist, home economics teacher, or special guest leader. The person handling a "special" group session should feel as comfortable as possible in relating the information. He should prepare himself with as much factual knowledge as possible. If the educator who handles the session on a particular subject is comfortable with the information, then the group members will usually accept the information matter-of-factly and will be able to investigate it with more interest and less anxiety.

As adolescents mature, they can handle more responsibility, both in the group counseling sessions and projects that may result from the sessions. This should be encouraged. Expectancy, as with the elementary school youngsters, is a significant reinforcer. If the counselor expects the adolescents to act like young men and women, they usually will. When stimulated with the right program and a positive attitude, the adolescents will often increase both their social and academic performance.

One of the difficulties that occurs in the secondary school group counseling sessions is the question of when the group should meet and the conflicts that occur with scheduling. It is easier to have children leave the classroom in the elementary school than it is in the secondary school. There are different ways that this can be handled. Some counselors scatter the sessions, that is, hold the sessions at different times on the same day during subsequent weeks in order that the youngster will miss one class of a particular subject (i.e., every five or six weeks). Other counselors scatter the days on which the youngsters meet. Groups may meet before school begins. The students report directly to the counselor's office for group counseling and attendance in place of the homeroom. The counseling session is held during that first half-hour of the day. Other counselors have found it more convenient to meet after school.

Most youngsters think that the group counseling sessions are important enough, and like them enough, that they are willing to come either after school or before school begins. The major difficulty that generally presents is that the teachers do not want the students to miss their classes. There are few scheduling difficulties that occur because the youngsters do not want to participate. There are teachers who, for one reason or another, do penalize the youngsters for missing class, regardless of the reason. In order to alleviate this problem, communication between the counselor and the teacher is necessary. It is important that the teacher not be apprehensive about a counseling session. This can only be accomplished by communication between the counselor and the teacher. It is the counselor's responsibility to give as much information as appropriate to the teacher. This is both indicated and reasonable. When the communication is adequate and the teacher understands the group goals, he will usually be willing to cooperate and be ready to excuse the student from class.

In many cases the teachers have reasonable complaints against the counseling sessions, especially when youngsters may be borderline in their work. The teacher may think that a decrease in attendance will "push" the youngster into a failing bracket. This consideration has to be weighed against whether an under-achiever will benefit more from a group counseling session. This is something about which both the counselor and the teacher will have to be reasonable. The decision should be as objective as possible. Usually when difficulties are shared by all involved staff, a reasonable solution is reached.

Scheduling is a difficult problem in the secondary school and accentuates the seriousness of the group counseling program. Group counseling should not be done just for "kicks." It should be done, like everything else in the school setting, with a definite priority: that is, that which will be most important to facilitate the basic goals of the school, i.e., the processes of teaching and learning. When something else, such as routine class work, appears to take priority in achieving this basic goal, then that class should have priority. If, however, a counseling session would benefit the child most in the overall achievement of these goals, then the counseling session should take priority. These are professional decisions which both the counselors and the teachers have to be cognizant of and willing to work out.

The adolescent has characteristics peculiar to himself. He is older and more mature than his elementary school counterpart. He is not as apt to take a suggestion, or even an order, as willingly as does an elementary school child. It is important that the counselor not put the adolescent in an embarrassing situation by giving a suggestion or an order that cannot be reasonably (or will not be reasonably) carried out. This is neither good for the stature and position of the counselor nor the well-being and growth of the student. In the army there is a significant saying that an officer should not give orders unless that officer is particularly sure they will be carried out. This, of course, is true of the adolescent. If he is testing and looking for more direction, the counselor should make sure that what he decides to do in order to meet the youngster's needs is something that the counselor is able to handle. Otherwise, the youngster will continue to act up until the counselor, or somebody else, gives him the effective direction necessary.

The average adolescent does not like to be pushed. The counselor must be patient. The leader with experience knows that it is much easier to accomplish something with adolescents if he first presents the ideas so that they can readily accept and incorporate it as part of the ideas that they have already considered. Adolescents do not like to be called children, especially in the early adolescent years. Some adolescents are quite sensitive about this. They will accept a challenge with a great deal of enthusiasm. They resent it when anyone, either their peers or the adults, hints that they may be "chicken."

Adolescents are an active, enthusiastic group with which the counselor must be patient and recognize that he cannot change, alter, or influence their personalities or cultural background in one session. Perhaps the most significant factor is that with adolescents, one must be frank and sincere. If the counselor attempts to "bluff" his way with an adolescent, he may not be able to readily develop a cohesive group effect (regardless of his technical knowledge).

## SUGGESTED READINGS

Akos, Patrick. (Jun 2000). Building Empathic Skills in Elementary School Children through Group Work. Journal for Specialists in Group Work. v25 n2 p214-23.

Baggerly, Jennifer; Borkowski, Tammilyn. (Dec 2004). Applying the ASCA National Model to Elementary School Students Who Are Homeless: A Case Study. Professional School Counseling. v8 n2 p116.

Barrett, P. (1998). Evaluation of cognitive-behavioral group treatments for childhood anxiety disorders. Journal of Clinical Child Psychology. 27, 459-468.

Brantley, Lenore S.; And Others. (Dec 1996). Transforming Acting-out Behavior: A Group Counseling Program for Inner-city Elementary School Pupils. Elementary School Guidance & Counseling. v31 n2 p96-105.

Brown, Beverly M. (Mar 1997). Psychoeducation Group Work. Counseling and Human Development. v29 n7 p1-14.

Coppock, Martha W. (Dec 1993). Small Group Plan for Improving Friendships and Self-Esteem. Elementary School Guidance and Counseling. v28 n2 p152-54.

Cox, Julie Elizabeth Jonson. (Dec 1994). Self-Care in the Classroom for Children with Chronic Illness: A Case Study of a Student with Cystic Fibrosis. Elementary School Guidance and Counseling. v29 n2 p121-28.

Dennison, Susan T. (1998). Activities for Adolescents in Therapy: A Handbook of Facilitating Guidelines and Planning Ideas for Group Therapy With Troubled Adolescents. 2nd ed. Charles Thomas.

Ergene, Tuncay. (Aug 2003). Effective Interventions on Test Anxiety Reduction: A Meta-Analysis. School Psychology International. v24 n3 p313-28.

Flannery-Schroeder, E., and P. Kendall. (2000). Group and individual cognitive behavioral treatments for youth with anxiety disorders: A randomized clinical trial. Cognitive Therapy Res. 24, 251-78.

Gardner, Richard A. (1999). Individual and Group Therapy and Work With Parents in Adolescent Psychotherapy. Jason Aronson: Northvale, N.J.

Grant, Debra S. and Irving H. Berkovitz. (Mar. 1999). Values of long-term group Counseling in middle and high schools. Journal of Child and Adolescent Group Therapy. 9(1), 17-25.

Guth, Lorraine J.; McDonnell, Kelly A. (Mar 2004). Designing Class Activities to Meet Specific Core Training Competencies: A Developmental Approach. Journal for Specialists in Group Work. v29 n1 p97-111.

Hagborg, Winston J. (May 1993) Middle-School Student Satisfaction with Group Counseling: An Initial Study. Journal for Specialists in Group Work. v18 n2 p80-85.

Hall, Kimberly R. ( Sep 2006). Solving Problems Together: A Psychoeducational Group Model for Victims of Bullies. Journal for Specialists in Group Work. v31 n3 p201-217.

Hayward, C., et. Al. (2000). Cognitive behavioral group therapy for female socially phobic adolescents: results of a pilot study. Journal of the American Academy of Child and Adolescent Psychiatry. 39, 721-26.

Herring, Roger D.; Runlon, Keith B. (Oct 1994). Counseling Ethnic Children and Youth from an Adlerian Perspective. Journal of Multicultural Counseling and Development. v22 n4 p215-26.

Kramer, Laurie; Radney, Chad. (Jul 1997). Improving Sibling Relationships among Young Children: A Social Skills Training Model. Family Relations. v46 n3 p237-46.

Mathias, Carlabeth E. (Feb 1992). Touching the Lives of Children: Consultative Interventions That Work. Elementary School Guidance and Counseling. v26 n3 p190-201.

McClure, Bud A.; And Others. (Mar 1992). Conflict within a Children's Group: Suggestions for Facilitating Its Expression and Resolution Strategies. School Counselor. v39 n4 p268-72.

McNair, Robert; Arman, John F. (Apr 2000). A Small Group Model for Working with Elementary School Children of Alcoholics. Professional School Counseling. v3 n4 p290-93.

Mehaffey, Joyce I.; Sandberg, Siv Kristine (Sep 1992). Conducting Social Skills Training Groups with Elementary School Children. School Counselor. v40 n1 p61-67.

Nelson, Ron; Mather, Sarup. (Fall 1997). Friends as Counselors: A Three-Step Group Counseling Intervention. Reaching Today's Youth: The Community Circle of Caring Journal. v2 n1 p46-49.

Nufrio, Randald. (1988). Elementary counseling: a program model. 16 p.

O'Dell, Frank L.; And Others. (Nov 1994). The Boost Club: A Program for At-Risk Third-and Fourth Grade Students. Journal for Specialists in Group Work. v19 n4 p227-31.

Page, Richard C.; Chandler, Joyce. (Jul 1994). Effects of Group Counseling on Ninth Grade At-Risk Students. Journal of Mental Health Counseling. v16 n3 p340-51.

Phillips, Theodore M.; Phillips Patricia. (May 1992). Structured Groups for High School Students: A Case Study of One District's Program. School Counselor. v39 n5 p390-93.

Rathvon, Natalie Wilson. (Mar 1991). Effects of a Guidance Unit in Two Formats on the Examination Performance of Underachieving Middle School Students. School Counselor. v38 n4 p294-304.

Reeder, Jan, Cordelia Douzenis, and James J. Bergin. (Dec. 1997). The effects of small group counseling on the racial attitudes of second grade students. Professional School Counseling. 1(2), 15-18.

Ripley, Vivian and Gary E. Goodnough. (Oct. 2001). Planning and implementing group counseling in a high school. Professional School Counseling. 5(1), 62-65.

Schectman, Zipora. (Summer 2002). Child group psychotherapy in the school at the threshold of a new millennium. Journal of Counseling & Development. 80(3), 293-300.

Schectman, Zipora. (Oct 1993). School Adjustment and Small-Group Therapy: An Israeli Study. Journal of Counseling and Development. v71 n4 p77-81.

Schectman, Zipora. (Jul 1996). Does Self-Disclosure in Friendship Increase Following Group Counseling/Therapy? A Different Case for Boys and Girls. v35 n1 p123-30.

Schmidt, John J. (2003). Counseling in Schools: Essential Services and Comprehensive Programs. Allyn and Bacon: Boston.

Shapiro, J.L., L.S. Peltz, and Bernadette Shapiro. (1999). Brief Group Treatment: Practical Training for Therapists and Counselors. Allyn and Bacon: Pacific Grove, CA.

Smead, Rosemarie. (2000). Skills for Living: Group Counseling Activities for Young Adolescents. Research Press: Champaign, IL.

Stewart, J., R. McKay, and R. Robichaud. (1995). Group counseling elementary school children who use aggressive behaviors. Guidance and Counseling. 11, 12-15.

Timmer, David F. (Jul 1995). Group Support for Teenagers with Attention Deficit Hyperactivity Disorder. Social Work in Education. v17 n3 p194-97.

Tomori, B. 1995. Small group counseling at the elementary level: theory into practice. Guidance and Counseling. 10(3), 24-30.

Webb, Linda D. and Robert D. Myrick. (Dec. 2003). A group counseling intervention for children with attention deficit hyperactivity disorder. Professional School Counseling. 7(2), 108-16.

# CHAPTER VIII

## *GROUP COUNSELING AS AN ADJUNCT TO THE TEACHER*

It is not uncommon to find within a particular school or school system a definite hiatus between the counselor and the teacher. Why this occurs is often difficult to determine, but it is one of the things that may keep the counselor from doing her job effectively. Part of the counselor's job is to be an important adjunct to the teacher, for the teacher is the key to the success or failure of the teaching program. Everything that the school system does, whether it is at an administrative or counselor level, must be directed toward facilitating the job of the classroom teacher. The more progressive and modern school systems utilize their counselors in efficient and applicable ways to achieve this goal.

The hiatus between the counselor and the teacher often revolves around the fact that the counselor who has been classically trained works on a one-to-one basis, whereas the administrator and the classroom teacher have to be oriented to group problems. The administrator is concerned with the school as a unit. The classroom teacher is concerned with twenty-five to thirty-five different youngsters who together form a group. A fascinating phenomenon occurs when the counselor is trained in group process and starts doing group work. Teachers who did not discuss classroom problems with the counselor start approaching the counselor to discuss classroom problems rather than just discussing the problems of individual students. Administrators start sharing responsibilities with the counselor when previously the counselor was not invited to participate.

The communication gap between the counselor and the rest of the school faculty is bridged by a common understanding and common sharing of group difficulties. There are probably two reasons for this phenomenon. The administrators and teachers recognize the value of the counselor by the group work she is doing, and the counselor herself recognizes her value to the school by the experience she has had working in groups. She starts to visualize innovative programs that can be utilized by the school and school system in a significant way that previously she had neither the techniques nor the opportunity to exploit. The counselor too often, especially when using the classical one-to-one approach in her work, has felt isolated in the school system. The counselor himself has helped to foster this hiatus between the counselor and teacher because she has never felt part of the general routine. Everyone else is concerned with group work except the counselor. When this happens she cannot share with the rest of the school staff the same problems and similar experiences.

When a counselor works with a child on a one-to-one basis, she usually relates one-to-one experiences to the teacher. When the counselor is able to work with the child not only on a one-to-one basis but also on a one-to-group basis, she is able to relate group experiences which can be correlated with classroom behavior.

Both the counselor and teacher should be oriented to the classroom as a unit, or as a group. Both have to recognize that sometimes the most efficient way to "reach" the child is through a group approach. The child who thinks she is part of a cohesive unit and an integral member of a group or classroom is apt to communicate more spontaneously. The child does not feel isolated; she is sharing an experience with other peers as an active participant. The counselor (and the teacher) who is not oriented to group work can isolate herself as a non-participant in the overall teaching program.

In order to defend herself, the counselor may say that counseling is not teaching. It is a separate phenomenon and a separate entity.

This is a battle of dogma which has no place in the school system. A school system has to be, by its very definition, an educational phenomenon. There are many ways to define education, and the definitions of education have been manifold. The author defines education very succinctly as the processes of teaching and learning. Any definition beyond this basic fact is perhaps important but has to be at least partially superfluous. If what is done within the school system is not oriented to facilitating the basic processes of teaching and learning, then it should be considered secondary.

One of the difficulties that often occurs is that programs are designed which are very good and worthwhile but the ultimate step is never taken to correlate the program to the educational process. The counselors frequently fall into this trap. In order to be effective the counselors should consider themselves a basic adjunct to the entire school program. They cannot, by defense or any other reason, separate themselves from the basic goals of education. When the counselor is able to recognize her part in the basic teaching and learning processes, she excavates areas of opportunity and innovation that perhaps she has never had. When the counselor is willing to utilize techniques such as group counseling along with the basic one-to-one counseling technique, then she is able to enhance the overall educational process that the entire system unit is concerned with: that is, the student, teacher, counselor, and administrator.

The counselor must review the basic goals of the institution that she is serving. Everything she does must be geared toward achieving these goals. When the counselor starts working with a group of youngsters, one of the first things that she should do is to define the goals that she would like to accomplish with the group with which she is working. The counselor in the school system has to do the same thing as does everyone else. She should first define goals of the institution and then try to define her role in the institutional structure. The counselor can then examine if her job is relevant to the basic goals. In most cases, this is fairly clear. When it is not clear, then it means the leadership of the institution, or the particular department that is involved, must redefine its position so that all the members of the department can see what their roles are.

When this review brings about differences in theory and/or defending of jobs or positions, it means that everyone concerned either has lost sight of the basic goals of the institution and/or does not have the techniques to help achieve the goals. This does occur occasionally because of the evolution of changing leadership, new techniques, new concepts, and new institutional goals. It is the responsibility of the respective members of that department to define what their needs are, what techniques are needed, and what areas have to be investigated further. They should then redefine their roles according to new goals, needs, and demands of the institution and new techniques that may be required. When this is done there is little room for questioning about what a person should or should not do. Practical aspects of meeting the needs of the institution are met in some reasonable way. The change that is brought about will help achieve the basic goals. Roles are redefined and the groundwork is laid for an opportunity to develop the techniques necessary for achieving those goals. This cannot be done in isolation. The counselor cannot define her role by isolating herself from the faculty of a particular school or school system. The counselor can only define her role after she reviews the roles of administrators and teachers. The counselor should evaluate and ask what their needs are as they see it and what their needs will be in the next five to six years. In this way she can design her program in a way that will meet the needs not only of the counselor corps, but also of the entire school system. When direct communication is established and everyone is working together as a team, sharing ideas with one another and trying to investigate each other's needs, then a more meaningful and innovative program can be established.

A counselor's job is to facilitate the basic goals of the school, which are the processes of teaching and learning. Sometimes the role of the counselor will be that of teaching. Occasionally there will be a hazy line differentiating counseling and teaching. The counselor should be flexible enough to participate in areas and overlap in areas that she has previously considered forbidden ground. The counselor should not be afraid of treading on the perimeter of the teacher's domain and the teacher should not hesitate to tread in the counselor's province. They should be willing to overlap their programs so that there will be a cohesive overall effect that will promote the process of teaching and learning.

Both the counselors and teachers should share techniques that will help each other and, most important of all, will help the children. For example, one project that has been developed is for the reading teacher and counselor to work together with groups of remedial readers who are reading below grade level. These youngsters often need to develop socialization and verbalization skills. The counselor works with the youngsters, giving them an opportunity to interact in small groups. The overall program is directed toward developing the socialization and communication skills which are necessary in a good remedial program. The reading teacher works specifically in the areas of reading but at the same time develops group techniques (shared by the counselor) to use within her reading classes. The counselor becomes a direct adjunct to the reading teacher, facilitating her program. The teacher eventually incorporates the group counseling skills into her regular lesson plan. The counselor can then withdraw.

The classical approach that the group counselor often uses to help the teacher is to work with a group of youngsters from her class who seem to be having either behavior or learning problems. The counseling sessions are oriented to the apparent needs of the youngsters. (The counselor may elect to work with the entire class.)

## THE LEARNING PROCESS

There are certain factors which do influence how the student performs and that appear to influence how much the student learns. These factors are little discussed but comprise an area in which the group counselor can be a direct adjunct to the teachers in stimulating the students' interest, motivation, and performance.

## THE NOVELTY EFFECT

The first factor is the "novelty effect." The novelty effect is usually characterized by the introduction of something new or novel to the student. It may be gadgets or audio-visual equipment. It may be a new idea or concept. It may be a new approach or technique in the classroom. It may be the introduction of a learning game, or a trip to the museum. When utilized in a unique way, the novelty effect can significantly influence the student's performance, especially when introduced in an otherwise routine curriculum. The teacher, for example, can ask a colleague who may teach a different subject to present her views or supplement the discussion. A history teacher might present a historical perspective in a literature course. A counselor may talk about behavior in a biology class. An administrator may reflect on the overall school system in relation to community activity.

The counselor can be very effective in helping to achieve a novelty effect. When the counselor coordinates with the classroom teachers and the administrator, she has the opportunity to inject new ideas or projects for a particular week, semester, or year. For example, a Baltimore high school utilized a novelty effect by having a goal-directed concentration on career planning. They called the project "Operation JEEP" (Job Entry Education Program). It was well planned with coordination of every segment of the school: that is, administrator, teacher, counselor, student, and maintenance crew. A novelty effect such as "JEEP" can stimulate interest in the classroom as well as in student councils and various other group activities. It gives the youngsters an opportunity to plan, create, and accept responsibility in many different ways.

## THE EXPECTANCY EFFECT

Another basic factor in learning is the "expectancy effect." This is little understood but seems to depend on the educator's anticipation and expectancy of the student's performance. When the educator expects a student to perform in a certain way (i.e., increased or decreased performance) the anticipated response is often fulfilled. This is apparent with above-average children as well as under-achievers and potential dropouts.

The author has often noted this phenomenon in the schools. Special curriculum under-achieving youngsters often do not perform as well as they are potentially capable because of an expectancy by the teachers and administration involved that these youngsters are not capable of performing better. The faculty does not expect them to perform well and they do not. The schools are reinforcing (either directly or indirectly) the poor performance of their students. If a counselor who works with youngsters from the inner city anticipates that these students will not be able to perform, or are not capable of keeping up with the routine middle-class academic program, then, in fact, these youngsters will not respond as well as they might. It has not been uncommon to occasionally find innovative inner-city school programs shelved because the sponsors felt that the youngsters would not be able to participate.

It is important that school officials not make the same mistakes that many of their predecessors have made in the past. The school staff must discard the impression that just because a child is not performing as well as she should (because of social, cultural, or emotional deprivation), she is "lost." Inner-city children who are capable can catch up and perform comparable with their peers who live in the perimeter of the city (provided that they are given the right remedial programs). It has also been noted that above-average youngsters (who were put in groups because they *were* above average) performed far beyond expectation because it was anticipated that they were above average and would do well, and they did.

Group counselors have been helpful by demonstrating that a teacher can program (and anticipate) the children's increased performance. Students will perform better when given the opportunity and the reinforcement that comes with success and recognition. In school systems where there has been effective coordination between services, group counselors have been successful in helping teachers to design programs that have enhanced the expectancy effect.

## THE SOCIALIZATION EFFECT

Another basic factor in learning is the socialization effect. (This is similar to the "Hawthorne Effect.") Students appear to perform better because they have the opportunity for increased socialization and acceptance by the leader. Just the fact that the group leader has shown some interest appears to increase the youngster's performance.

The effect of being accepted by the educator and the opportunity to interact, even minimally, in a well-structured and organized group cannot be underestimated. It may be sufficient for the student to simply attend the group with minimal participation. The counselor who demonstrates good leadership by directing all the events in the group, who is personally interested and feels comfortable in working with the students, usually enhances the socialization effect.

What the essential biological and psychological factors are (in the socialization effect) is still a moot question. Basically, humans are social animals. Humans need constant interaction with the environment and his fellow humans in order to emotionally and perhaps biologically develop and continue to maintain his basic faculties to an optimum level of performance. When socialization is enhanced, youngsters are often more alert and creative. The socialization effect appears to reinforce their performance in the learning situation.

Group counseling is one of the techniques that stimulate the socialization processes necessary to develop verbalization and communication skills. It has been recognized in programs like "Head Start" and "Higher Horizons" that youngsters need continual social nourishment. When a person is anemic the physician gives her iron therapy. Her blood level then increases to normal levels; but in order to maintain normal levels, the individual must have a minimum supply of iron ingestion or six months later she is going to become anemic again. This analogy is true of social stimulation. If a youngster is given the right social environment and stimulation, her social performance will improve. However, the same type of environment has to be maintained or the youngster will have a tendency to withdraw, become passive, and not participate in the classroom.

Occasionally, all that is necessary is for the teacher to understand that the youngster may have well-developed social skills but she is not able to adapt to the classroom which is foreign to her. When the teacher uses different techniques, including a group approach technique, these same youngsters, with minimal stimulation, will often respond. It is not uncommon to hear youngsters say that the way they relate to each other affects the way they learn. The same social skills necessary for them to relate to their peers are necessary to relate to the teacher and each other in the learning process. The youngsters in group counseling sessions often say that they want an opportunity to think verbally within the class. Verbalizing one's thoughts reinforces the learning process. The group counseling technique gives the educator an opportunity to stimulate a frank and open discussion with the youngsters.

Group counseling also gives the educator an ideal opportunity to accept almost anything appropriate that the youngster says. In teaching, this can be important. The educator should encourage discussion. Once the student feels accepted with reasonable guidelines, she is willing to test his ideas with others. Without the basic feeling of acceptance, the students may receive the didactic information that is delivered but often do not feel secure enough to test that information and utilize it in original or different ways than the context in which it was delivered.

Group counseling offers the educator the opportunity to be flexible. When there is spontaneous group interaction, the youngsters share with the teacher what they like and do not like, what methods and projects they seem to enjoy and what they do not. The teacher who is able to be flexible and build into her lesson plans flexibility of curriculum and methodology is the teacher who is usually able to stimulate and interest her students.

The psychological and biological implications of these three basic effects (that is, the novelty effect, the expectancy effect, and the socialization effect) is still a moot question. Why and how they function is still not completely understood, but that they are influential is evident. The counselor can coordinate her activities with those of the teacher to enhance these basic factors that do influence the learning process.

## WORKING WITH INEXPERIENCED TEACHERS

One of the difficulties that the new teacher has is that the administrative staff often expects her (regardless of her training) to be proficient in both subjects and techniques when she enters the classroom. Most administrators would deny this but at the same time would corroborate that their in-service training program for new teachers is not sufficient.

Unfortunately, in many of our large urban school systems, a significant percentage of teachers have not completed formal training. They are caught in the quandary of not knowing what they are supposed to know. The experienced teacher knows what she can handle and what she is not expected to handle, what the school is capable of undertaking and what it is not, where the school system as an organization is deficient and where it is not. As a result, the experienced teacher knows when to ask for help. She knows when a gripe is legitimate and when it is not.

The knowledge of what one should know (and should not know) is important. Many new teachers, because of their inexperience and/or because they have not had the training, do not know what to complain about and what not to complain about. What is even worse, when the inexperienced teacher is put with a difficult class, she does not know whether she is supposed to be able to handle that class. The lack of knowledge of what one is supposed to know is an inhibiting factor for the teacher and a significant obstacle to school innovation; it is one of the factors that contributes to the rigidity of the school system.

The group counselor can be particularly effective in working with new teachers. When she works with them in groups, she can relate new techniques and also give them an opportunity to share with each other difficulties that they are having. What may be just as important is that they have an opportunity to share with experienced teachers common problems that both they and their experienced colleagues are having. This should not be underestimated. The author has never organized a training seminar for teachers in which an inexperienced teacher has not said, "It certainly is a relief to know that these older, experienced teachers who have been around for a long time are having the same troubles that I am." When the new teacher is kept isolated from her peers and is not given an opportunity to sit together in "bull sessions" and/or training sessions to share her experiences (and the experience of others), she encounters unnecessary frustration and trouble. What is even worse the new teacher may be allowed to develop poor techniques.

The new classroom teacher is usually concerned with how to control the class in an effective way so that she can teach. Unfortunately, this has often been left to the teacher's intuition. She has been well prepared to plan a lesson. The teacher is already enthusiastic, but she may not have received effective training in class control. This, of course, is a basic part of a teaching program. Without effective organization, the school system might as well go out of business. Without controls, the youngsters will feel insecure and will act out until they get some kind of direction. Usually the direction they receive (when they act out) is an authoritarian, disciplined type of action that is not conducive to developing the best learning or teaching climate.

One program that has been effective is to organize training groups of new teachers (with support from experienced teachers who are willing to participate) prior to the beginning of the school year. Practical techniques of control and theoretical concepts of group dynamics that would be helpful for effective classroom learning should be given to the new teacher prior to student admission. The new teacher should anticipate what may happen in her class before the first student enters the room.

How the new teacher feels will be reflected in the students. If she is anxious, the kids will probably be anxious. If she feels comfortable, the kids will probably feel comfortable. But if the teacher is uncomfortable, she should probably share this with the youngsters. For example: "I am new at this job and will need your support." When the new teacher is able to do this (which may or may not be necessary) it indicates to the kids that the teacher is comfortable enough to share this particular information with them. When the new teacher is, in fact, able to share this information, she usually is comfortable enough to control her class.

On the first school day the teacher should be more direct with the youngsters. For example, she should tell them where to sit and what to do. The teacher should have a definite program outlined so that she can organize and start "shaping" the youngsters in the classroom behavior which she wants to develop. It is generally better if the teacher has prepared simple rules for the class. She should introduce these rules in the first class meeting. These may be developed around placement of books, storage of clothes, rules for going to the lavatory, homework assignments, etc.

The experienced teacher will often share the responsibility for the formulation of classroom rules with the youngsters. For example, she may ask the students, "How do you think we should run a classroom? What do you think should be the do's and don'ts in the classroom?" The experienced teacher may not outline any rules initially, but may simply ask the class members how they think the class should be organized. Invariably the students will enumerate all the rules that the teacher would have outlined. If the youngsters do this themselves, then the teacher is delivering the message that (1) there will be at least a minimal amount of organization and discipline within the classroom, and (2) she anticipates sharing this responsibility with the students.

The more advanced a class is, the more spontaneous the students will be. The more comfortable the youngsters feel, the more they are able to interact with each other and with the teacher in a favorable way. Groups in general will usually test a new leader in some way. Sooner or later the teacher will have to meet this test so that the students know that she does have things under control. If she does not recognize the little things that they will do initially, they may become more troublesome at a later date.

During the first week the counselor and administrator should give recognizable support to the new teachers. They should be "walking the halls," occasionally dropping in to say "hello" to the new class. The senior staff should inform the new teachers that at any time they have any questions about the general school routine, curricula, students, or control of the class, they are available. In fact, they should make themselves available in an organized way. They should meet frequently with the new teachers in small groups so that the teachers have an opportunity to share with the senior leadership the difficulties they are having.

If the counselor and administrator make themselves available, control of the school and of the classrooms will be significantly enhanced. The philosophy of the administrator that a new teacher is on her own, that she has to sink or swim, is a philosophy that is as archaic as the quill pen and has no place in a modern school system. The availability of help should be basic. It should be encouraged not only because it offers the new teacher techniques to resolve particular problems, but also because it decreases the task of the administrator. Most new teachers, when they have an opportunity to get together in groups and know that support is readily available any time they need it, will feel comfortable enough to handle most of their classroom problems themselves. It is when there has been no orientation that the teachers feel isolated and think that they do not have an opportunity to communicate with their administrators and counselors. It is the "isolated teacher" who is apt to get into the most difficulty and who will act out herself until she gets the needed support from the administrator or

It is not uncommon for the inexperienced teacher to ask about some irrelevant school routine when, in fact, she may be asking for a technique that will help her control the class.

When the counselor is oriented to doing group work, the inexperienced teacher frequently comes to her for information about how to be more effective in the classroom. Communication and direction are as necessary for inexperienced teachers (and for the entire faculty) as they are for any small group counseling program with students.

It is not uncommon for administrators and counselors to indicate that there is a lack of response on the part of the faculty, that they do not want to participate in teaching seminars; "they just want to come late and leave early." When this happens it is not due to a lack of sincerity on the part of the staff. It is usually due to the lack of support that the teacher has been getting. When the teachers get the support necessary from both the administrator and counselor corps, when they are secure in their jobs and think that they know how to do their jobs, and when they are given the techniques that allow them to do their jobs, they usually show a significant degree of enthusiasm, sincerity, and effectiveness.

Teachers as a group are no different than students as a group. They need good leadership. Their performance is not only a reflection of how they are trained, but also is a reflection of the school leadership. If the teachers present poorly trained, with little insight into the practical techniques of teaching and little understanding of the learning process, then the good administrator and/or counselor will program her teaching seminars at a level that meets the needs of the teachers as they present, not as she would wish them to be. The teacher who is a so-called "underachiever" should be supervised just as the student who is an under-achiever. The leader must meet the group at the level of performance at which the group is operating, then program the teaching seminars so that the teachers will have the techniques to reach the goals that the leader (administrator) and the group (the school system) have established.

It is particularly important for the counselor and the administrator to share with the teacher not only the guidelines for creating spontaneity within her classroom (in an organized way) but also to share with her the experience that the students may be having in group counseling sessions. This is essential because the students often become more spontaneous in group counseling sessions and then return to the classroom and attempt to be original in their ideas and spontaneous in their responses. If the class is run as a non-group-oriented class with little spontaneous interaction, then the youngster may be considered belligerent, out of order, or acting up. This is especially important with the under-achiever whose performance starts improving. All of us orient ourselves to people and adapt to each other in certain ways. If we are used to some youngsters not performing particularly well, we may misjudge improved performance for one of negative performance.

## THE TEACHER WORKING WITH AIDES

Most classrooms today have too many students. Because of the influence of many factors, including the Head Start program, there has been a significant "movement" throughout the country to increase and utilize the number of aides in the classroom. The Head Start program has recommended fifteen children with one teacher and one aide. This essentially amounts to two small groups of approximately eight each. This reflects the optimum group size for intense group interaction, which probably is the best number to develop socialization and communication skills. The same attempt is now being transferred to post-kindergarten levels, that is, other elementary school grades.

One of the things that should be done to help the teacher, both with personnel and techniques, is to develop small group skills for the class. When this is accomplished and the teacher and the assistants or aides are able to utilize small group interaction within the classroom, coupled with the classical didactic lecture, the performance of the youngsters and the quality of their education will be enhanced.

In order to increase the efficiency of the teacher-aide program, both the teachers and the aides should have close supervision. Group counseling sessions lend themselves particularly well to this type of training program. Bringing the aides together in a unit by themselves to share their own frustrations, problems, questions, and ideas can be helpful. At the same time meeting with the teachers who have aides will accomplish the same thing.

Combination groups of teachers and aides will give a good cross-fertilization of ideas and also relieves some of the questions and perhaps feelings of discomfort that each may share. When teacher aide programs are initiated, the administration should do as much as possible to develop training models for both teachers and their aides. This should be done to increase the efficiency of both groups and to continue to develop and investigate techniques within the classroom that might be helpful in facilitating the basic processes of teaching and learning. An inexperienced aide who has not had formal training may present practical ideas that may help considerably in the overall program. This has been noted. Aides have accepted significant responsibility for the teaching program and have innovated and contributed in significant ways.

It is important for the administrative staff in teacher aides programs to help to define the roles of both the teachers and the aides. Too much responsibility too fast can weaken the overall effect. Some teachers may not be as adept at training a less-qualified person. The basic responsibility for the teachers and the aides is and always will rest with the administrator. It is up to the principal to design her program in a way that will meet the needs of the aides and the needs of the teachers.

The group counseling technique can offer a significant tool in developing effective teacher aide programs. There should be "built-in flexibility" whereby what is anticipated of the teachers' aides initially may be completely reversed, subtracted, added to, or altered within the course of the first year of operation. It does not matter where the program is initiated as long as the leader of the program recognizes that she has the option of flexibility. When the leader is willing to be flexible, then she is able to develop a program to meet the needs of her school as well as the needs of the teachers and teacher aides who are involved.

## SUGGESTED READINGS

Anderson, Lorin W. (2001). Teacher Peer Assistance and Review: A Practical Guide for Teachers and Administrators. Corwin (Sage): Thousand Oaks, CA.

Bieschke, Kathleen J.; And Others. (Sept 1996). Training Group Counselors: The Process Observer Method. Journal for Specialists in Group Work. v21 n3 p181-86.

Branco, Madeleine. (Jul-Aug 1991). Concern Circles. Learning. v20 n1 p56, 60.

Dreikurs, Rudolf, Bernice Bronia Grunwald, and Floy C. Pepper. (1998). Maintaining Sanity in the Classroom. 2$^{nd}$ ed. Accelerated Development (Taylor and Francis): Philadelphia.

Erwin, Wesley J.; Toth, Paul L. (Summer 1998). Applying Skill-Based Curriculum to Teach Feedback in Groups: An Evaluation Study. Journal of Counseling & Development. v76 n3 p294-301.

Furr, Susan R. (Mar 2000). Structuring the Group Experience: A Format for designing Psychoeducational Groups. Journal for Specialists in Group Work. v25 n1 p29-49.

Gordon, Thomas, and Noel Birch. (2003). Teacher Effectiveness Training: The Program Proven to Help Teachers Bring Out the Best in Students of All Ages. Three Rivers: CA.

Hulse-Killacky, Diana. (Sep 1996). Using the Classroom as a Group to Integrate Knowledge, Skills, and Supervised Practice. Journal for Specialists in Group Work. v21 n3 p163-68.

Moracco, John C.; McFadden, Hope. (May 1982). The Counselor's Role in Reducing Teacher Stress. Personnel and Guidance Journal. v60 n9 p549-52.

Riva, Maria T.; Korinek, Lauri. (Mar 2004). Teaching Group Work: Modeling Group Leader and Member Behaviors in the Classroom to Demonstrate Group Theory. <u>Journal for Specialists in Group Work</u>. v29 n1 p55-63.

Robinson, Bonnie A.; Elias, Maurice J. (1993). Stabilizing Classroom-Based Group Interventions: Guidelines for Special Services Providers and Consultants. <u>Special Services in the Schools</u>. v8 n1 p159-77.

Rosenthal, Robert, and Lenore Jacobson. (2003). <u>Pygmalion in the Classroom</u>: Teacher Expectation and Pupil's Intellectual Development. Crown House.

Schmuck, Richard A. and Patricia A. Schmuck. (2000). <u>Group Processes in the Classroom</u>. 8<sup>th</sup> ed. McGraw-Hill.

Sprintball, N., E. Gerler, and J. Hall. (1992). Peer helping: counselors and teachers as facilitators. <u>Peer Facilitator</u> Q. 9(4), 11-15.

Sullivan, Jeremy R.; Wright, Nilah. (Jun 2002). The Collaborative Group Counseling Referral Process: Description and Teacher Evaluation. <u>Professional School Counseling</u>. v5 n5 p366-68.

Theodore, Lea A.; Bray, Melissa A.; Kehle, Thomas J.; Jenson, William R. (May-Jun 2001). Randomization of Group Contingencies and Reinforcers to Reduce Classroom Disruptive Behavior. <u>Journal of School Psychology</u>. v39 n3 p267-77.

Trubowitz, Sidney and Maureen Picard Robins. (2003). <u>The Good Teacher Mentor: Setting the Standard for Support and Success</u>. Teachers College Press: New York.

Velsor, Patricia Van. (Mar 2004). Training for Successful Group Work with Children: "What" and "How" to Teach. <u>Journal for Specialists in Group Work</u>. v29 n1 p137-146.

Wasielewski, Raquel A.; Scruggs, Martha Y.; Scott, Carl W. (Mar 1997). Student Groups Conducted by Teachers: The Teachers as Counselors (TAC) Program. Journal for Specialists in Group Work. v22 n1 p43-51.

Zirpoli, Thomas J. and Kristine J. Melloy. (2001). Behavior Management: Applications For Teachers. Merrill: Upper Saddle River, N.J.

# CHAPTER IX

## *GROUP COUNSELING AS AN ADJUNCT TO THE ADMINISTRATOR*

The most important member of a group is its leader. The most important and influential member of a school is its principal. He administers the school, helps to formulate student goals, and influences school attitude. If a program in the school is not successful, it can be due to different reasons including the lack of student participation, lack of qualified faculty, and the influence of the neighborhood. If a school program is successful, then that success is often due totally or at least partially to the chief administrator.

Many research teams have found that their programs cannot be successful without the obvious approval and involvement of the administrator. Educators occasionally think that they should initiate new programs "with or without" the consent of the principal. This is impossible. The first obligation of the school staff is to support the administrator in the tasks in which he would like them to participate.

There are administrators who do not efficiently utilize their staff. They may isolate teachers instead of uniting them. Administrators who do organize their staff for effective group work have found their general program enhanced. Every leader should periodically review his group techniques in order to ensure the type of group interaction which is necessary to stimulate professional progress, interest, and academic achievement of his staff.

## GROUP WORK WITH TEACHERS

One of the reasons for the lack of innovation in many public schools is the resistance of administrators to sit down, discuss, and work with teachers in small (and large) groups. Administrators have no difficulty in holding a staff conference or faculty meeting. They handle a "formal meeting" with little trouble; but they hesitate to allow spontaneous discussion. This is frequent in schools with large faculties and is probably an important factor in inhibiting the spontaneity of the staff.

There are probably several reasons that an administrator may hesitate to encourage spontaneous discussion in his staff. In many cases the administrator does not have the experience (or training) to do group work that emphasizes interaction and discussion. Part of the hesitation may be the fear of losing control (or direction) of the group members. There may be some validity to this concern. Many administrators have had no formal training for their jobs. Many teachers are not fully trained or accredited. Both are often frustrated and occasionally angry.

The administrator, as leader of the school, has to keep the school functioning as efficiently as possible. When the teachers are given an opportunity to get together and ventilate, which they should have the opportunity to do, the administrator must recognize that ventilation of anger and perhaps frustration if it comes (and it often does not come) is short-lived.

Teachers are often isolated and may recognize that they are not getting the support that they should in the classroom. There may be a negative attitude toward the complexity of the job. Coupled with this is the urgent need to move forward at a rapid rate which is being stimulated by the teachers' unions and the dedicated young teachers who are entering the teacher corps. It is important that teachers are not isolated. They should feel that their administrator is "backing them up" and is willing to share educational issues with them as well as with the parents of the children they teach.

## PRACTICAL GROUP TECHNIQUES

The primary consideration for the administrator is not to react angrily against the retort of the teachers. The frustration the teachers have is usually not directed toward the principal personally but towards the school system in general. Teachers are frequently asking for more direction and involvement. When the administrator reflects on the teachers' anger as one of a group dynamic rather than as a personal affront, he usually responds and is able to handle the situation more effectively.

If the administrator is patient the teachers will begin to work together in a constructive way. He should not try to engage the teachers in a one-to-group battle about their frustrations. The administrator must recognize and share with them that many of the frustrations they have are real. The problems discussed should be oriented to the problems of the classroom teacher.

The administrator should offer the teachers the opportunity to get together and share their experiences. The entire faculty should have the opportunity to resolve together the difficulties that they may be having within their classrooms as well as to share the successful techniques that they may be using. The program should be geared to both the needs of the children and the needs of the teachers as they and the administrators observe them. When staff meetings are designed to meet the needs of the teachers, the response is usually quite favorable. This is hopefully translated in terms of the needs of the children, which can be academically interesting and offer the individual teacher significant professional satisfaction.

The primary consideration for the administrator is that the group will not usurp his authority. If the administrator is patient they will usually rally around him and will, in fact, support his program (Chapter III).

Teachers who are involved as group members should be given an opportunity to express themselves. The best groups are usually those in which the teachers take an active part and can formally share professional considerations with their colleagues. When the teachers can be active participants they become particularly interested in faculty meetings, and look forward to them, and the meetings are usually well attended.

The general rule, when things are especially difficult and the task frustrating (as the teaching situation often is), is to allow group members an opportunity to express themselves so they can offer suggestions that may improve the general school program. This will offer the teacher a chance to express what he thinks might be indicated to alleviate the situation. The general concepts of group work, as outlined earlier in the book, are as applicable to group work with teachers as they are with children. The same basic principles apply.

If the administrator is patient and does allow the group to express itself and does pass the test of leadership (Chapter IX), then the teachers will usually unite and help him to develop a constructive program.

It is a mistake for the administrator to think that because he may delegate group leadership to the counselor and/or the master teacher, this will suffice. In many cases it does not. The administrator must still participate in an active way with his staff and co-leaders. The administrator should initially participate in an active way, minimal as it may be, or the same effect is not facilitated.

It is very important that the administrator become actively involved with the teachers in groups. Often the delegation of these tasks to master teachers and counselors is not sufficient, especially if there has been a traditional hiatus in the school between the administrator and the teacher corps. At a later date, if he wants, the administrator can transfer the leadership to responsible people on his staff: i.e., master teachers, assistant administrators, and counselors. If the administrator wants to eventually withdraw, he can, but he should be the one to start the initial groups.

The administrator can initiate staff meetings with the vice principal, counselors, or master teachers as co-leaders when the group is first organized. He can then transfer the leadership to his co-leader. This will, in effect, have an overall favorable impact because he can easily visit the groups for short periods of time and maintain interest and stimulation via his brief presence.

Personal involvement in the initial phase by the administrators is important. Once effective programs have been established and the groups are working well, then the administrator can withdraw. The administrator should be careful that if he does delegate this job to others and he does, in fact, withdraw, he maintains significant interest and support. Otherwise the momentum of the groups will not be maintained. During the initial formation of these groups, the administrator should slowly transfer the responsibilities of the groups not only to the delegated leadership that is going to in fact represent him, but also to the group itself. It is not recommended that the administrator plan to withdraw. One of the difficulties with many of the school programs is that the administrator does not become involved enough.

When initiating in-service training programs for teachers, the level of performance of the teachers usually follows a general pattern. Initially the teachers may be resistant to the idea of group involvement, especially if the program is being initiated for the first time. If the topics selected are pertinent and meet their classroom needs, they usually become involved much quicker and are more enthusiastic. This enthusiasm usually lasts from one to four sessions. If novel ideas are not continually presented, the teachers' resistance will usually increase, especially if they are not seeing any results within the classroom. (The administrator should caution the teachers against any immediate change in behavior on the part of the students, who have been conditioned to respond in a given way.)

The teachers reach a plateau in which they are assimilating information but their performance both in the group and in the classroom is relatively stable. As they test, try, and assimilate the new ideas that they have discussed, there is usually another increase in level of performance. It is at this point that a new plateau is reached and the administrator may face his greatest resistance. Teachers recognize that in order to do effective work in the classroom, they may have to do significantly more than they have been doing. Teaching is hard work. The administrator has to be patient and skilled in helping the teachers, both within the group discussion and within the classroom, in order to bring about any successful change.

It is often helpful to have parents or teachers' aides monitor the classes so that group programs involving, for example, all the first-grade teachers can be organized at a reasonable time during the day.

It is essential that if a program is initiated there should be a "follow through" so that the advantages and disadvantages of the program can be evaluated.

The concept of flexibility is important and should be built into every program. The administrator should be flexible enough to meet the needs as the program develops. One of the difficulties of innovation in the school system has been the inability to be flexible.

Because of the historical nature of American school systems and the independence of the teacher within the classroom, there is usually resistance to any group or team approach. This has been somewhat ameliorated by team teaching which has permeated educational programs. The positive results of team teaching usually makes a group approach within the school much easier.

One of the best ways to initiate group programs with teachers is to anticipate the problems within his classroom. Every teacher every year faces certain problems within the classroom. These are reproducible events that occur regardless of school area or school system. These problems can be discussed at the beginning of the year, and then the discussion can be used as a base upon which to share these same problems at a later date during the course of the year. For example: "Do you remember when we talked about this type of behavior problem during the second September meeting that we had?" Anticipation of problems helps to decrease the discomfort of handling those problems.

It is important that administrators be trained in how to work with groups of teachers because this type of work enhances the school program, allows the teachers to be more relaxed, and offers to the teachers an opportunity to continue to develop. It allows them to develop their own investigative spirit and research techniques, but insures that they no longer feel isolated. The school system that trains its administrators how to work with teachers will be significantly enriched.

Group work decreases the distance between the teacher

and the administrator and enhances the teachers' effectiveness by coordinating their work with the goals of the entire school and school system. This hopefully will enhance individualized instruction and general group programs for the children.

## THE CHICKEN STORIES

I was asked by an elementary school administrator to review a problem that both teachers and parents presented to her. The children were being encouraged to "run across the street" in front of oncoming cars in a "daredevil" stunt. If they refused, they were called "chicken" by the older kids. It was only a matter of time before one of the children would be seriously injured or killed.

There were several issues that presented: the safety of the children, the concern of everyone including teachers, parents and neighborhood, the pressure from the older children, the impulsivity of the children and their feelings of inadequacy.

When the administrator approached me and said what do you suggest, I replied, "Everything I do in the schools I do in a very prescribed way, to facilitate the teaching and learning process." So I suggested that we first present the problem to the counselors and obtain their suggestions after talking with the students. We then discussed the problem with a representation of the teachers (one from each grade). We subsequently designed an outline for a curriculum to be discussed in each classroom of the school (K-6). Each teacher was to use the outline and guide classroom discussion with his/her own teaching style but cover all pertinent points in the outline with suggestions for proposed discussion and questions.

We then started the chicken stories!

Once a week, every Tuesday morning, a student selected by the teachers read a chicken story to the entire school over the intercom. "What would you do if, for example, somebody told you to run in front of an oncoming car to cross the street?" "And if you refused, called you chicken?" The teacher in each class then discussed the story with their respective classes- with an outline of facts and suggestions by the joint committee (counselors, teachers and administrators). Everybody in the school discussed the same subject at the same time. The results were dramatic. The daredevil stunts (running in front of cars) disappeared, the teachers were able to improve classroom dynamics, the children became more spontaneous in a productive way, the spirit of the school was enhanced, and the group identity of the students (their concept of themselves as members of the school) improved. This was a vivid example of a system's approach facilitating the teaching/ learning process.

## SUGGESTED READINGS

Arrow, Holly, Joseph Edward McGrath, and Jennifer L. Berdahl. (2000). Small Groups As Complex Systems: Formation, Coordination, Development, and Adaptation. Sage: Thousand Oaks, CA.

Bauserman, Joseph M. and Warren R. Rule. (2002). A Brief History of Systems Approaches in Counseling and Psychotherapy. Rowman & Littlefield.

Carns, Ann W. and Michael R. Carns. (Jan. 1997). A systems approach to school counseling. The School Counselor. 44, 218-223.

Childers, John and Richard Podemski. (Nov. 1987). Implementing group work in secondary schools. Leadership Steps for Principals NASSP-Bulletin. 71(502), 83-88.

Crespi, Tony D.; Gustafson, Amy L.; Borges, Silvia M. (Mar 2006). Group Counseling in The Schools: Considerations for Child and Family Issues. Journal of Applied School Psychology. v22 n1 p67-85.

Dansby, Virginia S. (Nov 1996). Group Work within the School System: Survey of Implementation and Leadership Role Issues. Journal for Specialists in Group Work. v21 n4 p232-42.

Ehly, Stewart. (1993). Overview of Group Interventions for Special Services Providers. Special Services in the Schools. v8 n1 p9-38.

Glasser, W. (1969). Schools Without Failure. Harper & Row: New York.

Hickson, Joyce (1992). A Framework for Guidance and Counseling of the Gifted in a School Setting. Gifted Education International. v8 n2 p93-103.

Hulse-Killacky, Diana. (Sep 1996). Using the Classroom as a Group to Integrate Knowledge, Skills, and Supervised Practice. Journal for Specialists in Group Work. v21 n3 p163-68.

Johnson, David W. (2003). Joining Together: Group Theory and Group Skills. Allyn And Bacon: Boston.

Landy, S.; Menna, R. (Aug 2006). An Evaluation of a Group Intervention for Parents with Aggressive Young Children: Improvements in Child Functioning, Maternal Confidence, Parenting Knowledge and Attitudes. Early Child Development and Care. v176 n6 p605-620.

McElroy, Camille. (Dec 2000). Middle School Programs That Work. Phi Delta Kappan. v82 n4 p277-79.

Merta, Rod J.; And Others. (Sep 1995). Updated Research on Group Work: Educators, Course Work, Theorgy, and Teaching Methods. Journal for Specialists in Group Work. v20 n3 p132-42.

Napier, Rodney W. and Matti K. Gershenfeld. (2003). Groups: Theory and Experience. 6th ed. Houghton Mifflin.

Prapport, Hanna. (Mar. 1993). Reducing high school attrition: group counseling can help. The School Counselor. 40, 309-11.

Reiman, Alan J.; And Others. (Dec 1995). Counselor-and Teacher-Led Support Groups for Beginning Teachers: A Cognitive-Developmental Perspective. Elementary School Guidance & Counseling. v30 n2 p105-17.

Ripley, Vivian V. and Gary E. Goodnough. (Oct. 2001). Planning and implementing group counseling in a high school. Professional School Counseling. 5(1): 62-65.

Rye, D. and R. Sparks. (2002). Strengthening K-12 Counseling Programs: A Support System Approach. 2nd ed. Therapeutic Resource, Inc.

Trotzer, James P. (1999). The Counselor and the Group: Integrating Theory, Training, and Practice. 3rd ed. Accelerated Development (Taylor and Francis): Philadelphia.

Tubbs, Stewart L. (2001). A Systems Approach to Small Groups Interaction. McGraw Hill: Boston.

Vaught, Claire Cole. (Apr 1995). A Letter from a Middle School Counselor to Her Principal. NASSP Bulletin. v79 n570 p20-23.

Wesley, Donald C. (Feb. 2001). The administrator-counselor team. Principal Leadership. 1(6): 60-63.

# CHAPTER X

## *THE PROFILE OF SPECIALTY GROUPS*

The mechanics of group interaction are similar for all groups. Different types of groups, however, have their own "personality profiles" and retain distinctive characteristics. When the group leader is aware of these characteristics, she is often more effective in her job. Educators recognize that different classes have their own unique characteristics, and if they are to be successful in their teaching program they have to tailor the curriculum and the techniques to the class. The counselor would not consider working with all children who walk into her office the same. She knows that different children have different personalities. The same is true with groups. They have their own characteristics.

The following are a number of different specialty groups that the author has had an opportunity to work with in the school setting. A profile of group characteristics is included in each subsection. Recommended techniques that have proven successful in working with these groups are also included.

## *THE LEADERSHIP GROUP*

The leadership group has been a particularly rewarding group to work with. The members are selected from above-average youngsters with above-average IQ's and/or reading levels. They are youngsters selected by the counselors because the students have the potential to become leaders both in the school and in the community. Youngsters of above-average ability emerge at every level of the school system. As noted in chapter II, it is to the advantage of the inexperienced counselor to start working with an above average, or at least average, group of youngsters to begin his group counseling experience. Above-average youngsters interact more spontaneously and are usually more creative and original. A leadership group is usually more verbal than an average or below-average group. When above-average youngsters participate in group counseling, they have an opportunity to sharpen and develop their socialization skills and test their ideas with each other.

There have been several leadership groups in the Baltimore program. For example, a group of ten youngsters (five boys and five girls) from the inner-city of Baltimore were selected from a group of above-average students entering the seventh grade. The youngsters were selected by the school counselors on the basis of their elementary school records. The group was started in the early part of the first month of school (September). They met with the author and a female counselor for twenty-five minutes one time per week. Within six months it was recognized by the teachers that theses youngsters were performing in the classroom at a much more sophisticated and mature level than were ten equally bright above-average youngsters who had not had the experience of group counseling. The thought content of their ideas, the manner in which the students expressed themselves, their willingness to present material in the class, their willingness to have their ideas challenged, and their ability to challenge others (including the teachers) in a reasonable way revealed a more sophisticated level of social performance than did their peers.

These youngsters continued with the group, meeting the second year (eighth grade) once every two to three weeks for a half-hour with the counselor. The youngsters developed a sophisticated discussion group. They were concerned with current events which they formally (and informally) discussed with each other. They were invited to present a program to a local college (Morgan State College) and were amply rewarded for their performance by the enthusiasm of the audience. In addition to their social and intellectual performance, it was noted that the students appeared to have more confidence and more positive attitude toward school than did equally qualified students who were not participating in the group counseling program. The recordable IQ's of these youngsters when they entered seventh grade ranged from 106 to 120. These were not children who had IQ's in the "zillions." The format for these sessions was that the youngsters could talk about anything they wanted, whether it was international events, national issues, local school programs, subject material that they were studying, appropriate family matters, or experiences that they had in the neighborhood. Some insight into group mechanics was discussed with them during the first year (seventh grade).

Groups of above-average students can be organized at any grade level. The goals are usually to develop leadership qualities in potential leaders who seem to have the ability to improve their performance. The interesting phenomenon that often occurs with above-average students is that generally (except for a few) the grades that they achieve and the IQ scores that they achieved remain about the same. Occasionally students would raise their IQ scores 5 to 10 points, but this was unusual. What did improve was their socialization skills and their ability to present original ideas to a group. Whether they had these ideas or would have had them without group counseling is a moot question. Certainly the ability to present them, to interact with each other and to handle projects in an independent, responsible way was enhanced by the group counseling experience.

In our enthusiasm to ensure that all children have the opportunity to perform at least at grade level, a significant group of youngsters within our student population have been neglected. These are the above-average youngsters who have the potential to become leaders.

It would be a significant contribution if all administrators would take twenty-five minutes a week of their busy schedules and allot that time to ten youngsters who they think are above-average. If a school system had four hundred principals and vice principals and each spent twenty-five minutes a week with ten youngsters this would mean that every year four thousand above-average youngsters would have an opportunity to participate in small groups in order to share ideas and test themselves against others and a qualified educator. Within a ten-year period that school system would have exposed forty thousand above-average youngsters to a brief, intense, stimulating interaction that might significantly influence the students' development and indirectly affect the entire community. There would be additional benefits. The administrator would continually be involved with youngsters. She would have an opportunity to observe how at least one segment of the student population (although it would be an above-average group) reacted and thought about school-student-community matters.

## THE UNDER-ACHIEVER

The under-achiever may be defined, for our purposes in group counseling, as a student who the counselor and/or teacher thinks is capable of performing at a higher level of performance than she is currently achieving. She is usually a student whose IQ is in the normal to above-normal range but who is doing below-normal to unsatisfactory work.

There is another group of youngsters who are under-achievers. This group will be discussed in the subsection of potential drop outs. These are youngsters who have apparently below-average IQ's and are under-achieving in school, but the IQ scores are reflective of a cultural-gap rather than deficiency in the ability to perform. When given the right program these under-achievers usually score much higher on their IQ tests.

When working with an under-achiever group, the group leader should orient the goals first to the needs of the youngsters, and secondly to increased performance.

Lack of motivation is one of the major difficulties. Decreased motivation is probably a more significant factor in the students' poor performance than in not being intellectually able to do the work. The group leader should be as objective as possible. She should make an effort not to react in the same way as the frustrated parent. Patience on the part of the group leader is of utmost importance. Working with under-achievers takes time. Reinforcement should be of a positive nature: that is, the youngster's performance should be programmed in such a way that feedback to him will be as a result of what she does well and not what she does wrong.

Under-achievers may be a difficult group for the inexperienced counselor to initiate group work with. For example, one of the characteristics of an under-achiever group is decreased verbal interaction with `other students in the formal school or group setting. Under-achievers in the inner city may not have developed the socialization skills necessary to communicate and be comfortable *in the class*. Group counseling sessions oriented to general discussions will offer an opportunity to develop these skills.

One of the interesting facts that emerge in doing group work with the under-achievers is that occasionally the positive effects of the group counseling programs are not immediately apparent. In many groups that were organized for a six-week period there was essentially no apparent change in the students at the end of the six weeks. (The groups met during a spring semester.) However, when many of the students returned to school in the fall, they were significantly better students, academically and socially. It appeared that during the summer they assimilated the information and were able to utilize and test it. The percentage performing at an advanced level was higher than a comparable control group. *It is apparent in group work the results are not always immediate.* It takes an unknown period of time for the youngsters to assimilate information and to learn how to use it. The time varies with the ability of the student. The group leader working with under-achievers should be aware of this, or she may become impatient and frustrated.

When an under-achiever population is given the right program, the youngsters will respond, become motivated, and increase their performance. It should be noted, however, that these youngsters usually need a continually-enriched social atmosphere. If social stimulation and direction are withdrawn, these youngsters may revert to an under-achieving pattern, especially if the supportive program has been on a relatively short-term basis. Perhaps one of the reasons why similar programs have failed is that they did not build into the program the obvious need for continued enrichment throughout the school life of the students. People continuously need physiological and psychological nourishment. This is true of any group of youngsters, but particularly important with the under-achiever.

If the counselor wants to initiate a group program for under-achievers, the easiest group to begin working with is that group whose members have above-average IQ's but who are doing below average work. When the counselor initiates a program with a potentially capable group, she will feel comfortable "putting the pressure on." She will have an increased expectancy for the group. The counselor must not anticipate that in one or two counseling sessions the under-achievers are going to change a behavior pattern that has taken many months, perhaps years, to establish. This is unrealistic.

The group leader should avoid asking the question, "Why aren't you doing better? Your IQ scores are above-average, or average; why aren't you performing better in the classroom?" Most of the youngsters who are asked this question will answer, 'I don't know,' and in fact they do not know. When the counselor anticipates that they will know she is usually reflecting her inexperience. An estimated twenty to thirty percent of the students who are under-achieving (with average or above-average IQ's) probably need little more than some attention by a counselor. When students are allowed an opportunity to communicate and are given some direction by an educator, their performance often improves. This may result from the counselor merely saying, "Get on the ball." The counselor may elect to meet with the child in a group for an initial series of two to four sessions and then to meet once every three to four weeks. Follow-up support can be with her teachers, parents, or members of his peer group. A "get tough, get on the ball" approach probably works in no more than a third of the youngsters involved, if it works in that high a percentage. When the counselor anticipates better results from a get-tough policy she may reinforce the youngster's feeling of failure and increase the hiatus between the student and the adult world.

Two-thirds of the underachievers will need more than a brief contact with a counselor or teacher. They will need some type of sustained help until their behavior pattern changes and they feel confident performing at a higher level. By meeting just once a week (or once every two weeks) the students may gain some insight into their behavior patterns and how they and their peers react to different experiences. The counselor should convey the expectancy that they are capable of doing something worthwhile.

Effective group counseling must be coordinated with an effective classroom program. However, in order to be effective, group counseling must be coordinated with the classroom program. It is unrealistic for the counselor to think that she can, by herself, alter the behavior pattern of the under-achiever.

*The key to working with under-achieving youngsters (as well as with other youngsters) is to start at the level at which they are capable of performing.* If a student has an IQ of 120 in the sixth grade, but is only achieving at a fourth-grade level, it is unrealistic to start a program for that youngster at a sixth grade level. The program should be initiated at a fourth grade level in an upgraded program in which she can immediately be reinforced by the work that she is doing and allowed to progress at her own speed. As progress continues, then the work load should be increased. Group counseling should be correlated with an individualized approach to learning. Individualized programs and instruction in the classroom can be particularly effective. The total approach (that is, a combined group and individual opportunity) will often help to alter the behavior pattern and motivation of the youngster so she can increase her performance and achieve at a rate which he is potentially capable. *The counselor or group leader should note that counseling by itself may only prime the youngsters to be motivated. Group discussion may not be enough to sustain motivation. Some type of project that will allow the youngsters to become physically as well as mentally involved is important.* The students should have the opportunity, when possible, to transfer the enthusiasm and motivation generated by group counseling into an actual project. When they have this opportunity, personal satisfaction and learning are greatly enhanced. A group project does not have to be physical (that is, building something). It can be preparing a report, performing a skit, participating in a learning game, or involvement in a debate. When possible, under-achievers should be able to see that they can achieve by what they do.

Another group of under-achievers is the group who are truly bored. They are capable of doing more than the school expects of them. Their intelligence and capability may be above grade level. The routine school program may not be stimulating enough. Involvement in extra-curricular activities, increasing the work load, giving them group and individualized projects, are particularly important. There are different ways to program for this type of under-achiever. One group technique is to pick a subject or function of which she is fond and relate it in a direct or even indirect way to her classes. The program should be flexible enough to offer the bored student an opportunity to do individual or group research if she would like. The group should be designed so that the students receive immediate reinforcement and gratification from what they are doing.

Another group of under-achievers reflect difficulties at home, difficulties that the child internalizes and brings with her to the classroom as a constant concern. She may start daydreaming or may become preoccupied in her own world of troubled thoughts. This youngster (as well as other types of under-achievers) can be helped significantly by group counseling because (1) it gives her an opportunity to share the difficulty, either directly or indirectly, with her peer group which might give her support; (2) it stimulates interaction with her environment; (3) it offers an opportunity to express herself; (4) it offers an opportunity to be accepted by her peers and adults; and (5) it reinforces her ability to accept responsibility (i.e., the group) and handle it in an efficient, adult-like manner.

Many of these youngsters have or develop a pattern of not reacting to their environment. They have withdrawn from their environment to concentrate on their own difficulties. When they are in a group counseling program (which demands group interaction), they develop a socialization pattern which may stimulate them to be more aware of the activity around them and may enhance their performance.

There are cautions that the group counselor should note in working with a withdrawn youngster. It is not uncommon for a youngster who has been withdrawn for a prolonged period of time to initially be overactive or hyperactive as a result of successful group work. In some cases she has never been spontaneous before. A sudden change is unusual, and when it does occur the student is asking for direction and support from her environment. Individual counseling in coordination with a group counseling program can be helpful. The individual counseling can be by the counselor and/ or teachers or administrator. The second consideration is that youngsters who have been withdrawn and/or passive and suddenly become more spontaneous make it difficult for those around them. Their peers and their teachers are not used to reacting to them as active or spontaneous youngsters. If the teacher is not aware of what is going on in group counseling, she can consider this activity as negative behavior rather than as healthy, progressive improvement.

Perhaps the most important consideration is that some withdrawn youngsters are emotionally ill children. This represents a small percentage of withdrawn youngsters, especially in the inner city, but nevertheless it should be noted. Group counseling may increase their perception of their environment, which includes significant difficulty at home and in the neighborhood. As a result, they may become more hyperactive (and anxious) both at home and in the school stetting. If this cannot be handled in the group, they should be withdrawn immediately and given individual counseling. If the youngster's illness is severe, the child should be referred to a trained mental health professional.

A general characteristic of the under-achiever group is that the members often reflect angry moods or thoughts. It is not uncommon for the under-achiever to express her frustration some time during a group session. The members may reflect their frustration by discussing angry topics such as war, murder, and assaults that have been reported in the paper, or problems that have occurred in the neighborhood. The students eventually express angry feelings about the adults in their environment. Inevitably, the teacher or teachers receive the brunt of their difficulties. If the counselor is not "threatened" by the students' denunciation of teachers, and tolerates with some facility comments that may be said, the youngsters often discuss their problems (including problems with their parents.)

When the leader can adequately handle angry topics, the youngsters will often proceed to topics which they discuss in a positive and constructive way. Angry retorts are not inevitable. When the counselor is able to program a counseling session in an organized way, expressions of anger are sometimes averted; but with experienced counselors this occurs to variable degrees with most of the under-achieving groups.

The counselor should not anticipate that the under-achiever selected for a group counseling session will by some magical quality start performing at a higher level than she he has previously been performing. Under-achievers will initially have a tendency to under-achieve in the group. If a counselor anticipates otherwise she is being unrealistic. When group counseling sessions start, the youngsters will usually perform at the same level of performance as they usually do. If the counselor can work with the youngsters at their current level of performance (and not their anticipated level) and give them an opportunity to achieve at that level, they will have a chance to improve in a programmed, developmental way.

The counselor must be much more directive with youngsters who are under-achieving than those, for example, who are above average. The questions should be clear, concise, and simple. The leader should initially ask questions that will reflect the operational level at which the youngsters are performing. She should not initially "push" or test them beyond their apparent capability. The counselor's first questions should be within the realm of the children's knowledge and should be questions which they are capable of answering. The leader can then start challenging, but she should build on what the students know. She should be directive and be willing to set limits without hesitation. If the youngsters are to change, they are going to feel extremely comfortable. This can be accomplished by a well-organized, direct approach. As the youngsters' performance improves and they are capable of accepting more responsibility for the group session, the counselor should effectuate the transfer of leadership by increasing the opportunities for more responsibility. This will have a tendency to reinforce the youngsters' progress.

The under-achiever group is a worthwhile but difficult group to work with. If the youngsters do change and do improve their performance, it is the responsibility of the counselor to share the ideas, techniques, and concepts that were used with the teachers. When an under-achiever is classified by the school as an under-achiever, it is difficult for the teachers, and often for the administrators, to accept the fact that there is a change in performance. When the counselor or group leader is able to share the group experiences that she has had with other faculty members, it helps to facilitate a change in attitude of the staff, which can then reinforce the youngster's progress.

## *THE POTENTIAL DROPOUT*

The potential dropout is usually an under-achiever. Most of the material in the preceding subsection applies to the potential dropout.

The phenomenon of the high school dropout is not new in the United States. It is estimated that a large segment of the adult working force in the United States is comprised of dropouts. However, the consequences of the dropouts and of being a dropout are assuming new significance. The task of planning for this current crisis and the inability to cope with it reflect on every aspect of American education. The responsibility of the dropout does not rest solely with the schools, but the salvation of the dropout may.

A great deal has been done in describing "the profile of the school dropout." Large urban populations do not have difficulty recognizing who their dropouts will be. The records and profiles of the potential dropout are well known among the urban educators. Each geographic area, however, may have unique characteristics which are unlike other areas. The most notable differences are between rural and urban areas and inner city and perimeter areas.

Many educators note that they can identify the potential dropout population as early as kindergarten or first grade. Many of these youngsters come from families whose children have a history of absenteeism in the school. The predictions for their siblings are usually the same.

By the fourth grade a potential dropout population has been well defined. The school can generally note a significant increase in absenteeism of students in certain areas of the city.

When initiating a program for potential dropouts, it is important to note that dropouts are different. They form different groups; they have different characteristics. Overall they can be divided essentially into three groups.

*Group I* is composed of youngsters who are organically impaired and do not have the intellectual or organic capability to keep up with the average child. Special education and opportunity classes are usually designed for youngsters of Group I. They are often the most easily identifiable of the potential dropout group and usually receive the earliest attention. The author has noted that in many large urban school systems these youngsters are usually not placed in special education classes soon enough. These classes should really begin as early as kindergarten or first grade, with flexibility to transfer students as they improve or gain the skill necessary to do the required work.

*Group II* is composed of youngsters who have normal recordable IQ's but who are under-achieving in school. These youngsters form a large share of the potential dropout population in the elementary group and thereafter. (It is estimated that at least sixty-five percent of the dropout population have normal or above-normal IQ's.) This figure may be significantly higher. Their poor performance may be from not having developed the socialization and communication skills necessary to do the work in the early grades (and therefore getting behind) or to boredom because they are intelligent. Perhaps the most significant factor is the poor expectation by the parents, who themselves were often dropouts.

*Group III* includes youngsters who have below-normal recordable IQ scores and are below grade level in their academic performance. When these youngsters are given culture-free tests or well-designed academic programs, their IQ scores usually increase significantly: that is, increase to normal or above-normal scores. A large proportion of these youngsters are from lower socio-economic areas.

The programs designed for each of these groups should be

different. Group II and III are essentially similar but are operating at different levels of performance. Any meaningful program to decrease the potential dropout populations has to differentiate the sub-grouping of the potential dropout population.

In secondary schools the potential dropouts can also be defined by their attendance. Thus, the potential dropout population can be defined in terms of the groups noted above and also their attendance types. For example, the author has noted that at the seventh grade level the potential dropout population falls into three major types. *Type 1* is the potential dropout who does not become a major attendance problem until the end of seventh grade or the early part of the eighth grade. She may not be reading at grade level (and usually is not) but is willing to come to school and "stick it out." When she finds that junior high school has nothing to offer her, she starts to lose interest. The student starts to become a major attendance problem in the early part of the eighth grade. *Type 2* is the youngster who presents to the seventh grade and is willing to try the school for seven to ten days. If the school does not have a program designed to help, motivate, or retain her and/or give the student an opportunity to perform at a level she is capable of, the student will start becoming an attendance problem within the first two weeks of school. *Type 3* is the potential dropout who does not show up on day one and becomes an attendance problem before day one. Every school system should review its particular groups and types of potential dropouts and develop their programs accordingly.

In many large urban areas one significant statistic that seems to be reproducible is that about eighty percent of the fathers and seventy percent of the mothers of the dropouts were dropouts themselves. The statistic is important because any meaningful program designed to decrease the number of dropouts has to be coordinated with parent and community programs. It is estimated that at least two-thirds of the dropout population have normal basic intelligence and would probably record normal IQ scores if given a "culture fair" test. About six percent of the dropouts usually have IQ scores over 110. This means that in a ten-year period we are losing an estimated 400,000 to 500,000 children with above-average minds to the dropout pool.

A school program for potential dropouts should be designed at two levels. The first is to work with the potential dropout population that already exists, and second, to design a program that will prevent the creation of potential dropouts.

In describing the factors involved in dropouts, an educator might submit a list such as this: over-age, academic retardation, poor reading ability, low verbal intelligence, undesirable home environment, lack of participation in extra-curricular activities, poor school relationships (teacher-pupil, pupil-pupil), irregular attendance, and lack of interest in school. Lists such as this, which are described in many dropout profiles, are accurate but are not specific enough. The description is general and non-specific rather than a specific description of the skills or lack of skills and the ability to perform or not perform at certain levels. Because the investigators have been general and non-specific, the programs designed to meet the needs of the dropouts have also been general and non-specific. There should be more investigation into what techniques to use for the dropouts at their various levels of performance. When the school systems investigate the basic processes of teaching and learning of the dropout, they will enhance the development of a meaningful curriculum.

In designing a program for the potential dropout, the project directors should reflect on the way the potential dropout feels about not being able to perform in school the way she would like. This is something which the school often neglects. Consequently, the school often does not provide programs that are meaningful. The best example is the youngster who is a potential dropout, or in fact has become a dropout, and is hanging around the school getting into trouble breaking windows, and so forth. In order to understand these youngsters we have to reflect on what went on before the youngster became a school vandal. That youngster started school at kindergarten or first grade level at least two years behind in his socialization and verbalization skills. Instead of meeting the needs of the child and designing programs to give him skills necessary to learn, she was placed in a regular school classroom. The grade was not designed for individualized instruction (i.e., programmed learning). At the end of the first year the child either failed or was pushed ahead. If lucky, the child was referred to a special curriculum which was geared to the youngster's level of performance.

By the time the youngster has been in school two to three years, he was ready (perhaps for the first time) to start to learn. However, he has never seemed to be able to catch up; he remained one to three grade reading levels behind in his work. He became continuously more frustrated. He received little help from the home because, in many cases, his parents were also dropouts and may not have had the understanding or the expectancy to help. As the youngster became more frustrated with his inability to perform in the classroom, he started to become an attendance problem.

Along the way he gave many different signals of not being able to learn at the level at which the material was being presented to him. This becomes a crisis situation for the child. He becomes an attendance problem, which is another red flag that he is not able to perform at the level which the school expected. The staff did not recognize the signal. If they did, they did not have the programs designed to meet his needs, which increased the communication and socialization gap between the child and the school. The youngster began to feel more desperate and frustrated. In his search for direction and help, he went back to the school and started hanging around as a dropout delinquent. He initially started to pick on the younger children so that somebody might pay attention to him. When this did little good, the youngster started to throw rocks at the school windows in an ultimate effort to get the school to pay some attention to him and his needs. At this point the administrator and teachers reflected and said, "This youngster is nothing but a delinquent; he's a vandal destroying school property." There was no communication with the child except in a negative way. There was little insight into the fact that this youngster was just asking for more direction and perhaps hoping that the school would have some insight into his basic difficulties.

What the potential dropout is asking for is a chance to catch up on skills that he may have lacked when he entered school six to ten years before, in the kindergarten and first grade level. The school either indefinitely suspends the youngster (because of his vandalism) at which point he gets no help, or he is referred to a residential school because he is a so-called vandal. Hopefully, at a residential school he might learn a trade or receive some type of specialized learning. Unfortunately, even these institutions are not designed to meet the basic needs of the youngsters; consequently they help to increase the youngster's frustration even more.

The potential dropouts are not irrevocably lost, even at the junior high level. When the right programs are instituted, they are able to develop socialization and communication skills necessary for learning. Group counseling enhances these skills. I have seen youngsters whose IQ scores have gone from 85 to 110 when given the proper program that taught them how to perform. The potential dropout has to initially develop skills necessary to receive information from the teacher, to learn how to absorb the information, to communicate with the teacher, to listen to the teacher, and to listen to others. (It has been common to observe that inner-city youngsters have a tendency to work in isolation.) At the same time, the youngsters have to develop a positive concept of themselves. They have to think of themselves as capable of doing the job.

The counseling sessions should be programmed so that discussion will start at the level at which the students are able to perform. When the counseling session or classroom is designed so the youngsters can respond in a productive way, the counselor can begin to reinforce the work and performance that is given. As the youngsters, as a group and individually, continue to develop, the level of discussion and the sophistication of the discussion are increased. Dividing the class into small groups enhances the group effect. (Teacher aides, older students, and parent volunteers can help.) Smaller groups increase the socialization and verbalization opportunities for the youngsters and at the same time add the element of discipline helpful for group spontaneity.

Parent involvement is helpful. A positive community attitude towards the school and learning must be established. This is done by having the parents participate in programs during which they are actually told how they can help the child in the home in a stepwise fashion: that is, "If you do this with your youngster, this is what the effect will be. This is how your child performs now; this is how the average youngster performs. If you do the following things, you will be able to help him develop his verbalization and communication skills." The parents must have some insight between the relationship of what the school wants them to do in the home and how it will affect the child's learning. This should be graphically done so the parents understand what they are supposed to do. All too often we, as educators, are jealous of the knowledge that we have. We do not share it with people with whom it should be shared the most- the parents; and we hesitate to do things in a simplistic, clear way.

When working with potential dropouts it is interesting to note that their attendance problems often remain the same except on those days that the youngsters are to have a group counseling session, at which time they show up. Some youngsters attend the group counseling session and then leave school. This is indicative of the significant need for constructive, well-organized, positive interaction that these students so desire. When the school can design the classroom of the potential dropout for group interaction and opportunities for socialization, the school will have a much better opportunity to retain the potential dropout.

It is not uncommon for groups of potential dropouts to discuss angry things and express angry thoughts. This is usually a reflection of the frustration that the group members have about their own inabilities to perform as well as they would like and the anger that they have that the school has not given them the opportunities to perform in a productive way. They are looking for direction and are angry when they do not get it. Group counseling is effective when it gives the youngsters an opportunity to ventilate their feelings in a positive, constructive way. It is better for the potential dropout to verbalize her thoughts than to "act out" in anger towards the school or the community. Once the group members have expressed their angry thoughts (and the leader has met the test of allowing them to express these thoughts), the youngsters are usually ready to work in a constructive, positive way. Not all potential dropout groups will have angry thoughts or feelings. The leader, however, should be aware of this possibility. If the leader is capable (and willing) to handle the frustration of the potential dropout, then the youngsters will usually "settle down" sooner. The fact that they can be reinforced by doing well within a group is enough to given them a positive group identity, (at least for the group). The program should be designed to give them immediate gratification and an opportunity to increase their performance.

One of the difficulties that inexperienced counselors have in working with potential dropouts is that they often think that because the students have had a group counseling session (or sessions) the youngsters should be able to perform better in the classroom. The fact that the potential dropouts become more verbal and are willing to look at things in a constructive way does not mean that the teacher or the school system has designed programs to meet the needs of the youngsters in the classroom. If a remedial program is to be successful there must be close coordination between the group counselor, the teacher, and the administrators. The programs that have been designed throughout the country met with varying degrees of success depending upon the design of the program and the motivation and cooperation of the staff.

Another program that can be considered for the potential dropout is one designed to initiate help for the dropout by potential dropouts themselves. This is often done in an informal way in many schools. The potential dropout who has been retained in school tells the counselor of other potential dropouts. Some schools have organized this on a formal basis: a "Dropouts Anonymous." The members are recruited in special programs not only to help themselves but also to recruit others to join with them in a Dropouts Anonymous. The goal is to stay in school and enter in a special program designed to meet their needs. Significant insight can be gained into the dropout problem from the students. This should not be overlooked. It may be the first opportunity that they have had to accept some type of meaningful responsibility in an organized way. Group counseling can be utilized to facilitate this unique approach, to maintain the motivation and interest of the youngsters, and to help develop concepts of leadership.

In summary: Any effective program for the potential dropout must be done on a school-wide, grade-wide basis. If there is going to be a significant remedial change with "large numbers" of potential dropouts, this cannot be accomplished on a one-to-one, counselor-to student basis. The potential dropouts must have an opportunity to develop socialization skills and to be able to share their ideas with both the teacher and each other. These opportunities coupled with the opportunity to perform at the level that they are capable (programming their instruction and their lessons systematically) will decrease the potential dropout population as much as any other school program.

## *SPECIAL EDUCATION STUDENTS*

For the most part, the special education student should be considered an underachiever. A large segment of this group is culturally deprived. There are selected members of the special education group who do have characteristics which are unique to their group.

Many of the youngsters have organic impairments and neither the physical nor psychological controls necessary for group activity. Those within this category who are eligible for group work often have to be placed in smaller groups (i.e., two to four students). They cannot tolerate the stimulation of larger groups nor the intensity of the interaction.

Some special education students are reading at a primer or first grade level although they may be sixteen or seventeen years of age. These youngsters usually can verbalize; however, their ability to perform academic skills is so low that the counselor has to program the discussion at the level of interest and sophistication that the group members will understand. The use of audio-visual equipment, material aides, and elementary techniques are often helpful.

Many of the special education youngsters are restless and cannot tolerate an average group period (i.e., forty to fifty minutes). It is sometimes necessary to limit the group session to no more than twenty minutes.

It is not uncommon for the youngsters to go back to class very hyperactive and over-stimulated just from an average group counseling session. It is necessary to work closely with the teacher in order to develop the structure that will help handle the spontaneity after the group experience so that the students will be able to participate more appropriately in the regular classroom.

Special education students need group experiences. Their socialization and communication skills are often poorly developed. Their group identities are poor. They have difficulty relating to their peers and the community. They may have to literally learn how to relate. The concept of programming is essential if the group is to be successful. Refer to Chapter X (potential dropouts and underachievers).

## THE ADOLESCENT PREGNANT FEMALE

With foresight and vision, many school systems have organized special programs for adolescent pregnant students. The age range is usually from ages eleven to eighteen.

The group counseling experience that the author has had in working with these youngsters was both personally rewarding and extremely informative. In the younger age group (ages eleven to fourteen), it becomes apparent that the girls are not sure of what is happening. They are not fully aware of the consequences of their pregnancy nor the complications and responsibilities involved. These are eleven to fourteen year old children who are pregnant. They are working through the same basic concerns of any adolescent: those of body image, identity, and independence. All three factors may have been part of the psychological cause of getting pregnant.

It is a unique and sad experience to see a twelve-year-old child being concerned with what any twelve-year-old youngster should be concerned with and still facing the problems of having a baby. The educator has to be prepared to help the youngster work through normal development, as she would any adolescent. She also has the responsibility to share with the youngster information about pregnancy, birth, motherhood, and the responsibilities thereof. This is an extremely difficult task. The girls usually present somewhat surprised, concerned, and bewildered. The fact that they are allowed to participate in special programs for pregnant girls is perhaps one of the wiser things the school system has done. In special programs, they can identify with the other girls. This helps to relieve some of their guilt and pressure from the community.

The educator should not act as judge and jury on whether the youngster's action was right or wrong. The fact is the child is pregnant and the counseling program should be geared towards helping her in whatever way possible to make a suitable adjustment.

The older girls (ages sixteen to eighteen) usually do relatively well. Those who are still in school, particularly at the senior level, may want to complete their education, eventually marry or enter careers. It is not uncommon, however, for there to be a large percentage of girls who drop out.

The younger girls (the eleven to fifteen age group) are often confused about their futures roles and need guidance. School attendance among the pregnant girls is often a problem. The younger girls need more direction and more personal contact. Girls who have an attendance problem often come to school on the day of group counseling but may be absent for most of the week. The opportunity that group counseling offers for socialization, identification, positive group interaction, support from peers, a chance to express themselves and obtain information about particular subjects is significantly helpful.

Many of the common problems that are present in working with pregnant adolescents are concerned with pregnancy itself. The counseling sessions should be organized so that information about the problems can be discussed. The girls often use the difficulties of pregnancy as vehicles for expressing angry feelings about other things. For example, instead of complaining about a particular problem (i.e., pregnancy, parents, and boy friends) they may complain about their clinic visits. The opportunity to discuss personal problems in a general way is helpful. When indicated, the counselor can program the discussion so it will start with the question of boy-girl relationships and then, as the sessions progress, include discussion of more complicated topics: i.e., the responsibilities of motherhood, care and development of the baby, purpose of prenatal visits, delivery, etc. The many important topics cannot be discussed in one session but should be considered for discussion during the group counseling schedule.

The group counseling sessions should be organized to be a learning experience for the girls. It is helpful to invite a physician or nurse to the class or group to answer the girls' questions and explain to them exactly what is going to happen. If a number of the girls are being serviced by predominantly one (or two) clinics in the area, it is helpful to have a representative of that clinic visit the school. This will give the girls an opportunity to ask questions about the difficulties and concerns of pregnancy. It will enable the medical resource person to answer questions within the framework of the regular school routine. It is helpful to include in the curriculum lectures on delivery, care of the newborn infant, feeding schedules, routine care of a child during the first year of life, the normal growth and development of a child, and how the mother can help the child during the first year of life.

During the group counseling sessions the girls present a number of questions. The questions vary and reflect the concern of the youngsters. The following is a list of the most commonly asked questions. The questions are not in order of frequency or importance to the girls.

1. How is a baby born?
2. Can you explain methods of contraception?
3. How do you take care of a new baby?
4. How can you be independent and not depend on your partner?
5. What is the purpose of the babies' immunizations?
6. Can I finish high school and take care of my child at the same time?
7. When you are a teen-ager, what is the best way to say "yes" or "no?"
8. Why is it hard to say "no" instead "yes?"
9. What does a child expect from her mother?
10. How should a mother and father act at this time (age 15 years)?
11. How does a mother feel after she has a baby? Does she feel proud?

12. How do you handle the frustration of having to stay home with a baby when you would rather be out dating and having fun?
13. What is the best approach to handling uncontrolled emotions?
14. What are the tests for pregnancy?
15. How do you handle the fear of delivery of a baby?
16. Are spinals dangerous? Can they paralyze a person if not given right?
17. When should a teen-ager have a boyfriend/girlfriend?
18. When is a person ready for marriage?
19. How do you get along with your parents?
20. What should you expect from the father of your baby?
21. Can you give us more information about sexually transmitted diseases?

The girls often discussed their relationship with their parents. Some of the youngsters had a fantasy syndrome in which they thought, either consciously or unconsciously, that their parents would rescue them from involvement with boys and/or getting pregnant. During pregnancy the girls were both frustrated and angry at the parents because they had not been rescued. In the inner-city family there is often an absence of the father or adult male. The fantasy may involve the absent father. This type of interpretation was not made to the youngsters but was "worked through" indirectly.

Another consideration was that a small percentage of the girls (not all) were receiving an unconscious okay by the major matriarchal person in the family. The girls received tacit approval and encouragement for interaction that might lead to pregnancy. This was not overtly done by the matriarchs; but the way the children were managed at home, the conversations between mother and daughter, gave the youngster the impression that she had license (in fact, was encouraged) to become involved with the boys. The tacit approval that some parents apparently gave their youngsters to get pregnant seemed to come from the mother or grandmother, whose primary job was taking care of the children.

This was often culturally and traditionally influenced. In effect, if the young females did not present more children for the matriarch to take care of, the matriarch would be without a job.

There was a general feeling among the youngsters who become pregnant that they had let their parents down. Some cities have tried (with significant success) group meetings with both mothers and daughters so that they can develop together a program that will allow the teen-aged mother to assume responsibility for their child and to continue in school. Another successful program has been the involvement of adults from the community in "big sister" programs in which mature, usually married, women will adopt one of the pregnant adolescents as a "sister" and meet with her and share ideas and concepts.

If a meaningful preventative program is to be achieved, the school staff and the community agencies should design a plan that will also give the matriarchs some type of occupation or community involvement.

Economic factors which contribute to a large number of people using one to two rooms, poor housing and recreational facilities, lower incomes, all have a significant effect in encouraging youngsters to promiscuously have sexual relations.

Youngsters who have already become pregnant can be a significant help. Girls who are pregnant or have had children can share the realities of the situation with other girls. They can be informative. It is a myth that there is not hurt, guilt, or shame when youngsters from a lower socio-economic group become pregnant. It is true that in some peer groups the girls are not considered a woman until she has had a child, but this does not offset the inadequate, guilty and often shameful feelings of becoming pregnant. Many pregnant adolescents actually think that they will not be accepted by their peers because they are different: that is, they have become pregnant and will have a child.

One reason that some of the girls become pregnant was adaptation to the environment and their culture. Intercourse at an earlier age was prevalent. The girls were simply adapting to the routine socialization pattern of their peers. It is difficult to offset the environment and influence of the neighborhood. It cannot adequately be accomplished without the help of parents and involvement of the community. *School officials should develop within their curricula family planning and sex education courses that will include meaningful discussion of these topics.*

A large percentage of the adolescents who became pregnant were previously looking for closeness and involvement with another person. This is not uncommon with girls from homes in which there is a great deal of strife: i.e., poor interpersonal relationships. The need for acceptance and closeness with another person is important. Sex is part of the closeness and acceptance that the youngsters want. Sexual intercourse appears to be incidental. Some of the girls are looking for a close association rather then sexual intercourse. This has to be an important consideration in designing any program to help offset the high incidence of pregnancy in unmarried adolescents. Some youngsters appear to be very angry towards mother or towards the family and do become involved in sexual intercourse as a "spiteful" act towards the family situation, particularly the major parent figure.

Another factor is the universal concern of femininity (or lack of femininity) with the added peer pressure in some neighborhoods that in order to be a woman one has to become pregnant and have a child. Peer pressure is usually an important factor. Many of the youngsters in the neighborhood may be having sexual intercourse; in order to become one of the group members, the youngster also has to participate. Contraception is not the sole answer. Many of these youngsters know about contraception. They knew how babies are born. (A small percentage (five to ten percent) did not know how they became pregnant.) The remaining ninety to ninety-five percent knew and still became pregnant. Knowing about contraception and having it available are different things. Some meaningful program has to be coordinated with the community agencies and the parents. Group counseling can be a helpful technique.

Although the youngsters know how pregnancy occurs and understand the mechanical act of sexual intercourse and its implications, they have a significant denial of the possibility of becoming pregnant, with an "It can't happen to me" attitude. Some consideration has to be given to the Oedipal conflicts and the incestuous fantasies, usually at an unconscious level, that most youngsters in the Western world appear to reflect. The natural curiosity and experimentation of the adolescent are accentuated and reinforced when they are promiscuous.

One problem that often presented was that (especially with the younger girls) there was encouragement by the agencies that they give up their babies for adoption. It was the author's impression that this seemed to encourage the youngsters to become pregnant again. (This is of particular concern to the group counselor because in many groups one or more youngsters may be having her child taken away.) This is quite frightening to the other girls as well as the youngster involved. Avoiding the subject is not helpful and reinforces everyone's anxiety, but concentration on the subject also increases the anxiety. One thing that can be done is to bring in social workers or representatives of the courts and social agencies to discuss the issues with the girls. This does two things: it educates the girls who are pregnant, and it also educates the courts and agencies that service the pregnant adolescent. Decisions have often been subjective, made on the basis of intuition rather than good clinical judgment. This is unfair to the mother, the child, and the community.

A technical problem in working with the adolescent pregnant girl is that the girls present to the group at various times of the year. As a result there is no regular admission or discharge date for the students. Their schedules are superimposed on the regular school schedule. The counselor cannot plan on a given group staying together for a semester or longer. The author first tried an open-end group: that is, when somebody left another youngster took her place. It is more difficult to work with an open-end group because there are constant interruptions; different problems are constantly being presented by girls who are being discharged and girls who are coming into the group. Sophistication varies because some girls have been in group counseling for four to six months. They are mature and can handle selected problems that they have worked through quite well. The newer girls are frightened and unsophisticated about many of the questions that have already been discussed. In the open-end group the degree of unity and cohesiveness is decreased. An open-end group is more difficult for the leader and more distracting for the youngsters.

Whenever it is possible, it is better to work with a closed-end group: that is, the leader initiated the group with a given number of youngsters, all at about the same stage in pregnancy and all of whom have approximately similar E.D.C, (expected date of confinement). This facilitates the group counseling sessions because there is an ongoing group that lasts for a prolonged period of time. The leader can develop a cohesive group. The group members can share with each other the anxieties of their particular stage of pregnancy. The sessions can be programmed. Attendance is generally better with the closed-end group.

Some school systems which have a high incidence of adolescent pregnant girls have formed group counseling sessions for the youngsters when they return to their regular schools postpartum. When the girls return they often need support and direction. They need to be encouraged to continue their studies and also to identify with the school. Group counseling often helps them to re-adapt to the school routine. They can share the difficulties and successes that they are having with their babies and they can counsel each other. The questions they ask are varied but pertinent. The group counselor should not hesitate to bring in guest speakers when it is indicated to broaden the students' learning experience.

In summary, group counseling sessions can be a very useful technique with adolescent pregnant girls and the teen-aged mothers.

## THE BEHAVIOR PROBLEM

Every large organization has members who can be considered behavior problems; behavior problems, however, are probably more significant in the public school than in most other institutions.

Students usually have not developed the "internal controls" of adults. They often depend upon their environment for direction and guidance. When an administrator appraises the "behavior problems" of her school, she should first reflect on how much the administration and/ or staff is contributing to the prevalence of the behavior problem. A significant number of youngsters who are behavior problems have problems of adjustment because of the organization of the school. A professional educator who has had experience in several different schools is aware that a school which is identical in structure and architectural design can be completely different from a similar school two blocks away or on the other side of the city. The personality of the school appears to emanate not from a structural design (although architectural design does influence the personality of the school) but from it's leadership.

The administrator is the leader of the school and consequently will influence the performance of the group members (that is, the teachers and the students) more than any other single person. If an effective job is to be done in handling behavior problems, the administrator should initially work with her staff, who are the group leaders of the classroom. After the administrator has reflected on her own role, attitude, and style of administration she reinforces cohesion and unity of the school staff. Part of that program is to establish a routine system within the school to handle behavior problems. When possible, the entire staff should handle behavior problems in similar ways.

When the administrator establishes a school routine, she is then ready to handle the behavior problems that present to her office. Administrators and counselors should note, that when a youngster is referred as a behavior problem from a particular class, that youngster may have obvious problems; but the administrator must also reflect that the youngster may be utilized by the teacher as her ticket of admission for help in handling the entire classroom. When the administrator concentrates on the youngster who is being presented and does not reflect on the possibility that the teacher herself may be asking for help for her entire class, then the administrator will continue to get referrals from the same teacher. If the administrator is going to solve the student's problem (and other students in the class) and help bring about more effective teaching within the classroom, then she has to share with the teacher concepts of group direction that will "settle" her class.

When the problem is initially presented as a classroom problem (that is, the teacher is having trouble with her entire class), then it is important for the administrator to become involved with that class and give whatever support is necessary. If it is an elementary school this may mean participating in the class for short periods of time during the week. If it is a secondary school, then it necessitates a conference of all the teachers who work with the particular class, including the shop teachers, homeroom teacher, and instructors of minor subjects. The author has found that in the secondary school when teachers meet together as a team, the control of that particular class is brought about much quicker than if each teacher is supervised individually or if the administrator communicates with some teachers who handle the class and not with others.

There may be different reasons why a youngster is a behavior problem. The reasons can range from youngsters with severe internalized emotional problems that need intensive psychotherapy and/or medication to above-average youngsters who are simply bored and become restless. Hyperactive children and mentally retarded children have a tendency to act up or misbehave more when there is less than the desired amount of stability in the classroom (and school). As has been noted above, potential dropouts who are frustrated by not being able to perform often 'act up'. In summary, the counselor should note that in some cases behavior problems are a reflection of illness or severe emotional instability, when the youngster himself cannot control his own impulsive actions; however, sometimes the acting out or misbehavior may be a reflection of the student asking for more direction: i.e., the potential dropout may be frustrated and asking for help, or an above-average youngster may be asking for more work.

In general, misbehavior of a chronic nature is due to a request by that particular individual (or group) for more direction (Chapter III). When the individual is chronically restless and/or acting up, the individual (as is the group) is usually asking for more direction. The individual may be asking the school for guidance to be able to handle his work or asking for more work. She may be asking for a better program. Guidance and leadership may mean many different things to the respective individuals (or groups). It is the educator's responsibility to diagnose what the request is and to implement when possible whatever programs and goals are indicated.

Counselors have to be cautious about randomly selecting behavior problems for a group. The youngsters may identify themselves as a behavior problem group. This negative identification may reinforce their misbehavior. The counselor has to note the possibility that the youngsters may continue to misbehave in order to continue to be eligible for group membership. The kids may think that if they do well, they no longer can be involved in the group, especially if the group is designed only for misbehavior problems.

In working with a group of behavior problems the goals should be well defined, the expectancy of the group should be oriented in a positive direction, and the counselor must be aware that she should be reinforcing good behavior and not inadvertently reinforcing actual and/or related bad behavior.

A characteristic of the group members that occasionally occurs is an attempt to divide staff. For example, the group member may relate to a teacher one story and relate the same story to the counselor in a slightly different way, with just enough factual information in the story to make the responsible staff member very suspect. It is a characteristic of this type of student to try, either consciously or unconsciously, to divide staff. This, of course, must be recognized as part of the pathology of the individual student. It is important that the counselor and the teacher have direct communication with each other. The program should be coordinated with the teacher, counselor, and administrator working together. When there is direct communication and agreement among all staff members, the youngsters in the program will usually "settle down' quicker and respond faster.

There are different techniques that can be used with so-called behavior problem groups. One technique that is often effective is to work with a group of youngsters from the same classroom. Occasionally when a group of boys, for example, is organized for a group counseling session, the counselor is surprised that the youngsters cooperate and interact well within the group. She may wonder why the teacher is having a problem with the group in the classroom. Two factors may become obvious: When some youngsters are put in a larger group (i.e., the classroom or the playground) they have a tendency to become hyperactive because of the many external stimuli to which they are exposed. This is particularly true in the elementary school years. The second is that a group of boys from the same classroom may act differently because there are no female students in the group. When the counselor incorporates female students into the group, the same boys who preformed optimally within the group may revert to their usual pattern of acting out as they do in the classroom.

When it is feasible, it is probably best to avoid a homogeneous group of behavior problems. When possible, it is technically better to have a heterogeneous group including average youngsters who do not have similar problems. However, the goals of the group should be the same for all group members. The expectancy of the leader for the entire group may offset the youngsters' behavior. A group member usually attempts to adapt to the mannerisms and behavior patterns of the group. Her conduct within a good group, for example, has to be adaptive to good behavior. The youngster, by a process of reinforcement, participation, acceptance, and recognition by the group leader, may develop a positive group identity which can transfer to other group situations including the classroom. Placement within an average group is optimum because the counselor can handle the youngster's problems with the support of the group members, who also help to shape their colleague's behavior. (This does not, of course, work with all types of behavior problems.)

Since the Columbine school shootings, all educators have had to be more sensitive to the potentially violent child. Very often the potentially violent child is not a behavior problem per se. He (or she) may be withdrawn, angry or sullen. This type of youngster may not create a in the classroom. The teachers may observe this child as an unusually quiet youngster that may feel isolated in the class. But when placed in a group the youngster may be more spontaneous. Although not disruptive she may be the student who talks about angry/violent subjects often to the discomfort of the group members.

*The discomfort that the counselor feels may be reflective of the anxiety, anger and discomfort of the student.*

Students who have had behavior problems before becoming group members will still have them. The counselor who decides to work with a youngster is not going to automatically resolve that youngster's problems. Behavior problems in the school setting may reflect behavior patterns that the youngsters have learned as an adaptive mechanism. If the pattern of behavior is to be changed, it usually is a long process. When the counselor achieves one of those miracle changes of behavior which occur within a session or two, she should realize that the youngsters may need long-term support; for without additional reinforcement by the counselor or other staff members, the youngsters may revert to their previous behavior. Recidivism is common.

*As a supportive measure, the counselor can organize groups that meet periodically (i.e., one time per month).* The goal of the group is to reinforce the progress that the youngsters have made and to give them an opportunity to discuss any difficulties or frustrations that they may be experiencing. This is usually sufficient. It alerts the counselor to any impending difficulty that the youngsters may be developing since last seen. It allows the youngsters to feel that they will have periodic help that they can count on. This will often "take the edge off" so that a youngster will not have to "act out" with unfavorable or delinquent behavior in order to get the help and direction the student may think she needs.

Group counseling sessions which are used as support should be organized so that the counselor gives the youngsters an opportunity to talk. The counselor should not dominate the conversation and should encourage the students to discuss anything they want to bring up (positive or negative) that is appropriate to the group. Supportive group counseling sessions can help many youngsters and at the same time decrease the "chronic, difficult, problem case load" that the counselor may have. Everybody benefits. The administrator usually is relieved, as is the counselor, because the youngsters are being helped in a preventative rather than a remedial way. The youngsters are more relaxed because they know that somebody is ready and willing to give them the help when and if they need it. They have an opportunity to share their difficulties if difficulties present. The frustration and anxiety of a youngster may become considerable if she thinks that there is no one to give him any help. Some youngsters become anxious because they start thinking that if they do develop a problem there is nobody to help them.

The group counseling technique can often help the counselor to define a behavior problem by the behavior that occurs in the session. This type of description is reflective of the individual problems of the youngster as well as the problems that may appear when the student participates in a group. This information can be of considerable help to a referral clinic as well as to the teacher.

In summary, a behavior problem generally emanates from one of two causes, or both. One is an adjustment to the environment. Environmental manipulation (in the group and/or classroom) can be utilized so that the youngster can learn new behavior patterns and be given an opportunity to resolve some of the problems that she may have. The second is an internalized emotional problem that needs intensive counseling and/or medication. In some cases the youngsters will respond very quickly.

A significant percentage of youngsters may not need intensive counseling but often do need periodic support from some adult staff member (i.e., the administrator, teacher, or counselor). An important consideration is that the group leader should be patient. What seems to give the youngsters and the counselors the most difficulty is not what the counselor does (the counselors are usually very good technically) but rather the impatience of the counselor who expects the youngsters to change sooner than they are capable. The counselor should recognize that changing behavior is often a lengthy process. It is important for the counselor to recognize that behavior groups can be difficult.

One of the problems that group counseling had in its early stages was that counselors used their most difficult students to initiate group work. The author does not recommend this, especially for the inexperienced counselor. When the author first initiated group work within the schools, the staff had randomly selected ten girls. Five of the girls were borderline psychotic, two others were severely neurotic, one had a severe phobia for animals, and the other two were moderately severe adjustment reactions to adolescence. Even with his experience the author found the group almost uncontrollable at times. These youngsters were not candidates for group counseling in the school setting. Behavior groups should be well selected and, when possible, directed by experienced counselors. When the counselor cannot handle the problems of the group, the group should be disbanded and the youngsters either worked with individually or referred to the appropriate agencies.

## WARNING SIGNS OF YOUTH VIOLENCE

Many children and youth who behave violently have a long history of emotional and behavioral problems. Signs and symptoms of trouble usually have existed for years, not as isolated behaviors or single emotional outbursts. Consultations with a mental health professional should be considered for children who display behavior patterns incorporating one or more of the following signs:

- Frequent loss of temper
- Frequent physical fighting
- Significant vandalism or property damage
- Making serious threats
- Extreme impulsiveness
- Alcohol and other drug use
- Easily frustrated
- Hurting animals
- Preoccupation with violent or morbid themes or fantasies in schoolwork, artwork or choice of entertainment
- Carrying a weapon
- Name calling, abusive language
- Bullying or being bullied
- Truancy
- Excessive feelings of rejection or persecution
- Gang affiliation
- Depression, despair
- Low self-esteem
- Threatening or attempting suicide
- Extreme mood swings

- Deteriorating school performance
- Being witness to or the subject of domestic abuse
- Setting fires
- Preoccupation with weapons and explosive devices
- History of discipline problems
- Social withdrawal
- Blaming others for difficulties and problems

Note: These indicators are not necessarily reliable precursors or predictors of violent or delinquent behavior. They must be interpreted carefully and cautiously to avoid the risk of unfairly labeling and stigmatizing an individual. Just as important as responding to early warning signs is not overreacting, in what US Secretary of Education Richard W. Riley called "mechanical profiling of students." Stereotyping and labeling can have devastating and indelible effects.

(Sources: 32,33,39: David Fassler, MD, Commission testimony, March 2000) "From Youth to Violence" – Commission for the Prevention of Youth Violence Dec. 2000 pg. 11.

## CAREER PLANNING

Group counseling is a good technique to utilize in developmental programs emphasizing career planning. Career-planning programs should start in the early grades of the elementary school and should be programmed in a way that emphasizes a developmental approach: that is, the program increases in sophistication as the youngster matures. The essential goals of career-planning should be insight into jobs and job opportunities and the development of a positive self image so that the youngster feels that she can attain whatever she is capable. If the youngster thinks she is capable, the student will often be able to perform commensurate with her abilities. Expectancy of the teacher and the counselor is an important factor in influencing the career planning of the student. Youngsters in group counseling can see and hear other students in a group say, "I want to do this," or "I want to be that," and can share their own thoughts with their peers. They soon recognize that their fellow students have similar doubts and hesitations about the future including their future careers.

When students share their ideas, frustrations, and plans they are more ready to think that perhaps they, too, can "make it," especially when they can discuss with their peers how to overcome the reservations that they do have. A youngster who has some doubts about her own abilities and her future can gain more from a discussion with peers than she can from a classical one-to-one, counselor-to-student relationship, but it is very difficult (even for the experienced counselor) to enhance the student's group identity on a one-to-one basis.

Career planning is similar to many other programs that have been discussed in the book. It has to be "programmed"; that is, the group leader should start at the level at which the youngster is capable of understanding and performing and increase the sophistication of the discussion (and audio-visual materials) as the youngster develops her skills. For example, there is little reason to talk about going to college if the student has no idea what college is. There is no point in asking a youngster what she wants to "take" at college if she does not know what courses a college "offers."

The leader should not talk in general terms or concepts that the youngster does not understand. It is better to discuss particulars, especially with a less sophisticated group, and then program the discussion over a session or a number of sessions, according to the ability and understanding of the youngsters involved. For example, in a discussion about college the first question may be: "What is college? What do people do in college? Why do people go to college? What are the advantages and disadvantages of going to college?" The next consideration might be an actual visit to one of the colleges or junior colleges in the area, with a discussion with the college students and/or professors. The various types of colleges, scholarships available, clothes that are worn, and how to finance a college education might be discussed. The important part of the discussion would be to answer the so-called "bread-and-butter" issues. (A similar format can be used for discussion of other topics, i.e., jobs, training programs.) The concept that higher learning may take place in different settings, (college, work place, and trade schools) is an important realization to many youngsters. Many students think that it is college or nothing, or that it is a trade school or nothing.

It is helpful to compare and work with above-average youngsters as well as an average or under-achiever population. It will immediately emphasize the difference in approaching the youngsters at their level of performance and will contrast the sophistication of questions that can be used. Sometimes the questions are the same but the sophistication of the youngsters demands a more sophisticated or less sophisticated approach, depending upon the level of performance of the group members. In one career planning program called "Education and the World of Work" the topics discussed were similar in each group, but the involvement of the group reflected the social and cognitive maturations levels of the members. Some of the topics and questions that the sixth grade youngsters considered in their discussion were:

1. What is a good job?
2. What are the responsibilities of a job?
3. How do you get a job?
4. How do you apply for a job?
5. Are there any jobs that are not important?
6. Why do people drop out of school or drop out of jobs?
7. If one does drop out, what are the alternatives for furthering education or obtaining other jobs?
8. Interest in a job similar to father's.
9. Interest in jobs that are not similar to father's.
10. Value of training and education in relationship to a job.
11. How does one explore the various opportunities for different careers?
12. How does one investigate the possibilities of different careers?
13. What things would determine the selection of a career?
14. What influence do parents have in the selection of a career?
15. Why is it important to discuss and consider future career

planning at this particular age?
16. What should determine the final selection of a career?

A program in career planning should involve more than the opportunity of a group counseling program. The group program should be correlated with the use of available audio-visual material, field trips and discussion in the schools with representatives of the business community, and role playing sessions. The counseling sessions can be designed to allow each youngster to take part in a skit that is representative of a possible job or job interview. A varied career planning program offers the youngster an opportunity to broaden her knowledge of the mechanics of the business, and professional world. Thus, even if a youngster does not select a particular profession or trade, she has insight into the mechanics of that profession which might make her a more understanding citizen.

There are many techniques: i.e., provocative questions like "What would a fifteen-thousand-dollars-a-year salary do for you?" (also self-analysis questions as well as general topics) that stimulate the interaction and interest of the youngsters.

One issue that is frequently discussed by counselors in "career planning" is the so-called "cultural gap." The school staff may initiate career planning programs designed to bridge the "cultural gap" between inner-city and perimeter-city youngsters. This is a significant mistake. No one can measure culture. The youngsters of the inner city have their own culture, some of which is similar to the culture of the perimeter-city youngsters and some of which is not. The key is not to try to measure or close the so-called cultural gap. This is done most effectively not by a direct assault on something which cannot be measured, such as culture, but rather by "attacking" the gap between the performance levels of the students.

"Culture" cannot be taught. When the school staff orients itself to developing programs of culture for the sake of culture, they often do not reach their goal. When they orient the programs toward developing a cultural milieu with visits to the art museums, libraries, historical sights, and so on, they can then gauge what they are doing by the performance of the youngsters. If the youngsters visit an art museum and then return to class and discuss the art museum, the history of art, the biography of the painters, and a review of the decades in which the artists lived, then the teacher is able to measure the performance of the youngsters either on tests or discussions or projects that the youngsters develop.

Everything that is done in the school should be geared towards facilitating the basic process of teaching and learning. How can the child be taught career planning? How does he learn? What does a perimeter-city child do in the classroom that is different from the inner-city child? What skills does the youngster in one area have that make him a better student than the other? What does a trip to a particular place do for the child as far as his ability to learn and understand about career planning?

When projects are initiated that will orient students to planning their careers, the project developers should reflect on the performance level of the youngster. Culture or a cultural gap becomes a vague concept without having some understanding of what it means in terms of performance. When career planning programs are organized so that they reflect the needs of the students, the staff has a significantly better chance of reaching the program goals. When the program is designed to reflect generalities, it lacks the specifics necessary to find out exactly what the youngster is capable of doing and what he is not.

## STUDENT TEACHERS

In order to alleviate the current shortage of teachers, the school may have to utilize resource people who are readily available. There are two reservoirs that can be considered: the parents of the children who attend school and the students themselves. Both groups can be utilized as ancillary personnel. (The models for parent groups have been outlined in Chapter XIII.)

The students can be a significant resource. They are plentiful and readily available. When the older youngsters are utilized to help younger students, the programs have been of considerable help to the teacher, the younger students, and the student teachers themselves. When "trained" students help in the classroom it allows the teacher to work with smaller groups. When the class is periodically divided into small groups there is usually more group interaction. The interaction of a small group may stimulate more sharing of ideas than can usually be accomplished in the standard-sized urban class (thirty-five plus children). There are usually few problems with discipline because the younger children emulate and respect the older students.

There is little difficulty with the student teachers when they have been well prepared. They should be given a series of orientation sessions (as a group) by the staff advisor. For example, sixth grade tutors can be given a series of training sessions that allow them to identify as student teachers. They should be given the opportunity to discuss what might go wrong, what difficulties they might encounter, in what ways they can help, how to be patient, how to avoid being too authoritarian, the goals of the teacher, and what can be accomplished by utilizing small groups. Some schools have used third grade youngsters to help kindergarten and first grade youngsters. The fifth and sixth graders, however, are usually more effective. The school can use under-achievers as well as above-average youngsters to student teach. Sixth grade youngsters who are reading two grade levels behind can help first grade youngsters (and it helps them at the same time). Teaching increases not only their understanding of the skills which they are teaching, but it also increases their opportunity to interact and to learn communication-socialization skills.

The student teachers have an advantage: they can speak the language of the youngsters. When the youngsters do not understand a particular problem, the student teachers often have better insight why. Perhaps it is their age and conceptual framework; perhaps it is a common sensitivity. Whatever it is, the student teachers are particularly effective. They comprehend their assignment well and often give helpful suggestions.

The best way to learn is to teach. Every educator recognizes this. If the student does a good job that is approved by adults whom she respects, her teaching experience will usually have a positive effect. The opportunity to accomplish something that is worthwhile is extremely important. One of the difficulties today is that our youngsters do not have an opportunity to perform jobs that are meaningful and in which they can receive a positive feedback. Teaching offers an opportunity to do something which nourishes their wonderful, idealistic temperaments.

In initiating a student-teaching program there should be two basic considerations. The program should be started with above-average students. The first group of student teachers should be able to handle themselves with little difficulty. This will give the staff an opportunity to review the possible administrative and technical problems of the project. After this is accomplished, average (or even below average) youngsters can be used as student teachers. The second consideration is to make sure that the student teachers have an opportunity to learn what they are going to do by participating in group training sessions.

The anxiety that the students may have about participating can be minimized by giving them an opportunity to know exactly what their responsibilities will be, what the goals of the project are, and what possible difficulties they may encounter. It is important that the teachers involved also have training sessions. The teachers must be alert to what they are going to attempt to accomplish, what positive (or negative) feedback may be encountered, what the goals of the project are, and what they should do (in an organized way) if difficulties do occur.

If the youngster is selected as a student teacher who for some reason cannot handle the responsibility, then she should be withdrawn from the job, the positive work that she has done reinforced, and the unsatisfactory work discussed with her. The student should be referred to the teacher or counselor for additional counseling and perhaps training. Everything involving the project should be utilized as a teaching experience. If the youngsters do well at their jobs, then this too should be discussed and the project reinforced. The student teachers should be told why they did well so that they have some understanding of their performance and can subsequently duplicate their results.

Older youngsters have also been used as "big brothers" or "big sisters." The programs are designed to stimulate social interaction and to offer to the younger children support from an older student.

The student who is being asked to be a big brother or sister should recognize what her goals and responsibilities are and what they are not. This should be done within the school program. The camaraderie that has resulted from big brother and big sister programs and the help to some of the slower and/or behavior problems has been significant.

In summary, one of the significant resources that the school has is the older students, who can be utilized as teacher assistants. This enhances the entire teaching program. The success of student teaching often depends on the amount of training that the students receive prior to participating in their assignments. Programs should be designed so that the students receive didactic material, an opportunity to observe teachers in the classroom (before participating as teachers), and group training sessions that allow them to share with each other their experiences and observations. Those programs that have not been successful usually have not had careful training and support for the student teachers. Student teaching is an effective way of enhancing the school program and can be done at every grade level. One of the needs of our nation is to develop leadership opportunities. Student teaching is a "perfect" area in which to utilize youngsters.

## CHARM GROUPS

Most teen-aged girls are interested in fashion design, dress, and cosmetics. They do not often have an opportunity in school to discuss these interests with adults. Group counseling sessions or classroom discussion (i.e., home economics) can offer this opportunity. These sessions can be particularly meaningful to the girls. They have an opportunity to discuss with adult guidance current fashions of how to dress, how to use cosmetics, what is appropriate dress for a teen-ager (and what is not), what to anticipate at a particular type function, and other pertinent topics.

The counselor or home economics teacher can utilize these sessions to correlate discussions of dress with what kind of behavior is appropriate at a party, what is not appropriate for the particular age group, and so on. These groups have been very successful. The students enjoy them. They can broaden their experience by sharing ideas with each other and test their ideas against an adult who is not a parent. It also gives them an excuse with their peers if they did not participate in functions that they do not think are socially appropriate. For example, they can relate to their counseling group how they did not participate, and get the reinforcement they want, which they might not be able to receive in a peer setting that was not structured by adult supervision. This is particularly helpful to the students.

The groups will vary considerably depending upon the socio-economic status and the sophistication of the group. For example, in one rural county the "charm" group was oriented to literally teaching girls how to dress. This was a very practical counseling session which considerably enhanced the youngsters' self esteem. In other geographical areas where youngsters are more sophisticated about dress and socialization, the counseling sessions concentrate on general topics of interest associated with dress and behavior. The "what-to-do-at-a-certain-time" counseling session is particularly helpful. Youngsters going through adolescence may not be sure. They are uncomfortable about handling themselves in different situations. Practical pointers of what is expected and what is not, what adults expect of them and what they do not, can be helpful.

This emphasizes that group counseling sessions can serve many different goals at the same time. A charm group can be oriented to discussing practical pointers on dress, cosmetics, and hairstyles, and at the same time address itself to appropriate behavior for various functions. This is generally acceptable and encouraged by the youngsters. The counselor who is able to combine practical items with general abstract considerations can be considered an above-average counselor.

It is a mistake for a group leader to think that she must follow a classical model in which talking about abstract things is the only technique utilized. This is unrealistic for any kind of group counseling session with youngsters. The consideration of practical matters and the involvement of the group leader is important.

The youngsters inevitably will ask the group leader what he or she thinks about a particular topic and what they would do in that kind of situation. There are certain topics about which it is both practical and helpful if the counselor shares her ideas. However, there are other issues which cannot be resolved in a yes-or-no fashion and that involve many things, including the cultural background of the youngsters, their biological and physical maturation, and their awareness and sophistication about topics such as sexual relations. Many questions cannot and should not be answered with a "yes" or "no" by the group leader. It takes a skillful leader to stimulate discussion on these questions but yet not give a yes or no answer without incurring the anger of the group members. The group leader should hesitate to impulsively give her own thoughts about particular subjects. When the youngsters themselves can propose ideas and can handle the major part of the responsibility, then the sessions are usually more meaningful to the students.

## *ANONYMOUS*
## *(STUDENTS WHO APPROACH THE COUNSELOR)*

There are occasions when groups are formed because the group members present to the counselor requesting a confidential meeting and/or group. There may be many reasons for such a request. It may be that the youngsters in a class are having difficulty relating with the teacher and having behavior problems. Other students may feel uncomfortable in the school setting, not relating well to their peers, and feel that they would like some help.

These youngsters may have something in common which they think makes them different from their peers: for example, physical problems such as epilepsy, diabetes, or physical anomalies (i.e., arms, legs, or feet). They present to the counselor in confidence, requesting a counseling session individually (or as a group) so that the counselor might be able to share with them the difficulties that they have. They seek counsel and advice and/or a place where they can learn in an organized setting with professional guidance. The counselor, whenever possible, should not only tolerate but encourage it.

The most important step is that the youngsters themselves recognize that they have a problem and that they are willing to come to an adult in the school setting for help. The group has already achieved an element of success on which the counselor can build a reinforcement program. The mere fact that the youngsters handled the problem by approaching the counselor in a responsible way is indicative of success. This should be pointed out to the group by the counselor.

One of the considerations that has to be handled by the counselor in an appropriate way is the question of confidentiality. If youngsters are acting up in a classroom and want to come and talk about it, it is to the youngsters' disadvantage for the counselor to say that yes, she will concur with confidentiality. Although the youngsters are concerned about confidentiality, this usually is not a major problem. If the counselor says, "I will be glad to work with you and have counseling sessions, but I have to feel free to do whatever is appropriate and best for you," the youngsters will usually respond favorably. If they feel comfortable about coming to the counselor initially, then the question of confidentiality is not a real one. Sometimes a group that comes with the token of confidentiality is truly looking to see whether the counselor can handle the situation. If the counselor gets caught in the trap of agreeing to confidentiality, the group may never get started because the group members may think that the counselor is not able to handle the situation in a responsible way; whereas if the counselor establishes the "ground rules" that she will do what she thinks is appropriate, they will usually be more comfortable and recognize that the counselor has the necessary experience to handle whatever problems they are going to present.

There are some situations in which confidentiality can be utilized for the benefit of the group. For example, a group of youngsters presented to a counselor because they were all obese. The youngsters came to the counselor and said: "We'd like to form a Fatties Anonymous group and would like this to be confidential. We'd like to meet with you periodically." The counselor organized the group so that one afternoon a week, during lunch, the girls would get together with the counselor (in confidence). Of course, in a school situation it is difficult to withdraw eight obese girls and have it confidential, especially at noon hour. The girls related about their obesity, feelings of inadequacy, difficulties in identity and relating to their peers, what it meant to be obese, and what they had tried in order to lose weight. The counselor invited the school nurse and visiting physician to talk to the youngsters about diets and dieting. The girls were able to discuss their problem of obesity and also other problems relating to their peers and the adult world. These youngsters developed a very positive group identity which they had not had before. This carried over to the classroom and other school activities. Their obesity no longer deterred them from participating in group activity.

Groups such as this (that is, children with physical or other problems) can be initiated by the counselor. (In most cases the groups are initiated by the counselor.) The counselor does not organize the group as a confidential one but does not publicize it either. A tacit agreement of confidentiality is given by the counselor (because she is a counselor). No verbal commitment of confidentiality has to be given. When the students feel comfortable enough to approach a staff member with their problems (individually of in groups) the faculty has accomplished the prerequisite for establishing a positive attitude in the school.

## PSYCHO-DRAMA AND ROLE PLAYING

Within recent years there has been increased interest in the group technique called psycho-drama or role playing. Within this technique the group members are given particular roles which they are to enact. For example, the counselor may say to the group: "Suppose you were having difficulty in your work- that is, in your studies-and you wanted to talk to a number of people about this. Jack, you be the student; Mary, you be the teacher; Jimmy, you be the father; Betty, you be the mother; Jim, you be the friend; and Kathy, you be the counselor." The youngster would then play the part of a student and talk to each of these individuals in a role-playing situation. Each would react as they thought the student's parent, counselor, teacher, would react. The situations that can be enacted are numerous.

The group may be discussing career planning and the counselor may say: "Jane, you indicated that you wanted to be a nurse. Suppose we role-play what you think a nurse's role would be. Let's set the stage at the bedside of a sick patient." Or the counselor could say: "Jane, you indicated that you would like to be a nurse. Suppose we role-play an interview by the admissions officer of a nursing school. Betty, you play the part of the admissions officer. Jane, you play the part of the applicant."

A group may be talking about parents and the way parents handle particular problems, and the counselor could say: "Suppose we role-play a situation in which the son comes home later than expected. What would happen?" and she then indicated that one group member would be the son, another would be the sibling, and two group members would play the role of parents.

Role playing is an effective technique and can be useful in giving both the counselor and the group members' insight into how they and their peers would feel, think, and react about particular topics. It also gives the student members an opportunity to actually "play out" events that they have been putting aside. It is significantly different to think about how one is going to conduct herself in a job interview than to actually role-play how one would act.

After the role playing is enacted the counselor can ask questions about the events that took place during the role-playing or psycho-drama situation. For example: "Jim, do you think that when Bill played the part of the father he was being realistic? Is this the way you think the father would act?" or "Jane, do you think that when Betty played the part of the admissions officer for nursing school, that it was realistic? Do you think this is what would happen?" The students can observe how somebody played that particular role, and share ideas of what they would anticipate and what they would not. One youngster may say, "No, this isn't the way it would be. I don't think any adult would handle himself in that way." Another youngster may make a different interpretation. This clarifies in the students' minds many things that might happen under different situations and increases the student's awareness.

The group leader should be cautious, especially with adolescents, that the group members do not play the role too seriously and become too involved. Occasionally an adolescent will become particularly anxious or over-stimulated with the role she plays. If this occurs, the group leader should become directive in the discussion in an effort to decrease the student's anxiety. It is not uncommon for adolescents to over-identify in a role-playing situation. If after a few sessions the counselor finds that the student group she is working with seems to be over-enthusiastic with the psycho-drama incidents, then it is important that she change techniques or, if the counselor does continue to use psycho-drama, that she set limits so that the students will not be overactive in class, the corridors, club activities, etc.

Psycho-drama and role playing, like any group technique, should not be used to the exclusion of other techniques; however, to exclude role playing is to deprive the group of a good technique. The technique that is used should be as applicable as possible to the goals of the counseling session. For example, in career planning role playing is particularly effective. It can also be helpful with passive youngsters. The younger child who is not able to discuss something with the adult will often, through projective techniques and playing with toys, express her feelings. The passive youngster who is older may be more apt to participate in a role-playing situation than to express herself in a group counseling session.

The counselor should avoid giving the passive youngster a role that will require a more active part than she is ready or able to perform. The counselor should program the student's participation. For example, in one role-playing situation, a passive youngster could play the part of a butler. In the next role she might play a more verbal and perhaps more aggressive part; but to start a passive youngster in a demanding role may be unfair. Initially the role can be selected to fit the personality of the child. In subsequent sessions, it is better for the youngsters to enact different roles.

The counselor should be aware that in the role-playing situation there are usually two levels at which the discussion occurs. One is essentially an emotional or "feeling" level. The second is a more objective reflection of what is going on. Children learn and get better insight into the patterns of behavior if they handle it in a more objective way. This insight can be influenced by the course of the discussion after the role-playing is enacted.

## FOSTER CHILDREN

In the inner-city areas of our large communities there is often a high incidence of youngsters who have only one parent in the home, or are living with relatives (i.e., grandmothers, aunts, etc.) There is also a large group of youngsters who live in foster homes. The foster child may present problems that are unique.

One problem is that they have been separated from the primary group, the family. They feel that they are youngsters without a family, and they may be. Their concept of themselves as members of the primary group and their self-esteem and group identity may be poor. They often think that the world is against them and that nothing like this has ever happened to anybody before. They are sometimes frustrated and angry. Feelings of rejection may be prominent, and feelings of acceptance by others may be minimal. They are frequently suspicious; the question of trust is often discussed. *This is not true of all foster children.* Many foster children who are placed in foster homes are able to resolve the sequela of any emotional trauma they may have encountered. In good foster homes they can achieve a positive group identity which reinforces their individual self-esteem.

Group counseling offers to foster children an opportunity to see that other foster children are making it, and have the same difficulties and the same feelings as they do. It does not allow them to feel that they alone or isolated or that this is a one-shot, "once in a lifetime for-them-only" event. Once this fallacy is laid bare, the youngsters can identify with group members who may be oriented towards "making the grade." This is significant. When the youngster isolates herself, she is usually not able to effectively develop because she is continually combating the frustrated, angry feelings within her.

During the initial sessions the group members may talk about topics that reflect their anger. As the sessions continue, the youngsters usually start to review their position in a realistic way and orient themselves to real issues. Foster children in general are quite sensitive. They are quite aware of the difficulties that they and their peers are having. When they are given the opportunity to handle their difficulties in a well-structured, positive way they often do so and are usually willing to help each other in accomplishing these goals.

One issue that is repeatedly presented in foster children groups is the question of trust and acceptance. For example, the youngsters may discuss whether the foster parents have given them keys to the house and/or how long the foster parents allow them to stay out. There are many different ways that the issue of trust and acceptance are discussed. The youngsters often feel rejected.

When the school social worker elects to work with blood siblings it the same family, or in foster care, it is important to note the neighborhood effect (Chapter II). The loyalties and group cohesiveness that have bound these youngsters together previous to the group counseling sessions are stronger than the ties to the agency or institution with which they are now working. The author has not been successful in working with youngsters from the same genetic family who are in foster care (in the same home) as with children from the same family who are living with their biological parents. He has had even less success with siblings who are scattered in different foster homes. (this however, is based on his own sample which is small.)

Group work is usually more successful when one of the biological parents consents to act as co-leader (especially when the foster children are scattered in different homes and are all having difficulties in their respective homes). The group leader should initially accept primary responsibility for leadership of the group counseling session. The parent often needs initial support because of the anger expressed by the children for being placed in foster care. But as the group works toward some meaningful goal (i.e., getting together), the group usually becomes more cohesive. The sessions often become quite meaningful and a means of keeping the family united, at least in identity. It is important that the group leader and the parent work together so that there is direct communication and neither feels that the other is usurping her particular responsibility. The group counseling sessions will not be helpful if there is a "tug a war" between the co-leaders.

When the parent participates, it reinforces the neighborhood effect. The counselor utilizes the family ties of loyalty and interaction.

A positive group identity is working for the group. The author does not advocate a school social worker or counselor working with a family until she becomes an experienced group leader.

One of the technical problems that often present in working with a foster group is terminating the group. Because the youngsters have undergone traumatic separations from the major adult figures in their lives, whether by foster placement, death, or divorce, ending the group will create an anniversary of feelings and thoughts representative of another separation. It is for this reason that the group leader should organize the group so that termination is known beforehand and the group members can "work though" their separation feelings. Generally when the group leader is able to terminate the group at the specified time or date, the group members will respond accordingly and are able to terminate without difficulty. If they only have to handle their own thoughts they will do fairly well. If they have to handle their own thoughts plus the guilt feelings of the group leader, they may or may not do well.

In general, foster children respond well to group counseling sessions.

## *AUDIO-VISUAL AIDS*

Group counseling sessions can be enhanced by the use of audio-visual aids. Many counselors use tape recorders as an integral part of their program and often tape their sessions. The tapes can be used to let the kids hear themselves. In more sophisticated groups the student members can discuss how they thought group members reacted during the taped session. They can be helpful in training student leaders.

Projectors are commonly used: i.e., movies, computers, slides, charts, and less expensive "home-made" demonstrations. In the elementary grades word charts can be used to stimulate discussion. For example, a teacher holds up the word chart with the word 'classroom' and asks the students, "What do you think it represents?" or "What does a person do in a classroom?" The twenty-questions type of game showing the word chart first is frequently used.

Audio-visual equipment can be used to program a child (especially a passive child) who has difficulty communicating and expressing herself. She can receive information in a non-threatening way. It is surprising that more audio-visual demonstrations are not in cartoon form, especially for the elementary school. The children seem to like animated cartoons and respond enthusiastically to them. Audio-visual equipment can be used for a class presentation but is especially helpful when it is used as a stimulus for discussion.

One of the disadvantages of audio-visual equipment is that the counselor can use it as a "distancing" mechanism. By *distancing* the author means a method whereby the counselor or group leader uses either general topics or audio-visual equipment to keep from interacting with the group members. Unfortunately, many classroom teachers also do this. They may use a rigid classroom style whereby they never give the students an opportunity to interact with each other. When audio-visual aids are used as a distancing mechanism, the youngsters do not have the opportunity to discuss the material presented.

If the counselor plans a one-session meeting and has to deliver a given amount of material in a short period of time, audio-visual equipment can be very helpful. The teacher can cover considerable information in a condensed fashion that is acceptable to the students. However, exclusive use of audio-visual equipment, with little personal contact, will not give the youngsters an opportunity to develop other skills which are important in learning, skills which are primarily developed by interaction between students and between the students and the teacher.

## INTERRACIAL GROUP COUNSELING

Integration is of vital importance to the community and to the nation. It is vital to the growth of our school systems. Integration, however, must by its very nature be a two-way proposition. The white community must orient itself to participation in the African-American community and the African-American community must orient itself to participation in the white community. This means programs that will allow the traffic to flow both ways. When interracial problems that exist are presented to the students, the youngsters usually find very quick, lucid, and exemplary ways of resolving the problems that are presented. The solutions that are given are very direct and usually very simple. The reaction is "If there is a problem, lets' get together and resolve it," a good admonition for the adult leaders.

One of the major tasks is to find effective ways to facilitate the important job of integration. This task has become increasingly more difficult because of the concentration of the segregated population in the respective geographical areas (that is, white populations live in predominantly white neighborhoods and African-American populations live in predominantly African-American neighborhoods.)

A school system can facilitate the integration process in different ways. In one project five groups of four youngsters from predominantly African-American schools and four youngsters from predominately white schools (ten schools participated) were brought together for group sessions. The student members discussed their ideas about integration and several other topics which were of concern to them. The group counseling experience helped in many ways. It familiarized the children with youngsters from different schools. It reflected the interests and concerns of the students involved. It broadened the experience of the group members by giving them an interpretation and experience that many of the members had never had before. It also illustrated to the youngsters that they had similar interests regardless of the setting from which they came. It illustrated to the staff that capability, acceptance, and performance by the youngsters was not necessarily reflective of the environment from which the students come. This is particularly important in breaking down the barriers that are artificially created by our ghettoized societies.

Programs of this type can start to build a bridge across every section of the city. It can start to consolidate the city at its most important level, that of the children or future leaders of the community. It can have a mushrooming effect. The children who participate go back to their classes and schools and relate their experiences with other youngsters. It can build interest in future inter-school activity which can be used to expand the development of interaction between student councils, debate groups, dramatic societies, athletic events and so on. It develops city-wide (or area-wide) communication on which an integrated society can be built.

The group counseling technique alerts the faculty and the administrators to the possibilities that exist in working with groups representative of different schools. It offers a model to be used in the organized expansion of inter-school activities. It offers to the research-oriented person an opportunity to compare the strengths and weaknesses of similar groups of youngsters from different areas of the city. For example, an above-average group from one part of the city may be talented in one skill compared to an above-average group from another part of the city. By observing the contrast the staff can initiate programs of a compensatory nature, sharing with the teachers, administrators, and counselors significant and minor differences that may have been observed in the groups. *Interracial groups also re-emphasize the similarities of children in every part of the city upon which inter-school programs can be initiated.* It is recommended that an interracial group counseling project be started with average or above-average youngsters, and staff who are capable of handling the responsibility and of projecting many of their own interests and leadership qualities. One possible formula for beginning an inter-racial program is to organize small groups of eight youngsters, four white youngsters from predominately white schools and four youngsters from predominately African-American schools. The initial goals would be to learn as much as possible about the basic inter-racial problems that confront youngsters, community, neighborhood, family, and school.

The youngsters themselves resolve the interracial problems very quickly. It is the educators who have the most trouble. One of the great threats to education is that in many large urban areas there is still significant polarization between the races at the educator level. This presents a great threat to the integration and cohesion of our population because, as pointed out early in the book, the most important part of a group is its leadership. If the leadership (namely, the educators of our school systems) are polarized into separate groups, then the youngsters do not have a chance to make it. In smaller inter-racial groups, the author observed that when the groups were structured and organized in a positive way, the youngsters quickly (within the first one or two sessions) resolved the problems of race. When the educators involved were not cooperative and interested in the inter-racial project, or had negative feelings about "pulling together" within the system (and the community), then the youngsters had a much more difficult task. Sometimes they made it and sometimes they did not. Basically there was a neighborhood effect. The students had to identify with the leadership (which in this case was the educators) and did reflect the attitudes and mannerisms of the educators. When the educators were cooperative and wanted a good effect, this is in fact what the youngsters produced. When the administrators and other educators involved were negative about the program, then the youngsters' performance was less satisfactory.

The most important single variable appeared to be the attitude of the leader. As they responded, the youngsters seemed to respond likewise. A closer scrutiny of the group sessions revealed that when the groups were well organized, the youngsters came to grips with the concepts of interracial problems and resolved them quickly. When the group was not well organized they considered the question of differences but in a less direct fashion, that is, instead of talking about interracial differences, they talked about foreign movies, Indian populations, different types of music, etc. They talked about differences but not inter-racial differences. The factor that became very important was not the student readiness for a program like this, but educator readiness. The most influencing factor on the youngsters' performance, was the positive and productive attitude of the educator.

A preliminary interracial program is to learn about the administrative, logistical, and perhaps philosophical problems that may occur. If tested prematurely, the problems that do exist may never be resolved. Flexibility is extremely important, especially in the preliminary stages. The attitude of the leadership should be that they are going to learn about interracial activity at each step of the project so that the program might be expanded at a later date. Until the leadership has this insight, they are not going to be able to relate it to other administrators and teachers. (Administrators influence the teachers and the teachers influence the students.) A program developed for youngsters only is unrealistic. The initial consideration should be the staff and secondly the student.

When inter-racial group programs are well organized, the kids resolve problems (as noted above) very quickly; but unless there is a task or project on which they can work together, they quickly become bored. For example, one inter-racial project was organized for six weeks. The youngsters quickly resolved the problem and question of inter-racial differences. They then made it very clear that they wanted to talk about other things. The issues they talked about were varied: i.e., classes that they take, teacher attitudes, generation gap, adults in relationship to youngsters, etc. Some of the group members visited each other's classes to actually see what the differences were in the various schools. Another group went to a museum.

The program should be well organized by the staff with the concept of flexibility "built in" to allow for change. Discussion established the opportunity for communication; but once the communication is established, then the group should become task oriented to avoid boredom and to reinforce the significant meaning of the project. The question is not "How do you make it?" The question is readily resolved by the youngsters. The question is "What do you do when you do make it and establish communication?" This is the big problem that faces educators. This is the challenge that the youngsters are ready to "throw" at the adults. When communication is established, what has the community, society, and the school system to offer in meaningful projects that will allow youngsters to work together in a meaningful way?

## CLUBS AND STUDENT COUNCILS

The educator who is an advisor for a school club or student council often has different goals than the educator who is working with a group counseling session or a classroom. Although the goals may vary with each club, the overall purpose is to develop an opportunity of responsibility and leadership for the youngsters involved. A well-organized group counseling session can offer the youngster an opportunity to test her ideas and to share with other youngsters her concerns and successes. In club activity, however, the student gets another experience. When a youngster is elected to an office and has to assume responsibility that is well outlined, or when she joins a club and has to assume responsibility for fulfilling the obligations of club membership, the student is acquiring a meaningful experience that can only partially be obtained by verbal interaction alone.

An individual does not necessarily learn how to handle the responsibility of running a group, or directing a group, by a group counseling session. An individual cannot satisfactorily share the experience of being elected to office, or of being congratulated for a particular job that took considerable planning, time, energy, and interest, by a group counseling session. These things can best be achieved by actual participation in some type of organized activity. The students who do participate in meaningful school clubs and student councils and the youngsters, who participate in organizations "after school" (i.e., jobs, scouts, or church) enjoy an experience that is usually important in their psychological development.

The educator who is a student club advisor should orient her goals so that active participation by the students is part of the overall design. The leadership in student organizations is delegated to the student members, but adult supervision is important. Interaction with adults is a significant learning experience for the students. The student learns in the school at essentially two levels. The first is peer oriented: the student learns from fellow students. The second is adult oriented: the student learns from responsible adults of the school system. Both are equally important. The adult educator who "takes over" a student council is not giving the youngsters the opportunity to accept the responsibility that is theirs. In contrast, the adult who withdraws from the child and gives the entire responsibility to the students is also not giving the students the opportunity to test their ideas against more mature adult experiences. There has to be some meaningful compromise.

It is important to develop leadership at the student level. One of the disappointing things that the author has found in his work is that in some school systems there is a significant lack of opportunity for the students to develop the type of student leadership that they need. There are still many schools in the inner city areas that have a minimum number of club activities, offer few opportunities for the students to participate in student councils, and have little or no interschool activity. The lack of intra-and inter school activity denies the youngsters an opportunity to obtain from the school that which they need as individuals and as group members. In the inner city the need for the opportunity to develop meaningful relationships with one another and experiences within the school is particularly important. If the schools do not have programs that can involve the students, there should be a concerted effort to develop them. Student organizations enhance the esprit de corps of the school which in turn will often enhance the atmosphere for learning in the classroom. Club and student council activities interrupt the monotonous routine that many of our schools have.

When there are no extra-curricular activities and the youngsters have had no (or little) experience with club activities, then the counselor should be aware of the limited ability that the youngsters may have when the initial programs are started. Occasionally a principal will remark to the author, "Yes, we had clubs, but the youngsters couldn't handle the responsibility, so we closed them." This does not indicate that clubs are not necessary. It reinforces that fact that clubs are essential to the youngster of that particular school.

Club work, like any other activity within the school whether it be a learning situation or physical activity, has to be initiated at the level at which youngsters are capable of performing. When starting a club activity for the first time, it is important that the adult leadership be very directive and available for supervision. When the club activities fail, it is usually because the adults have given the youngsters responsibility for which they have not been prepared. For example, in one school there was an urgency for some type of group activity. The school organized a dance, which had never occurred in the school before. There was little preparation. The youngsters were given the responsibility but little direction for organizing the dance. The result was chaos and confusion. The administrator recognized the problem. He organized the next dance with significant adult supervision available to the youngsters. The dance went very well. Gradually, over a period of months, the responsibility was shifted form the counselor-teacher supervisors to that of the youngsters. As they learned how to handle an activity of this type, they assumed more and more responsibility. They did not have to "act out" in order to get the direction which was needed. This is true of most school activities. The youngsters should be given direction and supervision in the initial stages. The program should be started at a level at which they can participate. As the students learn more about the activity and running of groups, the adult supervisor can slowly shift the responsibility to the youngsters themselves, while retaining overall supervision.

The development of a student council should be programmed. When the youngsters present to the middle school for the first time in the sixth grade, they should be given a series of lectures (with the opportunity for discussion) about election procedures (national, local, and within the school), what an election means; what type of people should be selected as representatives; what powers the representative person should and should not have; and what his obligations should be. At the same time adult supervisors should be selected who are interested and want to work with student councils. After these preliminary steps the youngsters should be given an opportunity to select representatives of their homeroom for formulation of a sixth grade student council. They should be well supervised in order to enhance their leadership ability and to give them insight into the responsibility of being an elected official.

The next year, the new sixth grade students should be allowed to undergo the same type of training program with the ultimate election of their own homeroom representative to a student council. With this procedure both the seventh and sixth grades will have received a training program. As the youngsters are promoted, the new grade should have the opportunity of electing their representatives in a similar fashion. Within two years all three grades will have had an opportunity to undergo a similar learning experience. This will alleviate difficulties that may arise and at the same time give the students a meaningful experience in the development of leadership and the meaning of representation. This may significantly influence the attitude of the school. It can have a mushrooming effect on the school and, with some supervision, can occasionally affect the neighborhood.

Sometimes an opposite effect can occur. Adults can be very directive and supervise "closely" in the initial stages, as is indicated, but then never relinquish the responsibility to the youngsters. When the students reach that developmental stage of being able to accept responsibility, they may begin to resent close supervision which in fact they may not need. The question of increased responsibility should be discussed between group leaders and students. Where there are difficulties and they are openly shared with the students, some type of meaningful resolution can usually be achieved.

Another phenomenon occurs in the perimeter (suburban) areas in which the youngsters may have an important opportunity for group responsibility, leadership, and innovation. Adult supervision has to be careful not to inhibit youngsters who have had significant experience in group work. At the same time group leaders have to maintain supervision so that the youngsters do not extend themselves beyond their capability. Programming in these areas is equally important. Youngsters have a tendency to "feel their oats" and start to take on tasks for which they have neither the training nor the necessary equipment. The important consideration for the group leader is to maintain momentum by continuously upgrading the program so that the projects will continue to stimulate the interest of the students but will not extend beyond their capability.

Another problem that presents with club activities is that it is not uncommon for a few youngsters to be particularly skilled in organization work. It is the responsibility of the adult supervisors to make sure that everyone gets a "fair share" and that a few do not dominate the clubs to the exclusion of other members. Usually this is of more concern to the faculty members than it is to the students. The youngsters usually accept it relatively well. If there is any question of domination, one consideration would be to discuss it openly with the student members. It is particularly important to help the youngsters learn that sometimes their energies are diluted by over-activity into many different things. School clubs and student councils are a great opportunity for the youngsters to develop experience, responsibility, and the ability to participate with their peers and adults in group activity. It should not be underestimated and whenever possible should be encouraged.

## CLASSROOM COUNSELING

Classroom counseling is a technique that is being utilized more frequently in both the elementary and secondary schools. It can be described as counseling with the entire class. Counselors are leaving their offices and are becoming involved in many school activities including classroom guidance and counseling programs. Some schools have so many problems that it has been necessary to attempt to contact a greater number of students at one time but still encourage discussion in an organized setting. Group discussion within the classroom is often neglected in the large urban school systems since the classrooms have increased in population. Like the college professor, the classroom teacher has reverted to more didactic lecturing. The students have been less spontaneous and in some cases more angry. Teachers have often felt intimidated. Many have not been comfortable enough to allow spontaneous classroom discussion. Thus, many students have not had an opportunity for group discussion within the regular classroom, nor have they had an opportunity to discuss general problems about which they may want to have instruction and/or guidance.

The basic principles of classroom counseling are the same principles that apply to any group counseling session. The group mechanics and group processes are essentially the same except that the group is larger. Classroom counseling does emphasize the unique characteristics of a large group. A large group has the same difficulties that exist in a small group. However, the resolution of these difficulties is more difficult. The group leader quickly recognizes, when working with a very large class (i.e., thirty-five youngsters), that she does not have the eight to ten. All of the verbal and physical interaction cannot be perceived by even the most experienced leader.

A large group program that encourages spontaneous discussion has to be well organized. The youngsters should be familiar with the rules. The leader should continuously reinforce the rules until the group as a group can help her. The goals of a large group are usually different than the goals of a smaller group. The leader has to recognize what her goals, as well as the goals of the group, are. All goals have to be well defined. It is unrealistic for a leader to anticipate that every one of the thirty-five members of the class is going to participate during one class period. Discussion of personal problems with a large class can be difficult, especially if the discussion occurs before the group becomes a cohesive unit. It is usually best for the leader to consider general goals that she wants to accomplish rather than specific goals or personal issues of the youngsters. The leader will emphasize different things in different classes. If the topic is a particular war period, or science subject, or sex education, the general concepts of the particular subject should be considered first, and the individualized problems should be considered second. The classroom teacher in a social studies class will attempt to achieve different goals than would a home economics teacher. Their basic goals are (and have to be) different, although both may want to encourage spontaneous interaction within the classroom.

With a smaller class (i.e., twenty to twenty-one) it may be possible over a semester or academic year to work with the individualized problems of the students. This should not be attempted prematurely by the group leader. In large classes of thirty-five to forty this is unrealistic. If the group leader attempts to work with individualized problems prematurely, she may only increase the frustration of the students as well as herself. Some teachers compromise by dividing a large class of thirty-five to forty youngsters into two sections. On certain days Section 1 will have a group discussion with the teacher while Section 2 will either do work under the supervision of an older student, teacher aide, second teacher, student leader (i.e., the elementary grades), or will do independent work without supervision. On the second day of the week the teacher will have a group discussion with Section 2. This can be an effective compromise and can lead to more interaction, with allowance for personal questions that may arise and also for more detailed discussion of subject matter.

The group leader has to be cautious that she does not repeatedly utilize a small core group (i.e., seven to ten youngsters) who appear to be more spontaneous to the exclusion of the rest of the class. She should note that seven to ten students is not an indication that a class of thirty-five is spontaneous or the effective classroom counseling is being accomplished. The remaining twenty-five youngsters in the class may simply be patient observers (although they may be getting something from the discussion).

One of the difficulties that does occur in classroom counseling is that some youngsters have more effective group skills than others. This is particularly true in classes with heterogeneous grouping. There may be youngsters who are quite sophisticated about particular subjects and can spontaneously participate. Other youngsters may be more passive, have less ability, and be less sophisticated. This hiatus between knowledge and experience (and perhaps fantasy and reality) may cause some concern with group leaders. This would indicate that randomly working with a class is not indicated. Sometimes this is so. However, when the classroom discussion is developed around a definite curriculum, the youngsters usually adapt to it and the group leader usually is more comfortable. When the class has two distinct groups, one group of youngsters who are more sophisticated and one group of youngsters are less sophisticated, the class should be divided into separate groups. There are certain topics of discussion, i.e., family life and sex education, that predicate more careful member selection. It may be indicated that classroom discussions and randomly selected classes are helpful, but that random selection of topics or opportunities to discuss may not be indicated. The curriculum should be well organized and programmed so that it will be tolerable and acceptable to the participating youngsters.

When classroom counseling programs are initiated because of specific problems (i.e., behavior problems within a class), it is not uncommon after four or five sessions for the classroom sessions to become less spontaneous. When this occurs, it is often because the group goals have been accomplished and the youngsters have been able to discuss those things that are particularly troublesome to them. When the group members think that they have resolved their "problems" they may begin to wonder why they are still continuing these "spontaneous discussions" and quickly become bored.

One way to offset boredom in an ongoing classroom counseling group is to have a curriculum outlined so that different topics can be presented to be discussed. Both the leader and the students can indicate what they would like incorporated. A meaningful curriculum can be prepared by the questions and interests of the youngsters. This allows the teacher to keep her curriculum contemporary with the interests of the students. Every year the youngsters present slightly different interests than their peers did the year before. This can be particularly pertinent, for example, in the home economics classes that are involved with family life and planning courses. The students in history and social studies become involved with many current national and international events, as well as engage in the exciting and innovative changes in the areas of science.

When one teacher encourages spontaneous discussion within a class and the other teachers of the particular grade do not, it often leads to difficulty for the students. As they learn how to be spontaneous, they will become frustrated and often angry that other teachers do not allow the same type of participation and meaningful investigation in their classes and the methodology that is being used (that may either enhance or decrease spontaneity).

Classroom counseling and/or group discussion within the classroom should be part of the technical armamentarium of every educator. If meaningful discussion does not occur within the classroom, then it is the responsibility of the educators to review the particular reasons why it does not. Basic concepts of group process, as outlined in the earlier chapters for small group, are directly applicable to the classroom. The classroom counseling technique can help to avoid boredom, allow for more meaningful discussion, and develop opportunities to produce projects within the class that will reflect the interests of the students and the goals of the curriculum.

## SUBSTANCE ABUSE

Over the last ten years there has been a surprising increase in teenagers who are abusing drugs. There are very few high schools in the United States, that don't have some students who are either dealing and/or taking illicit substances. In the past twenty-five years, the percentage of eighth graders reporting illicit drug use during a one-year period has doubled. Alcohol and smoking are still considered "gateway" drugs, and the first age exposure has dropped over the last 35 years from age 18 to age 15. There are over one million new smokers each year under the age of 18. In a 2001 survey by the University of Michigan, 50% of high school seniors, 39% of tenth graders, and 20% of eighth graders reported using alcohol within the month prior to the survey. Ninety percent have experimented with alcohol or drugs by high school graduation. One-third has reported binge drinking. Teenagers, themselves identify drugs as one of their main concerns. There is a predisposition to and high rate of antisocial behavior among substance abusing adolescents, and there is a higher rate of suicide attempts in adolescents who are substance abusers. Over 54% of adolescents have tried an illicit substance by the time they have left high school, and there is a high rate of co morbid/dual diagnosis within the substance abuse adolescent population, i.e. psychiatric and substance abuse. Trauma is the leading cause of death during adolescence and there is a high correlation with substance abusers. The statistics are staggering.

There are three components to the way school systems handle the problem of substance abuse. With all of these programs it is necessary to keep in mind the major considerations in adolescent growth and development which include body image, *independence,* and *group identity.*

Traditional informational programs have not been shown to be particularly helpful unless the topics are motivated and/or suggested by the students. The same information may be presented by counselors, but it is the input of the students themselves which has the greatest impact. Group counseling has been shown to be particularly helpful as it reinforces a more positive group identity and allows the students the opportunity to present issues and topics of interest. At some point in the discussion the development of substance abuse should be discussed (exemplifying how drug use is a challenge to independence and has harmful physical effects (body image).

Role-playing as a counseling technique is both helpful and informative. Some of the topics should include peer pressure (see the chicken stories on p. 203) and how to cope with peer pressure. The students should be given an opportunity to discuss pressure/ stress situations that occur with their peers. Issues such as changes in self-image, feelings of insecurity, wanting to "belong", "need" to fit in, "what would you say if someone offered you a drug?" should be discussed. Role-playing situations regarding peer pressure should be practiced at each session as repetition is the best way for the students to develop the skills and internalize the concept of being able to handle their peers in pressure situations in a reasonable way.

Some of the things that should at some time be addressed is the concept of "losing control", "who is susceptible", "using drugs as an excuse," and "trying to solve problems in inappropriate ways." These are all issues and questions which should be presented to the students if they themselves don't spontaneously "bring them up" themselves. The natural development of substance abuse should be reviewed, including experimentation which is usually the first step. This is usually followed by more frequent use to a point where the student can't control the experimentation any longer. One of the difficulties that students have is recognizing a problem when they have it and "not denying" that it exists. One of the hardest things for a teenager is to be able to ask for help when they need it. "Asking for help" goes against "the grain", their self-esteem and sense of independence. Role-playing should include a discussion of asking for help, when you know you need it, and not losing your sense of independence.

Developing new interests, putting energy into more productive things, broadening one's sense of interest, are among the best ways to prevent substance abuse. Studies have shown that students who work at least part-time were less likely to use and abuse illicit substances. This is more difficult to discuss with students who are functioning at a borderline intellectual level when concepts have to be more structured and activities more directed.

Students need to be given information about drugs so that they know which drugs are the most dangerous and why. Both SAMHSA and NIDA have ample materials available for teachers, counselors and students and these are particularly helpful. Telling a student that marijuana has the potential for developing lung cancer in the future has less of an impact then telling a youngster that marijuana "makes you stupid" with a decrease in intellectual functioning. Using cocaine has less of an impact when you tell them that it "eats up your brain," then it can cause an immediate heart irregularity and can cause immediate death. This is what happened to Lenny Bias, the Maryland athlete who died from cocaine use. The Grant Dawson studies indicated that for each year adolescents delay use of alcohol, they decrease the odds of life long dependence by 14% and life long abuse by 8%. The Hawkins Graham, et al studies indicated similar results for drugs with a reduction of 5% for life long dependence and 4% for life long abuse for every year the student delays initial use.

Although, the content is important in the group counseling sessions, it is of paramount importance that the process of the group is driven by the students themselves. Studies have indicated that as few as 15 – 20 minutes of effective intervention can have an impact on many students. Systems approaches involving the entire school or school wide programs can be extremely effective in reinforcing a more positive group identity and making it easier for students to more effectively handle peer pressure.

## COMMUNITY/NATIONAL DISASTERS

Since 9/11, schools have been an important stabilizing factor for the preservation of emotional stability in our students. It is the one place (outside the home) that children have an opportunity to "work through" the emotional aftermath and the residual effect of a community/or national disaster. With the potential of terrorist attacks, and periodic natural disasters, schools should have a general plan of how to react and work with children in helping them to re-stabilize after a major traumatic event. Research has shown that children can have high rates of complicating post traumatic symptoms, which can occur immediately to several years post event. Group counseling has been proven to be one of the most effective techniques in ameliorating post traumatic symptoms.

When planning and/or coping with a traumatic event, the administration should initially consider a systems approach; that is working with the entire staff. Those children who were closest to or present at time of the traumatic event have the greatest risk of posttraumatic complications. Those children who had a close relative die in the event, had previous personality and/or learning problems before the event or have a poor support system will also be a higher risk for developing post traumatic complications. Teachers should have an opportunity to discuss the issues, be given an outline of what topics to discuss and the best approach with the children, in their respective grades. The students in different grades will react differently per their age, previous experiences, family background, and the traumatic impact of the disaster on the staff.

One of the major jobs of administration is to convey information that is as accurate as possible about the events. Administration should allow teachers to express their anxieties, anger and fears, and then attempt to refocus them on the principle roles of the school (teaching and learning). The focus for the staff will be three fold. Help the children work through the emotional effect of the traumatic event, refocus on teaching and learning, and identify those children who appear to be emotionally impaired by the event and should be referred to either the school counselor and/or a community mental health professional.

## HIGH SCHOOL

In high school, the children may overreact with anger, inappropriate behavior, withdrawal, increased restlessness, absenteeism, decreased in school performance, somatic complaints, sleep disturbances or feelings of anger, guilt and thoughts of revenge. Themes of death and dying are not uncommon. The staff has to be particularly sensitive to the possibility of anger against minorities and/or select ethnic groups with possibly acting out. Decrease in school performance and depressed mood is not uncommon. For some adolescents, there will be a greater tendency to experiment with drugs and/or alcohol.

As classes resume, within the usual schedule, adolescents may present issues spontaneously, and what appears to be at inappropriate times. For example: discussing the disaster during math class or diverting the conversation from the main theme in English. Identifying with the process and expressing inappropriate guilt in an unrealistic way may occur.

Intervention

The group counseling technique is extremely helpful. It helps to reinforce and reestablish a more positive group identity at a time when their group and self-identity may be low. It reinforces a group feeling of support, which can be used to mobilize their energy in appropriate ways, for example, in projects that may help the victims and/or their families, as well as working through significant feelings of inadequacy that everyone feels. It gives the adolescents an opportunity to express their feelings in a safe way in a safe setting. It gives staff a chance to facilitate ideas of safety, fostering a sense of security. It is very helpful to offer to the students an opportunity to discuss the events in an appropriate way, such as focusing their energy into productive tasks, which reinforces their wanting to be helpful. Group Counseling helps the students to learn constructive ways to cope and gives them an avenue to channel their energy in an appropriate way.

*MIDDLE SCHOOL*

In middle school, children are more vulnerable. Concept formation is not as well developed. Inappropriate and distorted thoughts of what happened may be present. Emotional liability may be increased. Spontaneous bouts of anger and liability of mood may be present. There may be inappropriate expressions of concern at inappropriate times. There is a greater tendency towards anger at minority and/or ethnic groups.

278 THE PRACTICAL HANDBOOK OF GROUP COUNSELING

It is important to have a more structured group and/or classroom discussion. For example,

- Give the students an opportunity to discuss events and their thoughts regarding the events.
- Clarify the facts that are known.
- Reinforce ways to ensure safety and feelings of security.
- Discuss ways that may help students relax, for example: music, art, and relaxation techniques.
- Discuss ways to handle anger and frustration in appropriate ways (anger management techniques).
- Handle inappropriate or indirect comments in a kind, supportive, but firm way.
- Be patient with repeated questions or comments about the same things or topics, particularly immediately post event.
- Program the educational material, so as to reduce the complexity of information until classroom stability has been reestablished, (noting that school performance may decrease immediately after a disaster or event.)
- Once stabilized, be patient but don't continue to recall or discuss traumatic events unless appropriate.

## ELEMENTARY SCHOOL

Depending upon the age and grade, children in elementary school vary in their reaction to major trauma. They are more reactive to their environment, including their parents, teachers and fellow students.

Anxiety may present in more physical ways, for example, aches, pains, headaches, nausea, and extreme cases of anxiety. Parents may report decreased sleep and appetite. In the earlier grades, the children may revert to earlier forms of behavior (thumb sucking, separation anxiety, oppositional behavior and baby talk). There may be increased irritability/temper tantrums, depressed mood, social withdrawal, loss of interest in classroom activity, and increase in aggressive behavior.

Group counseling can be very helpful. I am always impressed with how much children in kindergarten and first grade, both observe and comprehend things that are happening in the community, including national or community events. Distortion of the facts is common. One of the goals of the counselor/teacher is to delineate the information that is known in generally accepted appropriate ways.

Major emphasis should be placed on the concept of safety and security. There must be a reestablishment whenever possible of feelings of security. It is particularly important to allow the children to discuss their concerns, understanding, and frustration of the events. Once stabilized, it is important to allow and to manage discussion at appropriate times, but not continuously re-live the traumatic events. It is important to structure the classroom as much as possible. Well-structured programs, including group discussions, helps to decrease anxiety, increase the feeling of security and stability, as well as reinforce the spontaneous discussion of issues that may be bothering the children. In the event that some children may present with difficulty (decrease in performance, change in behavior, increase in aggressive behavior, increase in depressed mood) they should be referred to the school counselor and/or mental health professional in the community for further evaluation.

Reference – National Child Traumatic Stress Network (www. nctsnet.org)

## SUGGESTED READINGS

Albertson, Jim. (May-Jun 1996). While the Pendulum Swings: Activities for a Hard of Hearing Support Group. Perspectives in Education and Deafness. v14 n5 p4-5, 24.

Arman John F. (Fall 2002). A Brief Group Counseling Model To Increase Resilieny of Students with Mild Disabilities. Journal of Humanistic Counseling, Education and Development. v41 n2 p120-28.

Arman, J. and R. McNair. (Apr. 2000). A small group model for working with elementary school children of alcoholics. Professional School Counseling. 3(4), 290-3.

Arzin, N. H.; And Others. (1994). Youth Drug Abuse Treatment: A Controlled Outcome Study. Journal of Child & Adolescent Substance Abuse. v3 n3 p1-16.

Atkinson, Donald. (2003). Counseling American Minorities: A Cross-Cultural Perspective. 6th ed. McGraw-Hill: Boston.

Baca, Louise M.; Koss-Chioino, Joan D. (Apr 1997). Development of a Culturally Responsive Group Counseling Model for Mexican American Adolescents. Journal of Multicultural Counseling and Development. v25 n2 p130-41.

Balaban, V. (2006). Psychological assessment of children in disasters and emergencies. Disasters. 30:178-198.

Bauer, S., S.M. Remen, and D. Johnson. (2000). Group counseling strategies for rural at-risk high school students. High School Journal. 83(2), 41-50.

Becky, Debra; Farren, Peggy M. (Mar 1997). Teaching Students How to Understand and Avoid Abusive Relationships. School Counselor. v44 n4 p303-08.

Bemak, Fred; Chung, Rita Chi-Ying,; Sirosky-Sabdo, Linda A. (Jun 2005). Empowerment Groups for Academic Success: An Innovative Approach to Prevent High School Failure for At-Risk, Urban African. Professional School Counseling. v8 n5 p377.

Berner, Michelle L.; Fee, Virgniia E.; Turner, Andrea D. (2001). A Multi-Component Social Skills Training Program for Pre-Adolescent Girls with Few Friends. Child & Family Behavior Therapy. v23 n2 p1-18.

Berube, Elinor; Berube, Lionel. (Mar 1997). Creating Small Groups Using School and Community Resources to Meet Student Needs. School Counselor. v44 n4 p294-302.

Blatner, A. (1997). Psychodrama: the state of the art. The Arts in Psychotherapy. 24(1), 23-30.

Bradley, Carla. (Jun 2001). A Counseling Group for African-American Adolescent Males. Professional School Counseling. v4 n5 p370-73.

Brantley, L., and P.S. Brantley. (Dec. 1996). Transforming school guidance and counseling: a group program for inner-city elementary school pupils. Elementary School Guidance and Counseling. 31(2), 10p.

Braswell, Lauren. (1993). Cognitive-Behavioral Groups for Children Manifesting ADHD and Other Disruptive Behavior Disorders. Special Services in the Schools. v8 n1 p91-117.

Butler, S. Kent; Bunch, Lela Kosteck. (Jun 2005). Response to EGAS: An Innovative Approach to Prevent High School Failure for At-Risk, Urban African American Girls. Professional School Counseling. v8 n5 p395.

Campbell, Chari A. (Apr. 1991). Group guidance for academically undermotivated children. Elementary School Guidance and Counseling. 25(4), 302-307.

Campbell, Chair A. (Mar 2005). Closing the Achievement Gap: A Structured Approach to Group Counseling. Journal for Specialists in Group Work. v30 n1 p67-82.

Carr, A. ((2004). Interventions for post-traumatic stress disorder in children and adolescents. Pediatric Rehabilitation. 7:231-244.

Carty, Laurie; And Others. (May 1993). Youth Life Career Planning. Guidance and Counseling. v8 n5 p29-36.

Center for Substance Abuse Prevention, Substance Abuse and Mental Health Services Administration, U.S. Dept. of Health and Human Services (2002). Keeping Youth Drug Free.

Chemtob CM, Naskashima J. Carlson JG. (2002). Brief treatment for elementary school children with disaster-related post-traumatic stress disorder: a field study. Journal of Clinical Psychology 58:99-112.

Coleman, Hardin L.K.; Freedman, Albert M. (Nov-Dec 1996). Effects of a Structured Group Intervention on the Achievement of Academically At-Risk Undergraduates. Journal of College Student Development. v37 n6 p631-36.

Coppock, Martha W. (Dec. 1998). Small group plan for improving friendships and self-esteem. Elementary School Guidance and Counseling. 28, 152-4.

Court, Deborah; Givon, Sarah. (Nov-Dec 2003). Group Intervention: Improving Social Skills of Adolescents with Learning Disabilities. TEACHING Exceptional Children. v36-n2 p50-55.

Cummings, Anne L.; Hoffman, Sue; Leschied, Alan W. (Sep 2004). A Psychoeducational Group for Aggressive Adolescent Girls. Journal for Specialists in Group Work. v29 n3 p285-299.

DeLucia-Waack, J.L. (1996). Multiculturalism is inherent in all group work. Journal for specialists in group work. 21(4), 218-23.

Daratha, B. Michelle. (Fall 1992). Behavior Impaired Students: Putting Them on the Right Track. Schools in the Middle. v2 n1 p19-22.

Fairbrother, G., Stuber, Jr., Galea, S., et al: Unmet need for counseling services by children in New York City after the September 11th attacks on the World Trade Center: implications for pediatricians. Pediatrics. 113:1367-1374.

Fournier, Robert R. (May 2002). A Trauma Education Workshop on Posttraumatic Stress. Health & Social Work. v27 n2 p113-24.

Fremont WP: (2004). Childhood reactions to terrorism-induced trauma: a review of the past 10 years. Journal of the American Academy of Child and Adolescent Psychiatry.

Ginsberg, G.S. and K.L. Drake. (2002). School-based treatment for anxious African-American Adolescents: A controlled pilot study. Journal of the American Academy of Child and Adolescent Psychiatry. 41(7), 768-75.

Goenjiam, A.K., Walling, D., Steinberg, A.M. et al. (2005) A prospective study of posttraumatic stress and depressive reactions among treated and untreated adolescents 5 years after a catastrophic disaster. American Journal of Psychiatry. 162:2302-2308.

Goodman, Harriet; And Others. (Jul 1996). Group Work with High-Risk Urban Youths on Probation. Social Work. v41 n4 p375-81.

Goodnough, Gary and Vivian Ripley. (Jan. 1997). Structured groups for high school seniors making the transition to college. The School Counselor. 44, 230-34.

Grant, B.F. and D.A. Dawson. (1998). Age at onset of alcohol use and its association with DSM-IV alcohol abuse and dependence: results of the National Longitudinal Alcohol Epidemiological Survey. Journal of Substance Abuse, 10, 163-173.

Hawkins, J. David; And Others. (Aug 1989). Skills Training for Drug Abusers: Generalization, Maintenance, and Effects on Drug Use. Journal of Consulting and Clinical Psychology. v57 n4 p559-63.

Hoven, C.W., Duarte, C.S., Lucas, C.P., et al: (2005). Psychopathology among New York City public school children 6 months after September 11. Archives of General Psychiatry. 62:545-552.

Hyman, L.A. (1998). Introduction to the special theme section on school violence: the ecology of school violence. Journal of School Psychology. 36(1), 3-5.

Johnson, Irene H.; And Others. (Sep 1995). Issues and Strategies in Leading Culturally Diverse Counseling Groups. Journal for Specialists in Group Work. v20 n3 p143-50.

Kadish, Tara E.; Glaser, Brian A; Risler, Edwin A.; Calhoun, Georgia B. (Apr 1999). Counseling Juvenile Offenders: A Program Evaluation. Journal of Addictions & Offender Counseling. v19 n2 p88-94.

Kellner, Millicent H.; Bry, Brenna H. (Win 1999). The Effects of Anger Management Groups in A Day School for Emotionally Disturbed Adolescents. Adolescence. v34 n136 p645-51.

Kerr, Barbara,; Eth, Cheryl. (Jul 1991). Career Counseling with Academically Talented Students: Effects of a Value-Based Intervention. Journal of Counseling Psychology. v38 n3 p309-14.

Kim, Bryan S.K.; Omizo, Michael M.; D'Andrea, Michael J. (Jun 1998). The Effects of Culturally Consonant Group Counseling on the Self-Esteem and Internal Locus of Control Orientation Among Native American Adolescents. Journal for Specialists in Group Work. v23 n2 p145-63.

Kizner, Lori and Scott R. Kizner. (Feb. 1999). Small group counseling with adopted children. Professional School Counseling. 2(3), 226-29.

Kottler, Jeffrey A. (Mar 1994). Working with Difficult Group Members. Journal for Specialists in Group Work. v19 n1 p3-10.

Leveton, Eva. (2001). A Clinician's Guide to Psychodrama. 3rd ed. Springer: New York.

Linton, Jeremy M.; Bischof, Gary H.; McDonnell, Kelly A. (Mar 2005). Solution-Oriented Treatment Groups for Assaultive Behavior. Journal for Specialists in Group Work. v30n1 p5-21.

Lubit, R., Rovine, D., Defrancisci, L., et al: (2003). Impact of trauma on children. Journal of Psychiatric Practice. 9:128-138.

Marbley, Aretha Faye. (Sep 2004). His Eye Is on the Sparrow: A Counselor of Color's Perception of Facilitating Groups with Predominantly White Members. Journal for Specialists in Group Work. v29 n3 p247-258.

McNair, R. and J.F. Arman. (Apr. 2000). A small group model for working with elementary school children of alcoholics. Professional School Counseling. 3(4), 290-93.

Miller, Mark J.; And Others. (Mar 1995). Effects of Structuring on Students' Perceptions of Career Counseling. Career Development Quarterly. v43 n2 p233-39.

Milsom, Amy; Akos, Patrick; Thompson, Michael. (Dec 2004). A Psychoeducational Group Approach to Postsecondary Transition Planning for Sgtudents with Learning Disabilities. Journal for Specialists in Group Work. v29 n4 p395-411.

Moreno, Z.T. (1965). Psychodramatic rules, techniques, and adjunctive methods. Group Psychotherapy. 18, 73-86.

Muller, Lynne. (2000). A 12-session, European-American led counseling group for African American females. Professional School Counseling. 3(4), 264-69.

Mulvhill, D. (2005). The health impact of childhood trauma: an interdisciplinary review 1997-2003. Issues in Comprehensive Pediatric Nursing. 28:115-136.

O'Donnell, Angela M. and Alison King, eds. (1999). Cognitive Perspectives on Peer Learning. L. Erlbaum: Mawah, N.J.

Patterson, Jeanne Boland; And Others. (May 1995). The Process of Inclusion and Accommodation: Creating Accessible Groups for Individuals with Disabilities. Journal for Specialists in Group Work. v20 n2 p76-82.

Peng, Huiling. (Oct. 2000). Comparison of two group counseling approaches to enhancing confidence in planning careers. Psychological Reports. 87(2), 67-75.

Phillips, L. (2000). Youth and Violence, Medicine, Nursing, and Public Health: Connecting the Dots to Prevent Violence. The Commission for the Prevention of Youth Violence. American Medical Association: Chicago, IL.

Pickleslmer, Billie K.; Hooper, Denise Roberson; Ginter, Earl J. (Jul 1998). Life Skills, Adolescents, and Career Choices. Journal of Mental Health Counseling. v20 n3 p272-82.

Proehl, Rebecca A. (Spring 1995) Groups in Career Development: An Added Advantage. Journal of Career Development. v21 n3 p249-61.

Pyle, K. Richard. (Fall 2000). Career Counseling in an Information Age: The Promise of "High Touch" in a "High Tech" Age. Career Planning and Adult Development Journal. v16 n3 p7-29.

Quarmby, David. (May 1993). Peer Group Counseling with Bereaved Adolescents. British Journal of Guidance and Counseling. v21 n21 p196-211.

Riddle, J., J. Bergin, and C. Douzenis. (Feb. 1997). Effects of group counseling on the self-concept of children of alcoholics. Elementary School Guidance Counseling. 31, 192-203.

Rochlen, Aaron B.; Milburn, Lynne; Hill, Clara E. (Jun 2004). Examining the Process and Outcome of Career Counseling for Difficult Types of Career Counseling Clients. Journal of Career Development. v30 n4 p263-275.

Ronen, T. (2002). Difficulties in assessing traumatic reactions in children. Journal of Loss and Trauma. 7:87-106.

Rose-Gold, Marc S. (Nov 1991). Intervention Strategies for Counseling At-Risk Adolescents in Rural School Districts. School Counselor. v39 n2 p122-26.

Rosenbaum, Janet N.; And Others. (May 1994). Experiences of Adolescents Participating in a Developmental Peer Group Counseling Career Programme. Guidance and Counseling. v9 n5 p3-7.

Roth, Henry J. (1991). School Counseling Groups for Violent and Assaultive Youth: The Willie M.s. Journal of Offender Rehabilitation. v16 n3-4 p113-31.

Schechtman, Z., I. Gilat, and L. Fos. (Oct. 1996). Brief group therapy with low-achieving elementary school children. Journal of Counseling Psychology. 43, 376-82.

Schopler, Janice H.; Abell, Melissa D.; Galinsky, Maeda J. (May 1998). Technology-Based Groups: A Review and Conceptual Framework for Practice. Social Work. v43 n3 p254-67.

Sommers-Flanagan, Rita; Barrett-Hakanson, Tina; Clarke, Christie; Sommers-Flanagan, John. (Jun 2000). A Psychoeducational School based Coping and Social Skills Group for Depressed Students. Journal for Specialists in Group Work. v25 n2 p170-90.

Stringfield, Sam and Deborah Land, Ed. (2002). Educating At-Risk Students. University of Chicago: Chicago.

Stinson, Charles H.; And Others. (Feb 1995). Dysfluency and Topic Orientation in Bereaved Individuals: Bridging Individuals and Group Studies. Journal of Consulting and Clinical Psychology. v63 n1 p37-45.

Stuber, J., Fairbrother, G., Galea, S., et al. (2002). Determinants of counseling for children in Manhattan after the September 11 attacks. Psychiatric Services. 53:815-822.

Symes, Brent A. (Winter 1998). Group counseling for vocational decidedness. Guidance&Counseling. 13(2), 28-33.

Tartar, Ralph E. (2002). Etiology of adolescent substance abuse: A developmental perspective. American Journal on Addictions. 11, 171-191.

Taub, Deborah J. (Jun 1998). Promoting Student Development Through Psychoeducational Groups: A Perspective on the Goals and Proce Matrix. Journal for Specialists in Group Work. v23 n2 p196-201.

Topping, Keith J. and Stewart W. Ehly. Peer assisted learning: a framework for consultation. Journal of Educational and Psychological Consultation. 12(2), 113-32.

Torres-Rivera, Edil; Wilbur, Michael P.; Roberts-Wilbur, Janice; Phan, Loan. (Dec 1999). Group Work with Latino Clients: A Psychoeducational Model. Journal for Specialists in Group Work. v24 n4 p383-404.

Twemlow, S., P. Fonagy, and F. Sacco. (2001). An innovative psychodynamically influenced approach to reduce school violence. Journal of the American Academy of Child and Adolescent Psychiatry. 40(3), 377-379.

Twemlow, S.W. (2000). The roots of violence: Converging psychoanalytic explanatory models for power struggles and violence in schools. PsychoanalQ. 69, 741-785.

Waterman, Jill. (2000). Helping At-Risk Students: A Group Counseling Approach for Grades 6-9. Guilford: New York.

Weiss, Bahr; Caron, Annalise; Ball, Shelly; Tapp, Julie; Johnson, Margaret; Weisz, John R. (Dec 2005). Iatrogenic Effects of Group Treatment for Antisocial Youths. Journal of Consulting and Clinical Psychology. v73 n6 p1036-1044.

White, JoAnna; Edmondson, Joanne H. (Apr 1998). A Tutorial and Counseling Program: Helping Students at Risk of Dropping

Out of School. <u>Professional School Counseling</u>. v1 n4 p43-47.

Williams, Sarah, Verba Fanolis, and Gerald Schamess. (Sep. 2001). Adapting the pynoos school based group therapy model for use with foster children: theoretical and process considerations. <u>Journal of Child and Adolescent Group Therapy</u>. 11 (2-3), 57-76.

Zinck, K. and J. Littrell. (2000). Action research shows group counseling effective with at risk adolescent girls. <u>Professional School Counseling</u>. 4(1), 50-59.

# CHAPTER XI

## *PLANNED GROUP COUNSELING MODULES*

It is helpful and appropriate in the school setting to have organized/ planned modules of counseling specific to issues that present to the teacher, counselor, and school and are of importance to the students involved. Although planned, the dynamics/mechanics of these groups are the same for all groups. The content may vary, the group process is essentially the same.

The goals and objectives of each group will be reflective of the topic being discussed. The introduction, resistance testing, productive and termination phases will reflect at least at a content level the designated topic of the module being discussed. Although the groups will help to improve the communication and problem solving skills of the students involved, the specific goal and objective for the students is to gain a greater understanding of the topic being presented in a way that can either modify their behavior, improve their skills and/or help them to gain insight.

In general the selection of students for the respective groups has to be done carefully as the students selected for one planned group module may not be a candidate for another.

The following modules presented are based upon four sessions which can be done over a four week period of time, one session per week, or at the counselor's discretion be extended to eight weeks. The topics are presented as examples only. The counselor can develop several different modules that may be more applicable to the school or school system they are counseling in.

It is important for the counselor to note that some of the modules presented have topics that can increase the anxiety of the student. It is important when the group is initially formed that the group members understand that they can be referred between sessions for individual support and counseling. If the anxiety is too great or if the youngsters are uncomfortable, the counselor should feel comfortable withdrawing the student from the group for individual counseling.

## ANGER MANAGEMENT

Anger management is an issue that presents to the counselor at every level of the school system, but the etiology of the anger may be quite different for each student. In the elementary school attention deficit hyperactive disorder, domestic discord in the family, oppositional defiant disorder, and pre-disposition to lability and volatility by medical conditions may be the source of anger. In middle school and senior high, it becomes even more important to attempt to recognize the source of the anger. A common rule for the counselor is to see the youngsters individually before placing them in an anger management group, in an attempt to evaluate the dynamics that may be causing the anger. In middle and senior high school, youngsters who have a long record of volatility and anger may already have been conditioned and have learned how to react to precipitating events by becoming angry and explosive. Other youngsters may have a very negative group identity or feel inadequate in the school setting and may reflect their discomfort by being angry.

This module is designed to attempt to mitigate the angry response of the student and help him/her develop insight, and hopefully, skills that will allow the student to respond in a more mindful response.

While discussing anger management, there are both advantages and disadvantages in having a heterosexual group. With the most disruptive youngsters a single sex group may be easier to manage. These youngsters have a tendency to be more outgoing, sometimes with inappropriate and disruptive behavior when placed in a heterosexual group. For youngsters who are less disruptive, less labile and less volatile, a heterosexual group can be very helpful and enhance the development of a more positive group identity.

## MODULE FOR SESSION ONE – NEGOTIATION

Very often, simply asking the question of the group members – "Do you get angry easily?" – decreases the individual and/ or the group's tendency to become more angry. Perhaps it is a "defensiveness" that occurs. Easy introductory questions in the first session, are: What is anger? Why do people become angry? If you start getting angry, How do you control it? Is anger a natural response? When does anger become inappropriate?

At this point, it is often helpful to introduce the concept that everyone periodically has problems or concerns and may feel angry. "Rule of thumb" – one half of a person's problems may start with his or her self. "So if you start with yourself first, half of your problems may be solved."

It is often difficult for adolescents to admit that they are wrong. They are sometimes "struggling" to become more independent and to feel comfortable with that independence. Sometimes their expression of anger is a reflection of the bravados they feel they need in order to be independent.

Another question to be asked: Is it common to have arguments, conflicts and be angry at other people? What are the best ways to negotiate and to come to reasonable, mutually agreeable terms? Is there a question of pride in winning an argument, even though it may be inappropriate? Do you ever feel defensive about arguing about something that you know is either inappropriate or wrong?

Questions that can be raised with the group: How does one negotiate or work themselves out of a position in which they are arguing about something they know is wrong? Does it take courage and/or confidence to be able to negotiate with another person about something in which they are arguing? Have you solved an argument with another person? How did you negotiate to solve the problem?

It should be noted that at no time during this first session was anybody accused of being an angry person. All the questions were generic, and were neither argumentative, anxiety producing nor demeaning. The session should conclude with reinforcement by the counselor that "you discussed a very difficult topic and handled it very well."

## MODULE FOR SESSION TWO - RESPECT

During this session, the two primary considerations for discussion will be that of change and respect, respect of one's self and respect for someone else. The following questions may help facilitate this session. How do you define respect? What does it mean? What are the parts of respect? When you respect somebody do you hold them in high regard? Do you show them consideration? Are you courteous? When people respect you are they courteous to you? Can you respect somebody that you disagree with? What is there in somebody else that causes you to respect them? Can you be angry with someone and still show them respect? Is anger a lack of respect? When you disagree with somebody do you always get angry? When people do get angry in an argument, what do you think the reasons are? Do you get more frustrated when you disagree with someone you respect or someone you don't respect? When you disagree with somebody and feel yourself getting angry, what can you do to stop yourself from getting too angry, and getting angry too quickly? Why do people lose their temper? Why do some people get into physical fights when they are angry? What are ways that people can use to stop their anger from becoming physical?

What are some of the things that cause people to be frustrated and angry?

At this point in the discussion, it is often helpful to bring up the concept of change. You can raise the questions: How do you define change? How does one go about changing one's thoughts, patterns, or behavior? If a person has a tendency to become angry too quickly, how does he/she learn to change that way of reacting? Basically, how do you stop yourself from becoming angry too quickly? Usually the students have a very involved discussion during the session.

At this point, you can consider raising this question: What happens if you do learn to control your anger and you feel good about it, and then you feel someone disrespects you? The kids often consider this "dissing or being dissed". How does that make you feel? Are you able to handle your anger at that point? When do you feel comfortable in walking away? What is the problem with walking away? Can you still respect yourself and walk away? Are you able to remain calm? Are you able to continue with a positive attitude? This will usually be the toughest question that is raised, and you might share with the group members, this is a tough question. "I don't know if any of us have the answers. It is certainly something to think about and consider taking up at one of future sessions."

## MODULE FOR SESSION THREE – RELATING TO AUTHORITY FIGURES

At the beginning of this session, the counselor should raise the question: "Are there any questions from the previous two sessions that anybody would like to comment on before we get started on this module." This will give the group members an opportunity to discuss unresolved questions that may have been precipitated by the previous session.

Okay, can somebody define for us what they think an authority figure is? Is an authority figure the same as a leader? Would you describe a teacher as an authority figure, or a leader or both? Would you define a parent as an authority figure or as a leader or both? If not, what are the differences?

High school is a time in adolescent development during which the students are trying to become more independent from the parent figure and parent surrogates. There is a constant struggle between the dependant/independent fluctuation in adolescents. This topic is worth exploring. Do you think that an authority figure should stick to the rules? Do you think that the members of a group or a class should stick to the rules? If so, why? When do you feel you can disagree with the rules and if so, how should you handle it? If an authority figure tells you to stick to the rules, do you get angry? How do you feel? How do you express it? What do you do? How can you disagree in a reasonable way? If you disagree, should you still follow the rules? Should you still follow the rules if you don't like the authority figure? If you should follow the rules, how do you handle your frustration and anger? Should you show respect to an authority figure that you disagree with?

This is often difficult particularly for high school students. There is a high truancy rate (particularly in the 9th grade) and a high drop-out rate in senior high school. Students often report that they didn't like the teacher(s) as their excuse for being truant or dropping out.

This module should end on a positive note. The counselor should give adequate time to summarize the group in a positive way before the group ends.

## MODULE FOR SESSION FOUR – WE ARE JUST HUMAN

Introduce to the group that they have really done well and have tackled some difficult questions. If the group has been established as a four module/four session group, then the students will often ask questions about termination.

One of the questions that may come up is: Are we going to meet after this group? The counselor should have a plan to follow-up with each of the group members at some time in the future. If that schedule has already been established and the students know when their follow-up appointment is, then the termination phase will be much easier.

The following questions may help to facilitate the group during this session. Have you ever been in a situation when other people have forgiven you when you did something wrong? How did it make you feel? Was it still difficult to accept the support and/or forgiveness of the other person? The discussion should be followed with the question: Do you find it difficult when you are told that you are wrong? How do you handle it? Everyone either misjudges or makes a mistake at some point about something. We all know that being human is not being perfect. Do you feel defensive when somebody tells you that you were wrong? Do you reply by retaliating or telling the other person that he/she is also wrong? With some people do you feel that you are never good enough?

This can be followed by a discussion with these questions being raised: Is it difficult when people disappoint you? Does disappointment lead to your feeling angry? Are you able to forgive or understand when others make mistakes?

When someone else becomes angry, are you able to remain calm? What are the things that you do that allow you not to react with anger? What can you say or do to deal with the situation? What can you do to handle the situation? Do you have the confidence to just walk away? Do you recognize when you are becoming angry? When another person starts to get angry, what do you do? Have you learned to recognize when you are becoming angry?

It is very common for the group members to refer to or bring up in the last session topics that they have discussed in the previous four modules. It is often part of the process of "working through" the last session. The group members may make suggestions to the counselor about future sessions or topics they would like to discuss. The counselor has to make a decision according to the needs of the students, the counselor's schedule and whether the students would be best served by continuing the group for another module or being seen individually. This particular session/module can be summarized by congratulating and reinforcing the progress that that group members/students have made; noting that it is difficult to control how other people think, feel or behave but that we can control what we do and say when we focus on our own ability to resolve problems.

## *STUDY SKILLS*

Every counselor has been referred youngsters who have at least average intellectual capacity but are under achieving. There can be multiple reasons for underachievement including, attitude, short attention span, poor study skills, negative group identity, dysfunctional family, medical illness and\or psychological problems. It is the responsibility of the counselor to evaluate each youngster individually to gain some insight to what may be helpful. A group counseling session on study skills is one vehicle for helping the youngster compensate and/or work through their respective problems. It may offer the youngster an opportunity to then relate to the counselor on an individual basis or if appropriate within a group. The objective of a group would be to provide the students with both a conceptual frame of reference as well as actual skills that may improve their study habits and subsequently enhance their learning.

One of the variables that the counselor should be aware of is that modifying behavior often takes time. Involvement of the group and the personal attention that the youngsters are receiving in the group by being selected will often improve their attitude, their self esteem and a more positive group identity. However, actually changing their behavior patterns may take more time than allotted in the group sessions before they can internalize enough information to change their behavior patterns.

This module represents an opportunity to gain some insight into the advantages of actually doing as well as discussing study skills during the group sessions.

## MODULE FOR SESSION ONE – CREATING THE RIGHT PLACE TO STUDY

The counselor should understand that everyone has their own frame of reference of what maybe helpful. The important element is the comfort of the student and not the frame of reference of either the parent or the counselor. The fundamental issue isn't always how one studies; but what is retained and what is accomplished and finished. One person may feel comfortable studying with the music playing, another student my need absolute silence. The individual's frame of reference of what they need is as important a variable as how or where one studies.

The initial discussion may start with: What kind of a place do you like to have in order to study and do your homework? What makes you most comfortable? There will be a great deal of discussion about this with many varieties. Nothing should be considered appropriate or inappropriate. The major question is: What gets the job done? What helps you get your homework finished? What helps you remember best? What helps you get your homework assignments in on time? The different answers from the group members will be the source of much discussion. The counselors will find that some youngsters need a neat, tidy place and other youngsters are more comfortable "with things all over the place." The next question that may be raised is, Where do you study best –

at home, in a library, in the school? How do you find the place that best suits you? Another question is, What's the best time for you to do your homework? How do you handle all of your responsibilities in a short period of time?

The next question that may be raised is, Is it hard for you to study, and if so what makes it so hard?

Before the end of the first session, the Homework Study Schedule and a Weekly Study Form should be presented and discussed. The first is to help the student organize themselves on a daily basis by simply writing down their daily assignment. These are schedules that they can make up on any lined sheet of paper. The second concept is a weekly study schedule that gives them the concept of planning their work on a weekly basis so that they can anticipate what they have to do and obtain a frame of reference of what time allocation may be best for them.

During this first session, one can also suggest the first specific recommendation of how to approach their homework or study assignments. The counselor should encourage them to "look over" their work assignments. First, skimming over their assignment and then encourage them to reread the assignment in detail, line by line. The emphasis on both the schedules and the reading will encourage them to conceptualize looking at the "big picture" first, emphasizing that the retention and comprehension will be much greater if they do.

## *MODULE FOR SESSION TWO – UNDERSTANDING THE "BIG PICTURE"*

The counselor should initiate this session by asking if there are any questions or general comments. The counselor should ask whether it was difficult to write out the daily assignments using the work schedule and whether it was difficult doing the weekly assignments and whether there were advantages or disadvantages to doing both.

One of the variables that the counselor should be aware of is that with some youngsters, parental involvement has revolved around what they do wrong and so they are inadvertently reinforced for either not doing their homework, not getting 100% or discussion about the difficulties that they are having. The basic concept during these modules for study skills is to reinforce what the youngsters have done well and what works so that the "payoff" is about what goes well and not what goes wrong.

The counselor should recognize that some youngsters will start to respond just by involvement in the group, regardless of what is being discussed, but other youngsters because they have literally learned not to perform will take a longer period of time to internalize and modify their behavior. It should be recognized that many youngsters in the group will have not done their homework for the group, duplicating their previous performance which can be the focus of discussion in a positive way.

One of the questions to raise during this session would be: Did you handle your homework differently this week? Was classroom activity any better or easier? What was the most difficult part, this week, in terms of homework and study? What is the hardest subject for you to study for? Do you do your toughest homework assignment first or do you leave it to the last?

One of the things to suggest is that they start with their toughest homework assignment first and leave their easiest or most enjoyable to the last.

One of the questions to be raised is: Do you find writing down the assignments on a daily and weekly basis helpful? If so, how? If not, why?

This second session will be the resistance testing session, so a great deal of discussion should be allowed. It should be less structured, more spontaneous, because they will be testing the counselor and resisting the change as they have done with teachers, parents and friends.

Before the session ends, one of the things the counselor can consider doing is having the students list five things that makes study easiest for them and five things that makes study hardest for them. The counselor should inform them that before the third module/session the counselor will be reviewing the items that they present to see what may be helpful. This offers the students an opportunity to feel that the counselor is concerned, but at the same time will evaluate what they feel is important to help them.

## MODULE FOR SESSION THREE – SUMMARIZING TEXTBOOK MATERIAL AND TAKING NOTES

There will be some "working through" the resistance testing issues that occurred during session two and some testing of the counselor initially. The counselor should begin the session by asking if there are any questions. The counselor should then review the list that the students made out and submitted during session two. The discussion will help to facilitate moving into the productive phase where more meaningful learning and hopefully behavior modification takes place.

The counselor should refer back to suggestions and comments that were made during session one. That is, skimming over material first and then reading the material in a more detailed way. One of the questions raised is: Has anybody had a chance to use that? and What do you find are the advantages and disadvantages of skimming the material first? and then reading the material in a more detailed way. This discussion will help to tie the big picture together in terms of approaching work, study and lesson plans. One of the questions to be raised is: When you do approach your school work in this way, do you find it more interesting and more understandable? Do you find that you are able to finish the work quicker and understand it better? Does it make it easier to get your work done? At this point the counselor should present to the students two pages of text, either from a story, a magazine, or a newspaper for all the students to review. The first instruction should be for the students to skim over the article, and then discuss it. What does the article say? What do you think it means? What is it trying to get across? What is the big picture? And then let them take a few minutes to read it in detail and ask them whether it was easier to understand? Did the meaning change? Do you think you will remember it more easily? One of the things that can be emphasized with the students is that when they understand material they will remember it and be able to use it much easier.

I would then review with them that when a newspaper reporter is writing an article, they always think about five things: who, what, where, why and when. And, when reviewing material they have a question about, they can raise those questions for themselves.

One of the questions to raise with the group is: Do you find that you have trouble either following the teacher or taking notes? One of the things that should be discussed is that the more they keep up with their homework, the more they will be able to understand the teacher because in many subjects new information is often based upon the previous information that has already been presented. Suggest that when they start taking notes that they date the top of each page. Emphasize that note taking has to be practiced. They will learn to take notes on what appears to be the main ideas that the teacher is trying to present. Each teacher will present information in slightly different ways. Some will say this is important to remember. Others may say these are the reasons to do this. Others could simply say this could be on a test. Material placed on the board with the teacher's comments are often material that should be copied. Handouts that the teacher gives you should be placed in your binder so that you can place them in the order that they are presented. With each suggestion to the students ask them what their thoughts are about the suggestions, and the difficulties that they may have in doing it. Let the students take ownership and make the suggestions when possible of what is helpful and what is not.

One of the questions that you can ask of the students is: Have they ever gone over the homework and asked yourselves the question, What material would I put on a test if I was making up the test?

One suggestion that the counselor can make is that those notes that are taken and reviewed the same day by the student is the information that is remembered the best, so going over the notes that the student takes on a daily basis is a very good way of both learning and retaining the information.

## MODULE FOR SESSION FOUR – TEST PREPARATION

At the beginning of this session, ask if there are any questions about any of the material that you went over in the previous three sessions. There will be some anxiety of about this being the last session. However, because it often takes several weeks to internalize information and modify behavior it is helpful to have a follow-up session already planned in which you see the youngsters in four or five weeks as a fifth session. If this is being planned, than this should be discussed with the students. For example, "This is the last of our four sessions, however, I will be seeing you in four weeks as a follow-up." This will reduce the anxiety and allow them to discuss the most anxiety producing issue for this group of students; "taking tests." One of the questions raised is: As you prepare your homework and study more effectively do you find it is making any difference in your test taking? And then raise the question: What do you find is the most difficult part about taking tests? Being tested is difficult for everyone whether it is on the athletic field, playing sports, participating in groups, discussing with friends or taking tests in the classroom. What do you find is the easiest way to prepare for a test? Do you go over class notes prior to your test? Do you think of possible test questions that the teacher may raise in the test? Do you ever discuss material of the class with your fellow students?

One of the exercises that can be done during this last session is to reintroduce a magazine article. Have the students skim it first and then read it line by line. Let them take notes on the article and then let them submit questions that they would (if they were the teacher) ask. Have them discuss the questions orally. At the conclusion of the discussion, reinforce the fact that they are getting the concept, that they seem to be more attentive, and that they should practice skimming material and then reading it in detail.

Reinforce that the group will be getting together again in four to five weeks.

During this time the counselor should communicate with the teachers to see how the students are doing so that in the follow-up meeting there is some realistic understanding of whether the youngsters have been able to improve their school performance, and to what degree.

## *ART COUNSELING TECHNIQUES*

A planned module that is often very effective with selected students is art counseling. It is particularly helpful for the socially withdrawn or isolated child, the child with limited social skills, and children with expressive or speech impediments.

It is also helpful as a unique technique to enhance spontaneity of expression and facilitate open discussion of feelings.

The "key" is to create an atmosphere in which the student can express him/herself.

The precaution is to allow the child to do the interpretation and not the counselor.

## PREPARATION FOR USING ART COUNSELING TECHNIQUES

The counselor should create a comfortable environment where the student can express feelings without judgment and can use the art materials freely without arbitrary or restricting rules. This is usually accomplished once the counselor becomes comfortable with art counseling techniques.

The counselor should become aware of the potential impact that various art mediums may have on the students. When a student draws with a pencil and is able to erase his errors, he is using a medium that encourages control, for he is able to make deliberate marks and also eliminate them.

Each media, movement or reaction by the student to other students' work is reflective of the students' feeling and behavior by others.

## THE "UNFOCUSED" STUDENT

If the counselor is working with a student who has difficulty with attention and concentration, drawing with a pencil on 9" x 11" paper will enable him to feel that he can organize this small space successfully. If the counselor wanted the student to use a material that would allow him to be more expressive, color pencils would provide a wide range of color, but also enable him to erase an error, thereby continuing to reinforce his ability to manage his environment. As the student progresses, he/she could be introduced to colored markers.

# THE "INHIBITED" STUDENT

If the counselor is working with a very inhibited student, it would be advisable to provide art materials that would allow for freedom of expression, such as pastels, tempera paint, or clay. Providing large paper for drawing and painting supports and encourages self-expression.

The counselor should begin with pastels, for this material allows for the greatest control. Since the inhibited student may resist relinquishing control, it would be necessary to introduce a medium that would allow the student to have both control and free expression. Once the inhibited student becomes comfortable with pastels, the counselor could introduce a looser material such as paint, then eventually clay.

If the student becomes frustrated with the medium, the counselor could assist him in learning techniques to control the looser media. If this did not resolve the student's frustration, the counselor would return him to a more restrictive material.

The transitions from one material to another should be based on the counselor's clinical judgment and used as a counseling technique.

# FINGER PAINTING

Finger paint may seem like a material that could be fun to use, but unless it is being used with a young child, it can stimulate unwanted behavior in older children and adolescents.

Clay can also lead to infantile behavior, so it is necessary to provide adequate instruction (structure and direction) when introducing clay to the student. The counselor should provide the student with several handfuls of clay, tools for sculpting, and water to help in molding and smoothing. Although the clay has a tendency to become dry, if the counselor observes the student making the clay unnecessarily wet, the counselor should intervene by showing the student how to regain control of the clay. This type of intervention is instructive and preserves the student's self esteem.

# *THE STUDENT'S INTERPRETATION*

The counselor should listen patiently as the student tells the story behind his artwork. The counselor may ask open-ended questions to help the student expand his narrative. The counselor should neither tell the student her interpretation of the student's artwork, nor quiz the student as she analyzes the students' work.

A counselor's inquiry or misinterpretation can increase the student's withdrawal or inhibition and decrease the student's spontaneity.

The counselor should be supportive of the student when he is ready to share his feelings verbally. The counselor may respond to the student's feelings by making reflective statements. The counselor should not tell the student the feelings she thinks are emanating from his artwork. As the student becomes more comfortable with the experience, the student will become more expressive and more open to his own feelings. The counselor should guard against inhibiting this process.

The counselor should not focus on or judge the aesthetic quality of the student's artwork. This could result in the student wanting to please the counselor by trying to execute his best drawing rather than expressing himself spontaneously. In addition, it may also create competition among the other students who are also vying for the counselor's attention. The counselor should be mindful of her comments about the students' artwork, and be aware of the uniqueness of each piece of artwork and the heightened sensitivity of each student to her comments.

The student should not be placed in a situation where he is feeling anxious. It is the counselor's job to focus on the student's affect, to monitor his responses to the topics being discussed and the imagery being revealed, and to observe him in the process of developing his art. It is essential that the counselor be vigilant about providing the necessary interventions to maintain stability and safety for each of the students.

# ART COUNSELING WITH THE WITHDRAWN CHILD

## MODULE ONE

There are many reasons that a child or adolescent may be withdrawn, including depression, poor social skills, lack of confidence, and family dynamics.

The goal of the counselor using art counseling techniques is to increase the psycho-social skills of the student in order to enhance the learning process in the school setting. Art counseling techniques will be new to most students and has a tendency to both excite as well to initially inhibit the withdrawn child/adolescent.

Initially structure and specific direction is helpful to decrease the student's anxiety. Instruction should be very simple.

The first module is to help the child learn to become comfortable with a new experience (using art materials).

In the first module, discussion and instructions are related in the 3$^{rd}$ person. Discussion is about materials and art exercises. Personal issues resolve around the reaction of the students to their exercises.

The first step is to give the student a box of multi-colored oil pastels and 19" x 24" paper. He would be asked to cover the entire sheet of paper with pastels and to apply the colors heavily. It should be explained to him that when the oil pastel becomes warm it will blend easily and feel as though the pastel is sliding across the surface of the pastel-covered paper when he draws. He should be reminded that since he is expected to cover the edges of the paper with the pastels that it is "alright" if the pastels get on the table.

For this first drawing, the student should be encouraged to experiment with color blending and make different kinds of lines, such as swirling and angular lines. Once he has thoroughly covered the sheet with pastel, he will find that new, unexpected colors will emerge, an insight that can be reinforced.

The counselor can suggest that the student use shades of yellow, orange, red, green, blue, and purple, and delay giving white, grey, brown, and black, when initially applying the pastels. The counselor will demonstrate to the student that he will be able to create brown himself by blending yellow with purple, orange with blue and red with green. The counselor should suggest that his artwork will remain more vibrant if the brown combinations are avoided, or used minimally. These directions will give him a sense of control that will allow him to feel more confident manipulating these materials.

The goal is for the student to find pleasure exploring and experimenting with the colorful pastels and trying new things. He may become discouraged if what begins as a bright color field becomes a dismal brown drawing. When this occurs the student may have lost control of the color blending. This can create frustration for the student. In the event this occurs, the counselor should use it as a learning opportunity for the student to cope effectively with his frustration and an aesthetic problem. The counselor can explain that the beauty of using art materials is that if you make a mistake you can toss it aside and start all over again. Or if you are really frustrated, you can tear it into little pieces and try again. You can always try again. "Each time you draw, you learn more about your own creativity and the media." The counselor can also ask the other students if they have any suggestions to help "Johnny" out.

Another option with a pastel error is to learn to stop drawing when the pastels begin to blend into unwanted colors. The student would take a pallet knife (found in most art classes), and scrape off the unwanted material from his drawing. Once this is done the drawing can be completed. This is a satisfying task for it allows the student to continue working on his original piece of art with only a minor interruption.

The counselor should give the students a demonstration on another piece of paper by applying the pastel thickly and then scraping it off gently (applying pressure to the broad edge of the pallet knife which is parallel to the pastel-covered paper). Enabling the students to do this will give them a sense of mastery over resolving their own problems, controlling their frustration, and maintaining the integrity of their artwork.

Towards the end of the module, the students can discuss what they enjoyed most, what was the most difficult part, what materials were the easiest to use, and what were the most difficult?

The foundation for more spontaneous discussion will have been developed.

## MODULE TWO & THREE

Module two and three will reinforce the work and techniques of the 1st module and emphasize the 2nd and 3rd person.

## EXPLORING THE UNIVERSE

The student would be given a box of large, multi-colored chalk pastels along with a 3' x 4' sheet of brown paper taped (on all four sides) horizontally to the wall. He may create people flying, in addition to flying cars, flying ships, and maybe even a castle in the sky! He can draw civilizations on the other planets and include himself with friends as he explores these imaginative places complete with shooting stars. The goal will be emphasizing drawings in the 2nd or 3rd person.

It's purpose is to conceptually reinforce involvement with others.

It enables the students to project themselves in an imaginary non-threatening way.

The student will be asked to use the colors to draw himself in his fantasy universe. He can be encouraged to be creative. He can draw himself in a rocket ship shooting across the sky, or living on Jupiter with all his friends and family. The student is being given the freedom "to be free."

The student would be given tempera paint in a variety of colors with brushes that include small and large brushes. He will be asked to draw his own personal tree on the 3' x 5' sheet of brown paper taped (on all four sides) vertically to the wall. He should be urged to take his time and enjoy the experience.

The counselor should suggest that the student begins by painting the ground line which will later become either grass or dirt, and then everything above the ground line as sky. Since the sky is background, the sky should be painted before the tree.

## PHYSICAL EXPRESSION RELATED TO ART

Once the sky has been completed, the painting of the tree will become the focus. The counselor should encourage the students to stand up with their feet firmly planted on the floor, to spread their arms, and to think of their body as the trunk of the tree and their arms as the branches. The counselor can provide ideas to stimulate the students' creativity. She may ask if the tree is strong enough to climb, or if the branches are broad enough to create shade. She could ask if it is a flowering tree or if the tree bears fruit. The counselor might say that after the thick roots emerge from the earth, the tree trunk tapers but expands again when you reach the branches. She may recommend that the student experiments with the color and the application of the paint by adding purples, blues, and oranges to tree with bold strokes and whimsical details to enhance the texture of the bark and leaves.

When the painting has been completed, the student and the counselor should stand far away from the tree and appreciate its presence, and discuss.

## MODULE FOUR

Module Four is the continuation and reinforcement of the previous module.

Clay is introduced as the medium. It should be pointed out that clay is the most difficult of the materials that they will use and because of their progress they are now ready to "tackle the next exercise." Questions and discussion at this point should be encouraged.

The counselor should provide a demonstration to the student, showing techniques used to connect pieces of clay together when constructing anything from a bowl to a figure. Questions should be encouraged.

The students will be provided with several handfuls of clay, tools for sculpting, and water to be used to keep the clay moist enough to mold. The counselor would explain that the first step in working with clay is eliminating the air bubbles. This is accomplished by condensing the clay into a large ball and forcefully throwing it onto a flat surface, such as the table, several time. A canvas placemat should be placed on the table where the clay is to be thrown. This is done to avoid the clay from sticking onto the table. Generally the student finds this practical task funny due to the loud sound that is made when the clay hits the table.

The student will be asked to gather the clay from the placemat and knead it back into a ball. The student should be warned that his hands will feel chalky, but that as long as he keeps his hands damp, he will not feel that sensation. Students often find it oddly amusing that an adult would encourage them to get their hands dirty! The application of water to the clay to avoid the clay from being dry and/or from being mud-like.

The counselor will be sure that the student has a generous amount of clay that should now be in the shape of a ball. She will explain to the students that together they would each construct their own bowls.

Each would stand, look down on their own clay balls, and with both hands holding their balls apply downward pressure to create a flat surface on the bottom of each one, creating their bowls.

The counselor will demonstrate on her clay ball how to begin to form the inside of the bowl. This is done by inserting her forefinger into the top center of the clay ball. The student would copy this task.

Questions should be asked by the counselor to the group. For example, What do you think the next step should be in making the bowl? Are there different ways that you would suggest that we do this?

The counselor could suggest the next step is to knead the sides of the bowl by reinserting her forefinger back into the original hole and gently pressing the clay together with forefinger and the thumb while rotating the clay ball.

After the student and the counselor do this they will see a bowl form right before their eyes as the opening of the bowls will widen. The counselor will urge the student to keep the sides of the bowl strong and slightly thick while the student gains confidence experimenting with the clay material.

The withdrawn student will have shared an enjoyable and

somewhat messy experience with the counselor that resulted in the construction of a well-built bowl.

Open discussion should follow. Positive reinforcement of their work, their involvement, and their suggestions should be made by the counselor. Questions of the students can be generalized to, Why do you think different artists choose different medias, some are sculptures, some are painters, and some are architects. Which material did you enjoy working with best?

The general concept is moving the inhibited withdrawn student to a more spontaneous creative youngster.

Plans for follow-up with the youngster, both as an individual and a group, are very helpful. In general, follow-up should be no less than 3-4 weeks following the last module. Coordination with the students' teachers is always helpful.

## *SUGGESTED READINGS*

Betensky, M. (1973). *Self-discovery through self-expression.* Springfield, IL: Pearson, Charles C. Thomas.

Kramer, E. (1979). *Childhood and art therapy.* New York: Shocken Books, Inc

# CHAPTER XII

## *GROUP THEORIES*

There are multiple psychological theories that have been applied to group counseling, most of which have influenced our thinking. The in-depth discussion of these theories is beyond the scope of this book, but a brief summary of these theories will emphasize the contributions, advantages and disadvantages to each.

It is important to note that no single psychological school or theoretical frame of reference is ideal for the school setting.

The "best" approach I have found is the developmental approach that every counselor has learned as an educator tailored to the student, school, immediate community and frame of reference that the counselor is most comfortable with. Although the theories and content may be different, the process and dynamics that influence groups are the same.

## *BEHAVIOR MODIFICATION AND GROUP COUNSELING*

Behavior modification is probably the most applicable theory to the school setting. If we define education as the processes of teaching and learning and our goal is to modify behavior and thinking to enhance the learning process, then behavior modification is certainly a frame of reference of choice. It is goal oriented, it is well structured and organized, it defines the problems, and reinforces the progress in order to modify the targeted behavior and/or to reward the desired attitude and motivation. It is time limited.

Because it is goal oriented, it can both enhance and reward the desired goals of achievement. It is a frame of reference that every good teacher utilizes. It emphasizes that "good" group production is accomplished by decreasing the anxiety of the group, as behavior modification does. It allows for a well organized approach which is the basis of any good lesson plan.

It emphasizes positive reinforcement and capitalizes on the concept of extinction ("no longer presenting a reinforcer"). It is hopeful that the learning process will generalize to other things in a positive way, helping the individual to discriminate so that they can react differently to different situations and/or problems. By utilizing the concepts of positive reinforcement, generalization, extinction and discrimination, we hope to shape the students' behavior and learning process.

Its main drawback is that it may not allow enough freedom to explore troublesome areas that a group member may have. This limitation may be a direct result of the primary concentration being on the student's target behaviors, rather than on his/her overall experience. Therefore, initial selection and assessment of each youngster prior to the group is critically important. A second concern that the group therapist must be aware of is that the increase in organization and structure of the group will decrease the anxiety of the students and as a result might facilitate the release of repressed material which the leader must be prepared to handle. (It is at this time that referral for individual counseling may be helpful to the student.)

Another disadvantage that may arise is that there may be too much emphasis on strict adherence to goals and objectives. This may isolate some group members, particularly in the resistance testing phase, making it more difficult for the group to move into a more productive phase, where more meaningful learning takes place. (Ref. Suggested Readings)

## ADLERIAN THEORY AND GROUP COUNSELING

The Adlerian frame of reference does have a place in group counseling in the schools. Alfred Adler re-organized the value of using group techniques and introduced the concept in Vienna in the 1920's. He felt that each individual is influenced by his social environment, while still striving to accomplish individual goals. He was more comprehensive than his colleagues including all the variables that influence one's behavior. Adler's frame of reference is that the individual wants to move to a state of health. He emphasized that the way to modify behavior was to learn (the skills of/or insight) for new behavior. At the very least, his was an educational model.

Group identity (the concept of oneself as a member of a group and/or part of a larger social system) was fundamental to his frame of reference. Adler's basic theme was one of "growth and development," both an appropriate and applicable frame of reference in the school setting. His theory was that perception was more important than reality and was particularly relevant to understanding students in the school setting. He believed that the fundamental strengths and assets of the individual would reinforce the student's ability to "self-determine" his/or her behavior and growth. Adler's emphasis on the social interest in others is something that the adolescent can identify with.

Adler believed that one's style of life influenced how a person handled the difficulties in his/her life and the way in which he/she resolved problems and achieved goals. He felt that there were common types of lifestyles, dealing with one's activity. There was a "social useful type" which had high social interest, high activity, and concern for others being both positive and mature. The second category was the "ruling type" who he described as having little social interest, but dominating and often antisocial. The third category was the "getting type," little social interest and waiting for others to meet their needs. The fourth he described as the avoiding type, who are usually isolated, unsuccessful, with low social interest.

Perhaps Adler's weakness in the school setting is seeing psychological problems (including maladaptive behavior) as a "failing in life" rather than as a result of the many variables that may contribute. His need to over emphasize social relationships including the family, if not programmed in a developmental way, may increase the anxiety of the student, and inadvertently increase a negative group identity. (Ref. Suggested Readings)

## EXISTENTIAL THEORY AND GROUP COUNSELING

Existential theory is applicable in concept to group counseling in the schools. Its essence is that nothing is predetermined (for example, by the unconscious) but that everybody has a self-awareness that gives them the freedom to choose what to do. It emphasizes that the individual has the responsibility to make their own choices. It is a very appealing concept to adolescent students because the adolescent has a constant "ying and yang" between dependence and independence. It is an especially helpful and appealing frame of reference for those students with a negative group identity and feel a sense of isolation and or dependence. It helps to give individual students an opportunity to confront the reality of the situations and experiences that they face every day.

The potential problem with an existential approach in a school setting is that the counselor/group members may move too quickly to confront the defenses of the student with resultant increase in the students anxiety which may increase the anxiety of the group with "acting out" of that anxiety by the students in the school setting. It is particularly important that the leader maintain a sense of stability and security within the group emphasizing his/her role as group leader while reinforcing a student's right to choose. By decreasing the group's anxiety the students are able to experience a greater sense of stability that will enable them to express themselves with increased spontaneity and authenticity. (Ref. Suggested Readings)

## RATIONAL EMOTIVE BEHAVIOR THERAPY AND GROUP COUNSELING (REBT)

Rational Emotive Behavior Therapy (REBT) (originally Rational Emotive Therapy) is applicable in concept to group counseling in the schools. REBT was developed by Albert Ellis, who in the mid to late 1950's was one of the original therapists to develop a cognitive oriented therapy. It was the precursor to Cognitive Behavioral Therapy (CBT) and more recently Dialectic Behavior Therapy (DBT) developed by Marsha Linehan. Ellis emphasized behavioral treatment with direct techniques (such as desensitization), doing actual exercises which will alter the individual's "way of thinking" particularly changing one's "culture." REBT emphasizes that the way the student obsessively thinks about something is often self defeating and irrational. REBT would encourage the student to challenge his self-defeating thoughts in order for him to learn to discriminate the healthy, logical parts of his thinking from his exaggerated, self-defeating thoughts. This would enable him to alter his irrational beliefs so that impending difficulties could be averted.

Ellis presented an ABC Theory of Personality. A – a person's goals are activated either by positive or negative influences; B – there is a response to the activating event; and C – there is a reaction to the activating event with a new perception.

Ellis emphasized that a mixture of Cognitive Behavioral and Emotive Techniques will decrease reoccurring self defeating "thoughts, feelings and behavior." It is easily translated into an educational format with specific instructions.

Although the adolescents may present with a negative self identity and a negative group identity, it is important for the group leader to recognize that this is developmentally a common occurrence among adolescents and not prematurely "push" them beyond their cognitive and emotional capabilities. The skilled group leader in the school setting offers leadership with a REBT frame of reference by structuring the group with a good lesson plan while protecting the group members as they attempt to alter their cognitive, behavioral and emotional frames of reference.

Among the many attributes that Ellis had was his sense of humor which relaxed the group members and decreased the actual and potential anxiety that change (and tasks) may bring about. (Ref. Suggested Readings)

## GESTALT THEORY AND GROUP COUNSELING

Gestalt Theory originally developed by Fritz Perls was developed primarily as a one to one therapist to client model. Perls basically believed that the individual "is best understood" in relationship to his/her environment. The environment includes past experience. Gestalt Theory was a prelude to systems theory, "the whole is greater than it's parts" (Latner, 1986), the emphasis being on the relationship of the parts to each other as well as to the environment. Gestalt Theory emphasizes that the environment is in a state of constant change and it's importance is how the person contemplates the environment at the moment. This basic concept is certainly applicable to the adolescent who views his/her environment as an important part of their group identity. Their perception of themselves and others has an important impact on them. This awareness in relationships is a fundamental concept in Gestalt Theory.

One of the earlier drawbacks to the application of Gestalt Theory was its confrontative technique seen in the 1960's in encounter groups, the "hot seat approach" which often appeared to become more destructive than helpful. A Gestalt therapist George Brown has said "Of all the therapies, Gestalt has the most potential for somebody really being cruel and hurting other people." Subsequent models were less confrontative and more supportive.

Gestalt Theory emphasizes the importance of the group leader and the group member trusting one another as well as trust being shared between the group members. However, the techniques used in the school setting may be too anxiety producing and should not be attempted by the novice counselor. (Ref. Suggested Readings)

## PERSON-CENTERED THERAPY
## AND GROUP COUNSELING

Person-Centered Therapy, previously called Client-Centered Therapy was developed by Carl Rogers. Its basic concept is that of being "non-directive" in counseling, which is also characteristic of the way the group leader facilitates the group. The leader's influence in the group is one based upon the relationship of the leader to group members rather than the group leader's ability to direct based upon the dynamics of the group. It is based upon the anticipation that group members have the ability to change based upon their own "self understanding." The movement is away from the concept of control (direction of events) to one of self realization. Person-Centered Therapy is similar to Gestalt Group Counseling and Existential Group Counseling (part of what has been referred to as humanistic psychology) as it stresses the importance of self awareness.

Roger believed (similar to Existential Theory) that the human has a tendency of growth to a healthy state and has the capacity to be "responsible and caring" in relationship with others. There is an emphasis on the subjective feelings of the individual, rather than an objective goal oriented frame of reference. The group leader must be genuinely empathetic with "non possessive warmth."

The basic tenants of Person-Centered Therapy certainly has a place in the school setting. Every educator should have a genuine caring and respect for the students, but the basis of an effective school program is to provide the feeling of stability in order to not only facilitate meaningful learning, but to decrease anxiety and enhance the feeling of security. Leadership in a school setting must provide the supervision necessary to facilitate the growth of the students. Every successful school/or school program provides this. An effective educator can be both genuinely empathetic and understanding and at the same time directive. (Ref. Suggested Readings)

## PSYCHOANALYSIS AND GROUP COUNSELING

It is helpful for the counselor to reflect on the psychoanalytic frame of reference both for its contributions and for its inherent disadvantages and potential difficulties in the school setting.

Psychoanalysis has contributed meaningful insight into resistance to change (which with our students we often reflect on as oppositional behavior). With change comes a natural resistance because we do not always know how events, both internal as well as external, will develop or relate. It is this lack of ability to predict the future that causes our increase in anxiety. In psychoanalysis increased anxiety is desirable to work with our repressed thoughts, but in a school setting our goal is to decrease anxiety in order to increase feeling of stability and security in our students to enhance the learning environment. It is one reason that the psychoanalytic technique in almost all cases is contraindicated in the school setting.

Although Freud's structure of personality (Id, Ego, and Superego) is rarely utilized or applicable in the school setting, his description and application of his ego defense mechanisms are certainly something that every counselor should be familiar with. Repression, regression, projection, intellectualization, denial, reaction formation, displacement, sublimation, rationalization, and identification are all observed in the students that we work with in the school or other settings.

Freud's psychosexual stages of development, although at times may be helpful in understanding the students perception, have little practical application in the school setting.

The concept of transference, however, is something that every counselor should always be aware of. Transference is the feeling that the student may project upon the counselor that is reflective of experiences, attributes, or feelings that the student may have that represents someone in his/her past or current experience. The concept of counter-transference is of equal or perhaps even more importance to the counselor. Counter-transference is the feeling of the counselor towards the student that may reflect or be reflective of the counselor's current or past experience that he/she projects on to the student.

The emphasis in the school setting is on the here and now, not the unconscious. Increasing the student's awareness of repressed material may be too anxiety producing for many students, particularly in the latency and adolescent periods. In the educational setting, our goal is to decrease anxiety, in order to increase performance and meaningful learning. (Ref. Suggested Readings)

## *CHOICE THEORY AND GROUP COUNSELING*

The basic premise of Reality Therapy which evolved to Control Theory and subsequently Choice Theory is appropriate in the school setting. It is particularly applicable to adolescents because it emphasizes that the individuals see their environment in terms of their own world rather than the world as it is, a frame of reference that is necessary to understand when working with adolescents.

Glasser, who developed Choice Theory recognized that

"control" is an important variable, particularly when working with adolescents who are going through significant physical and psychological changes in just a short period of time. Control (or the ability to direct the events in the environment) becomes an important frame of reference. By enabling the adolescent to make their own choices and helping them develop the skills to do so, the counselor is empowering the adolescents by reinforcing the positive choices made. Group counseling is a natural way in the school setting to enable the student to develop the skills necessary to make their own choices, as well to develop meaningful relationships.

During adolescence, the adolescent's social needs and group identity is as intense as any time in their development, a variable that Glasser emphasizes when he advocates that the basis of most people's problems is the lack of meaningful or satisfying relationships. Glasser's frame of reference is particularly helpful in the school setting because his Choice Theory emphasizes that the individual has control over what he/or she does.

The advantage of Choice Theory is that it gives a frame of reference to work with that is compatible with the adolescent. The disadvantage is that like any frame of reference, strict adherence does not accommodate the needs of all students. (Ref. Suggested Readings)

## SUGGESTED READINGS

### BEHAVIOR MODIFICATION AND GROUP COUNSELING

Bandura, A. (1969). *Principles of behavior modification.* New York: Holt, Rinehart & Winston.

Bandura, A. (1997). *Self-efficacy: The exercise of control.* San Francisco: W. H. Freeman.

Kazdin, A.E. (2001). *Behavior modification in applied settings* (6th Ed.). Belmont, CA: Wadesworth.

Skinner, B. F., (1953). *Science and human behavior.* New York: Free Press

### ADLERIAN THEORY AND GROUP COUNSELING

Adler, A. (1958). *What life should mean to you.* New York: Capricorn.

Carlson, J., Watts, R. E., Maniacci, M. (2006). *Adlerian therapy: Theory and practice.* Washington, DC: American Psychological Association.

Mosak, H. H., & Maniacci, M. (1999). *A primer on Adlerian psychology.* Philedelphia: Brunner/Mazel.

### EXISTENTIAL THEORY AND GROUP COUNSELING

May, R. (1961). *Existential psychology.* New York: Random House.

May, R. (1989). *The art of counseling.* New York: Gardner.

Yalom, I. D. (1989). *Existential psychotherapy.* New York: Basic Books

## RATIONAL EMOTIVE BEHAVIOR THERAPY AND GROUP COUNSELING (REBT)

Bernard, M. E., & Jpyce, M. R. (1984). *Rational-emotive therapy with children and adolescents.* New York: Wiley.

Ellis, A. (1973). *Humanistic psychotherapy: The rational-emotive approach.* New York: McGraw Hill.

Ellis, A. (1992b). Group rational emotive and cognitive-behavioral therapy. *International Journal of Group Psychotherapy, 42,* 63-80.

## GESTALT THEORY AND GROUP COUNSELING

Perls, F. S. (1973). *The Gestalt approach.* Palo Alto, CA: Science and Behavior Books.

Perls, F. S., Hefferline, R. F., & Goodman, P. (1951/1994). *Gestalt therapy.* Highlands, NY: Gestalt Journal Press.

Shetherd, I. L. (1970). Limitations in the Gestalt approach. In J. Fagan & I. L. Shepherd (Eds.) *Gestalt therapy now* (pp. 234-238). Palo Alto, CA: Science and Behavior Books.

## PERSON-CENTERED THERAPY AND GROUP COUNSELING

Boy, A. V., & Pine, G. J. (1999) *A person-centered foundation for counseling and psychotherapy.* (2nd Ed.) Springfield, IL: Charles C. Thomas.

Glauser, A.S. & Bozarth, J.D. (2001). Person-centered counseling: the culture within. *Journal of Counseling and Development,* 79, 142-147.

Rogers, C. R. (1942a) *Counseling and psychotherapy.* Boston: Houghton Mifflin.

Rogers, C. R. (1961) *On becoming a person.* Boston: Houghton Mifflin.

## *PSYCHOANALYSIS AND GROUP COUNSELING*

Bion, W. R. (1963). *Elements of psychoanalysis.* New York: Basic Books.

Freud, A. (1936). *The ego and the mechanisms of defense.* New York: International Universities Press.

Freud, S. (1923). *The ego and the id.* (Standard Edition, Vol. 19).

Freud, S. (1926). *Inhibitions, symptoms and anxiety.* (Standard Edition, Vol. 20).

## *CHOICE THEORY AND GROUP COUNSELING*

Glasser, W. (1998a). *Choice theory: A new psychology of personal freedom.* New York: Harper Collins.

Glasser, W. (2000a). *Counseling with choice theory.* New York: Harper Collins.

Glasser, W. (2000b). *Every student can succeed.* Chatsworth, CA: William Glasser Institute.

# CHAPTER XIII

## GROUP COUNSELING WITH PARENTS

Education is still the basic responsibility of the parents. School systems have been reluctant to allow parents to take an active role. Regardless of past history, current attention has to be directed toward parent involvement.

School systems are (and will be) using more paraprofessional personnel. The need for more staff has been accentuated by the increase in student population, the scholastic needs of the students, and concerted requests by the teachers and teacher aides for more academic involvement with their students. The two most readily available sources of extra personnel are parents and students. The counselor's role in initiating parent programs can be very influential. This is a role which the counselor should assume as part of his overall duties (with the consent of the administrator).

One of the difficulties of initiating parent programs is that the majority of educators have not been trained in how to work with parents, how to initiate parent programs, or how to utilize the resources which parents have to offer. On numerous occasions (i.e., lectures, classes, faculty meetings) the author has asked educators how many have attended either a training seminar, a faculty meeting, or a lecture on how to work with parents. It is not uncommon to have only three to four percent indicate that they have received this type of training.

If parent programs are to be initiated, then educators should develop and share with each other techniques and ideas of how to work with, counsel, and involve parents. Many hours of training are spent on how the student learns and how the educator should teach, but very little time (if any) is allotted to how to communicate with and involve the children's parents.

The first consideration in initiating a parent program is to collectively, as a faculty or school system, train the staff in how to talk and work with parents.

The next consideration is to outline those school activities in which the parent might be able to participate. In designing an effective program, the basic rule is to first outline those activities that the staff truly thinks would be helpful. The purpose is not to artificially create jobs or opportunities for parent participation that will be a significant nuisance to the school. The object is to review the overall school program, class by class and grade by grade, to find the essentials in which there is a need for additional manpower. It may be washing and ironing the children's smocks, repairing and building toys and equipment, being present in the nurse's office on the day that he is absent, being an assistant on the playground, doing secretarial work, or assisting in the class supervising a small group while the teacher works with another group. The opportunities are limitless. There are real needs within the schools. Part of these can be met by parent participation.

*The key in developing a parent program is to make sure that the school builds its program around the needs that the school officials think is indicated.*

It is not fair to the teachers, the children, nor the parents to ask the parents to design jobs for themselves for the school setting. The parents do not know what the needs of the school are. They usually do not know what the school routine consists of. This is a job and role for the professionals. It is therefore necessary for the professionals to outline the program in which they would like the parents to participate. There are exceptions. When parent organizations have already been established, the parents should participate in innovative projects of their own decision. They should be given an opportunity to develop more sophisticated programs.

In schools in which the neighborhood has not participated, the school should offer an opportunity for the parents to help in the planning of the early stages. The parents should not be excluded. However, if the program is to be successful, the leadership of the school (that is, the administration and teacher corps) has to be involved first. If the educators develop a program around the needs of the school, then the staff will be enthusiastic and can share this enthusiasm with the parents. The parents will feel that they are contributing something "real" to the school program. If the staff designs a program that does not fulfill the needs of the school, then the school officials will not be enthusiastic about it and will not encourage parent participation. The parents may become less interested and/or frustrated, and parent participation will either drop or not be initiated.

Too often a program is designed for the parents for the sake of having a parent program on record. Little enthusiasm is given to it. When there is a poor parent response, the remark of the administration is, "The parents don't want to participate." Parent programs are basically the responsibility of the school. Part of the responsibility is to develop participation in a programmed way, meeting the parents where they are (reflecting their attitude and ability) and programming their participation in a way that insures involvement and is helpful. When programs are hastily put together for the sake of having a program on paper, the results are usually poor, attendance is minimal, and the overt message to the neighborhood is that "We don't care whether you participate or not."

When a parent program is designed, it should be as "personalized" as possible. For example, the classical approach is to have a general school PTA meeting. The parents are able to identify as a parent group in support of the entire school. This has a beneficial effect on the parent, the school, and the youngsters. The general PTA meeting is easier to organize when there has been a well-established parent-teachers association. When the tradition of the neighborhood is for parent participation, a large PTA meeting reinforces a neighborhood effect. However, in areas where the neighborhood traditionally has not participated, then it is often helpful to have a general PTA meeting and then divide the large parent group into smaller units. The smaller parent groups should be organized according to the classrooms or grades of their youngsters. The grade meeting can be designed around the needs, problems, and natural development of the youngster at that particular grade level. For parents of first graders, the staff could present a program describing the curriculum for the coming year, what the natural growth and development of a first grader is, and the problems that the parent may face during the coming year in a home setting.

The program can be organized so that the parents can observe the children in a program or in the classroom. The teacher can then review the developmental characteristics of the particular age, what the parents observed, and what he hopes to accomplish relative to those characteristics. For example: "At an early age youngsters may want to play more independently than youngsters at another age." The teacher may comment on what the youngsters did and how they communicated with each other, then portray to the parent how he would hope the children would communicate and participate with each other. The teacher would point out to the parent that the reason he was trying to create more interaction with the youngsters was to increase socialization skills, which in turn will help the youngster's development with concept learning, ability to generalize and to be more original and creative in their thought. This gives the parents an opportunity to initiate and encourage the same type of activity in the home. The educational process becomes complete when the school can teach the parent how to stimulate learning in the home.

One of the best ways to encourage parent participation is by having programs that involve their children. Many principles have told me that when the children actively participate, the response by the parents is often one hundred percent better than if it is just a routine PTA meeting.

Another way to stimulate parent interest is to design programs that will allow the parents to see the advancement of their children on a developmental basis in the classroom. Parent meetings are usually held periodically throughout the year. At a meeting early in the school year the parents are given lists of things to look for as they observe their youngsters in the routine classroom. At subsequent meetings (for example, eight weeks later) the parents are given similar lists with additional questions: "Is your youngster performing any differently than he did eight weeks previously? Is he responding more? Is he able to read at a different level? What is his social interaction? Is he paying more attention to the teacher? Is he as physically active as he was?" These questions not only make the parents aware of what the teacher is trying to do in the classroom, but also attempt to give the parent some insight into the development and progress of the child. This is usually stimulating and interesting for the parent. It is often helpful to have a place on the questionnaire for the parent to make note of any observation that he has experienced. This gives the parent the opportunity to express herself about her child and also make observations that may be helpful to the teacher.

Another technique that encourages parent participation in the school is to give the parents an opportunity to share problems, successes, concerns, and programs with which their children have been involved. It is always reassuring to parents to know that other parents are having the same problems that they are. It is also easier for the children if their parents know that perhaps they are not the problems (or the geniuses) that their parents thought they were. Parents who can participate and share concerns and experiences obtain a socialization effect which increases their desire to participate in school activity and to return to future parent group meetings.

It is perhaps in this area that the school has been reluctant to become involved: that is, establishing opportunities for parents to express themselves and to share ideas with each other. Some of the reasons for this reluctance are reasonable. The school does not want to lose control of the organization of the school. However, when the program is designed in a reasonable way, the administrator does not have to "worry" about losing control. Parents do not want to run the schools, but they do want to be able to influence the schools to meet the needs of their youngsters and give their children the best educational opportunities available.

## HOW TO GET PARENTS INTO THE SCHOOLS

One of the important factors of getting parents into the school is to develop a climate within the school – that is, within the faculty (counselors, teachers, and administration) – that will be favorable towards the parents, an atmosphere that will encourage parents to participate in an organized fashion (organized, that is, by the staff). The development of this climate is the responsibility of the administrator and his representatives.

Programs should be developed to familiarize the teachers with techniques to satisfactorily work with parents. Unless this climate is developed, any program that is initiated will meet with, at best, only partial success.

The next step is to have a well-organized plan for parent participation.

Once these two basic factors are developed (the proper climate for parent participation and a well-designed program) the administration can then orient itself to inviting the parents into the school. It is obvious that most schools that develop parent programs start at the point of trying to get the parents into the school, and then belatedly develop a favorable climate and stimulating programs. This is unreasonable and is the main reason why many parent programs fail.

There are many different ways to issue invitations to the parents. The classic way is to send the invitations home via the youngsters. This is a precarious method but is not very expensive. If the notes reach home (that is, if they are not in the mail boxes, sewers, lawns, or garbage cans) then part of the message will be delivered verbally by the youngster. How the youngster has been prepared carries a lot of weight. For example, if a teacher says to the youngsters, "Here are some notes I want you to take home to your parents," there is little information that the youngster can share to encourage his parents to participate. However, if the teacher takes ten minutes to explain what is in the note, why the school and the teacher would like the child's parents to come to school, and encourages the youngster to be enthusiastic about the parent program, then the chances of the note reaching home are significantly better. The "sales job" by the youngster when he delivers the note will be immeasurably enhanced.

Another way of delivering an invitation is by having teachers "comb" the neighborhood and go to the homes of parents to invite them to school meetings. This has been done, for example, in areas where parents have been reluctant to come into the school because of the traditions of the neighborhood, especially when the school has been regarded as another unpleasant authority figure. This makes an impact on the parents that the school does want parents to participate. Personal contact supersedes the routine "we have a job to do" invitation. In those areas where telephones are available, phones by teams often helps.

Parent participation, perhaps more than anything else, is particularly helpful: that is, organizing teams of parents to contact other parents to participate in the program. In most cases parents seem to be able to contact parents and to initiate and stimulate parent participation better than faculty can. Often parents cannot participate because of the lack of baby-sitters or baby-sitting facilities, because both parents are working, or because of illness or other commitments which are important to the family. The school should consider both evening and day programs. In some neighborhoods the parents do not participate in evening programs because they are afraid to leave their homes. Many schools have initiated baby-sitting service during the day provided by older students.

Older students can also be used to call parents. For example, in the elementary schools fifth and sixth graders can be used. In the middle and senior high school, students of any grade can be used. When the neighborhood by tradition supports the school, then the school generally has no problem in expanding current programs when it thinks it is indicated.

Major problems present when participation by the parents in the neighborhood has been traditionally poor. The schools have usually not given enough credit to the parents that they could be of significant service. This is unfortunate. When parents are allowed to participate they do contribute. When the parents have "traditionally" not been encouraged to participate, it is often difficult to initiate programs and get the parents "in."

One of the difficulties that some schools have is that after an enthusiastic attempt to initiate parent programs, they meet with only minimal success and at this point, out of frustration, drop the idea, saying that the parents do not want to participate or that "We just can't reach the parents."

The parents usually want to participate. They may, however, be suspicious of newly-initiated programs by a school that has not involved the neighborhood before and previously designed parent programs that were guaranteed to fail. It is unusual for a school to initiate a new parent program and receive an overwhelming, consistent response. It takes time to develop neighborhood support, to train the teachers to cooperate, and to train the parents to participate. A program that starts with enthusiasm and expects a one-hundred-percent return the first year is doomed to a discouraging let-down. It is anticipating too much too soon.

What is important is that the faculty take the gains that they have achieved, whether they are large or small, utilize them, and build on what has been accomplished. Too often school officials will say, "Well, we tried, but we didn't get much of a response" and subsequently dropped the programs. This is unfortunate and indicates a lack of insight. It is egotistical to expect entire neighborhoods to suddenly adopt a new program because it has been initiated by the schools, especially when the schools have not been as productive for their children in the past as perhaps they would have liked. It is the obligation of the schools as part of the educational process to alert the neighborhood, to educate the children, and to train the staff so that there will be a positive attitude towards the development of a community approach to education. This takes time.

Most of the new programs that have met with only fair or poor success have been a so-called "shotgun" approach. They were designed to get as many parents into the school as possible. This is perhaps the most difficult program to initiate for a school that has not had an active parent group. Although a shotgun approach is a less satisfactory way to initiate a new program, it can be relatively successful with the proper preparation and organization. One of the difficulties with the shotgun approach is that the primary goal is to get the parents into the school. There is a hidden notion that if the parents present to the school, they will be able to participate in a meaningful way and will carry with them something that will transfer to the youngsters. This can be misleading. However, when the goal is to involve the parents in educational projects, it usually is more successful.

When a school has not had much parent participation, it is probably best to initiate programs in a small way and build from that point. For example, initiate a program when children are registered for school for the first time. The parents are invited to participate in an information program that same day or given a specific date in the future. The youngsters are watched by volunteers, other teachers, or older youngsters. The parents at this time are given a lecture of what to anticipate from their children during the following year, what the school is going to do, and how they, the parents, can participate in the school activity. A definite date should be given for a follow-up parent program. At this first meeting parents should be given an opportunity to express concerns about their own children, difficulties that they had, and things that perhaps they would like to share with other parents. At this time recruitments can be made for the parent organization and discussion of future projects.

Concomitantly, there should be an ongoing in-service program to train faculty members in how to work with parents. Community organizations, such as neighborhood churches, Community Action Agencies, and prominent citizens in the area, should be involved to develop a positive neighborhood attitude towards the school. From a small beginning in the early grades (pre-kindergarten, kindergarten, and first grade) the program can be expanded to involve the entire school. There are several advantages to starting parent programs in a small way. The staff can learn what the reaction of the parents may be and what projects the faculty can handle. When the program expands it does so as a result of previous experience. From a small project developed at a slow rate will come an opportunity to develop larger projects at a faster rate.

When the program is working well, both faculty and parents who were initially involved can be utilized to help train additional faculty and parents.

Simultaneously the opportunity for parents to participate and to assume more responsibility is increased. After the parent programs have been initiated, the parents should assume more responsibility for the organization of their projects. Part of the responsibility of the school is shared with the parents, but never the professional responsibility. The primary responsibility of the child is still the parents'. The school should allow the parents to exercise that responsibility in well-designed school programs.

When the school involves the parents and increases their opportunity for participation, many things should be noted. A parent should not be assigned to a job with the simple instruction, "This is what we'd like you to do." As simple or as sophisticated as the job may be, it is the responsibility of the school to explicitly point out and train the parent to do the job that is required of him. The job may only entail answering the telephone. It is the responsibility of the educator involved to explain to that person exactly how the procedure is done: i.e., how the telephone is to be answered. In the classroom this is even more important.

Explicit instructions should be given for many reasons. When there are many parents involved in the same program, sharing the same tasks, an established format adds a consistency to the school program which facilitates the overall educational process. Consistency is important to the function and organization of the parent program and is important to the stability of the school. It is often taken for granted that parents, because they are parents, are capable of doing routine things. Many of the parents will be above average, whereas other parents may be below average in both experience and intelligence. They may not have had an opportunity to do some of these so-called "routine" jobs. For the more aggressive parent who may want to initiate on his own, instruction serves as a monitoring device. For the parent who has not had the experience, it allows him to review methods to be used without embarrassment.

People who have worked with parent groups have noted that parents may be hesitant to become active within the class because they may not know the lesson material. This is unfair to the parent and unfair to the children. Parents should not be placed in embarrassing situations. They should feel free to question, ask, or (when appropriate) suggest. (But this should be done at a time that will not conflict with the routine school program.) The best way to lose parent participation is by giving them responsibilities for which they are not trained. This can only be avoided by careful instruction. When the parents are given a review of what they are to do, it gives them an opportunity to suggest that perhaps they might like to participate in something else, or that they do not feel qualified to do the particular type of work that has been suggested. This should be considered by the school as a sign of intelligence and insight rather than a reluctance to do the job.

If the stated needs of the school demand complicated and sophisticated tasks and this seems to represent the needs of the school, then the primary consideration should be whether the parents can accomplish the stated needs. It is the responsibility of the school to simplify the required tasks and to program parent participation. Parents can initially work with less difficult tasks. As the school and the parents become comfortable in working with each other and as the parents gradually learn the tasks involved, parent responsibilities can be increased.

Tasks are given to the parents at the level of performance at which they are capable of participating.

## GROUP INTERACTION

The first consideration that the educator should have in doing group work with parents is to understand that the parents are usually more nervous about coming into the schools than the schools are about having the parents participate. In many areas parents have not participated for many reasons: poor communication, perceiving the school as another authority figure, a belief that they were not competent to contribute, and a "feeling" that their participation was not wanted. The author has seen Ph.D.'s, M.D.'s, industrial-type executives stay out of school because they did not want to face their children's teachers. He has known men who have given lectures before large professional groups, have handled acute medical emergencies, and have been responsible for the direction and alleviation of large crisis situations who have told him that they never had quite the same type of anxiety as when waiting for their youngster's report card or to participate in a routine activity in the school program. This is reflective of many parents.

When parents are given the opportunity to participate with each other, they usually do and enjoy it. There are difficulties that sometimes occur. These should be noted. Basic rules for group interaction, such as a definite time and place of meeting, establishes the goals of the meeting, testing by the group members, anticipated reaction on the part of the group if the leader does certain things, are true of the parents' group counseling sessions as well as the children's. The basic concepts of group work with various groups are usually the same. The maturation level of the adults does influence group reaction. Parents in general are more sophisticated and "usually" have a greater tolerance level.

Occasionally, parent's groups that have been organized for the first time may "test" the leadership, become angry, and require more direction from the school officials. This is one of the reasons why it is important for the educators to know the goals of the program and have things organized prior to the parents' participation. The parents should be asked to participate in a definite, organized way that has been preplanned prior to the parents' participation, although the parents' initial participation may be to plan larger programs.

Throughout the nation there has been considerable parent frustration with the public schools. They want to participate; they want to help their children; they want to help the school to improve itself to give their children a better education; but they don't know how. As a consequence, they try different things in which they are not prepared, such as curriculum planning, methodology, and selection of principals. These are not the factors in which the parents are truly interested in. What they are interested in are educators who can communicate with them and tell them (the parents) what they can do to help. When this is done, there is minimal frustration (and anger). The parents are delighted to have direction from school staff and the opportunity to help in a meaningful way.

Group members reflect their own personalities. Parents are

no exception. But if the group can become cohesive, the parents become incorporated into a constructive unit. This is meaningful and helpful to the parents because they can adapt and identify in positive ways, which tends to influence their participation and gives them an opportunity to help each other as well as their children.

Another difficulty that occasionally occurs is when there is a significant difference in the group members. For example, one of the major differences the author has found is not a racial or ethnic difference but rather an economic difference. When there is a mixture of races, it makes little difference. When parent groups have a mixture of upper middle class and lower middle class parents (regardless of ethnicity), this seems to initially present the most difficulty. It is hard for the group members to identify with each other. However, as the group progresses, it becomes apparent that all parents have the same wishes for their children - "a good education," and there is a cohesive "feeling" that develops.

Too often when parent groups are organized, the only emphasis is on verbal interaction. One of the ways to overcome the economic difference or hiatus that may exist is to decrease the verbal interaction type meeting, at least at the beginning, and increase the actual task-oriented participation by allowing the parents to join in projects within the classroom: i.e., directing group activity while the teacher is involved with another group or, for example, repairing of toys. The parents become involved in activities that will help the children. They start working with each other before they have an opportunity to note any differences. They are working toward the same goal. Most parents share the same interests, that is, to improve the school curriculum for their children in a well-organized way.

After the parents share a common activity involving their children, a discussion group should be organized so that they can share their experiences. Each parent should have the opportunity to contribute. When parents work together, they have an opportunity to understand and respect each other and each other's position.

Some educators hesitate to work with parents because they think that they will be confronted by the parents with questions that they (the educators) will not know to answer. Actually, this should be the least of the educator's concerns. Most parents recognize that no one has all the answers. When the teacher can share with the parent that he may not know a certain question, then the entire school program becomes more realistic. When the educator can share that he does not know an answer and asks the parent what he may think about a particular subject, it can be helpful to both the educator and the parent. Parents do not expect the teachers to have all the answers. They do expect the teachers to try to understand and attempt to communicate with them and, when indicated, give them some direction in professional way.

When the educator wants to stimulate interest and discussion within parent groups, it is helpful to present information that will be meaningful to the parent. For example, the educator can explain what the school is attempting to do, what programs the children are going to be involved with in their respective grades, what the school hopes to accomplish, what difficulties the school sometimes encounters, and what opportunities the parents may have in assisting them. This will generally stimulate many questions. In addition, the educator may ask the parents what techniques they use to stimulate learning at home and how this might be translated to the classroom. The teachers may elect to share with the parents the successes that they have had in the classroom and how this might be transferred to the home situation. When parents are being prepared to assist within the classroom, the educator can teach them how to observe what the children are doing and how this information can be used to stimulate learning.

## CONFLICT BETWEEN PARENTS

It is not uncommon in group counseling sessions to have conflicts between group members. Personality differences and conflict of ideas increase the possibility of occasionally having a disagreement between parents. Unlike the child and adolescent, the parent conflict is usually more complicated and unfortunately can be more destructive to the school program. Perhaps the major difference is that youngsters have a better resiliency: that is, they are more apt to "forgive and forget." The adult is less flexible and tends to "remember and burn" a little longer.

The educator should attempt to avoid inter-adult conflicts. He should avoid partiality unless it becomes a question of school policy or routine. When an argument interferes with the school program, the educator should state what the school policy is and react accordingly. He should not allow himself to be in a position of allying himself with one segment of the group against the other. This does nothing but increase the hiatus between the educator and the parent members and between the parents themselves. If possible, the educator should not become emotionally involved, as many parents do. When the educator loses his objectivity, the parents have lost an important semblance of reasonable direction. Parents often test the leadership of the group by a major or minor conflict. When an issue that has become a source of conflict is presented to the group leader, the group leader should hesitate to "rush in" and try to resolve it, especially when there is no apparent solution for the problem. It is usually better to ask that everyone consider ways of resolving the question so that it can be discussed at the next meeting.

## PARENT PROFILES

One of the reasons for the reluctance of the school staff to work with parents is the different reactions that they anticipate they may get from various parents. The following is a list of the more common personality types that the counselor who deals with parents may encounter. Many parents, of course, may be a combination of the profiles discussed.

(1) *The Recalcitrant Parent* is the parent who presents to the school very angry over the school's failure to cope with, teach, and/or meet the needs of the child. This is the parent whom the average educator fears most: the parent who is angry and is willing to vent his anger on the person who represents the school. How vehement this anger may be, how he expresses the anger, and whether the parent will in fact be able to control that anger, are things which most school people feel quite anxious about.

There is another factor that is important to consider.

The primary responsibility for the child is always the parents. When the educator becomes involved with children's problems, he may be infringing on that responsibility. One of the things that most people working with children will occasionally wonder is whether the parent may present in an angry way by saying: "That's my job; let me do it. I don't like the way you are doing it and you have no business...." This may or may not be true but puts the educator in an awkward position. How to cope with and how to anticipate this parent is perhaps one of the many reasons that school officials hesitate to initiate parent programs. Consequently, how to deal with angry parents, both individually and in groups, is important.

When the parent presents angrily, it may be for a number of reasons. The parent may be a very pleasant person who "got up on the wrong side of the bed that morning" and has been irritated since he awoke. The parent may be angry for reasons of domestic difficulties, difficulties with his job, or difficulty with work and responsibility at home. There can be a number of reasons that have nothing to do with the school. When the parent is angry toward the school, it is often not directed toward the teacher; it is usually directed toward the institution at large. It is not uncommon, for example, when working in the inner city to find parents who come in quite hostile and very angry, reflecting their own frustrations and anger against the school for not giving them an opportunity when they were youngsters to "make it" (a consideration for which they may be partially if not totally right). There are times when the recalcitrant parent is right and has good reason to be angry. When the educator can share with the parent that he recognizes that the parent may be right, then some meaningful deliberation can begin.

A major objective in handling an angry parent, whether individually or in a group, is to allow that parent to vent his feelings (as long as it is appropriate for the school setting). The "key" is not to react in an angry way against an angry parent. This does not help the child, it does not help the educator, nor does it help the parent, who basically wants to cooperate.

If the educator is willing to listen, he may find an element of truth in what the parent says. It does not have to be totally accurate; it does not have to be even partially accurate. But there is usually a microscopic speck of truth (if not totally true) that the parent relates. It is on this bit of information (that may be only partially true) that the educator may find some mutual agreement and attempt to develop some rapport. In this way he offers the parent the respect and insight due him by indicating at least part of what he says may be true. Upon this common ground the parent and educator can build a relationship that can help both the school and the youngster. The educator should not reject the angry parent in the group, nor should the educator allow other parents to totally reject the recalcitrant parent. The school should be willing and technically ready to convert the energy expressed by an angry parent into constructive proposals or programs.

It is not uncommon for an angry parent to be frustrated because his youngster is not performing the way he would like. When the school has the same difficulty that the parent is having at home, the parent's frustration may be accentuated because the parent anticipates that the school should be able to "make it" where she is not.

Another reason for angry parents is feelings of guilt. Parents may think that they are not doing the job they should. These guilty feelings are often expressed by anger. When a child is performing poorly in school, the parents think it is basically a reflection of them. Each parent reflects on the difficulty of their child in a different way. The mother usually looks to the seed and reflects, "What have I done wrong?" Consequently her guilty feelings are often greater. The father generally looks to the future: "What are we going to do to get this kid corrected?" The father's anger may be accentuated if the youngster, especially a son, is a "miniature" of himself.

It is often easier to handle an angry parent in a group than it is on a one-to-one basis. The other parents usually share with the angry parent the frustrations that they also have had. This tends to minimize the severity of a problem. The other parents will often help the recalcitrant parent unless that parent is asking for more help than the group (or the school) is prepared to give.

(2) *The Over-Helpful Parent.* This is the parent who presents to the school "willing to help in any way, be cooperative in any way, and come every day." In general, this particular parent is "overly-helpful." He wants to cooperate and may be found helping in the school and also in churches, Girl Scouts, Boy Scouts, Red Cross, and charitable drives, perhaps all at the same time. This parent can be utilized and may be very effective but needs to have work that is well organized by the school. His tasks should be limited. The teacher should be sure that he organizes the parent's tasks so that it will not interfere with the routine of the classroom. This is the type of parent who may become a "buddy" of the teacher to the point of interfering with the usual school routine. "Limit setting" is particularly helpful and aids this particular parent in being more constructive and efficient in her job.

(3) *The Professional Parent.* This is the parent who either presents with twenty diplomas following her name or feels that he should have twenty diplomas. He has read every leading educational journal, including Oprah, Time, and Newsweek. He can participate in the most progressive program and still feel that he has a suggestion that may be helpful. The professional parent has a talent for offending the professional teacher.

The educator should attempt to be objective and reflect on the ideas: "I'll be glad to refer your suggestion." Once the professional parent has been accepted as an "equal" but not given the responsibility of an "equal," he usually "settles down" and often can contribute something. The professional parent is more task oriented than relationship oriented and needs considerable reinforcement.

*(4) The Guilty Parent.* The guilty parent presents with misgivings that he should have done "this" for his child or he cannot provide "that." The parent's youngster is only getting six A's instead of seven because of something that he is doing. This is the parent who feels that what is wrong with the child is his fault. Sometimes the parents are guilty for a good reason. There may have been emotional, physical, or situational trauma within the family that has contributed to the youngster's poor performance.

It is not uncommon for the guilty parent to be an angry person. What presents as guilt may really be anger, not infrequently against the child. This parent has to be reassured but not overly reassured. One has to accept at face value the information that he projects and not be too quick to come to the parent's defense. The educator should attempt to cooperate with the parent, accept the information that is delivered, and give the parent the respect due by intimating that he will utilize the information in whatever way may be professionally helpful to the child. Particular emphasis should be placed on reinforcing what has been done well for the child rather than concentrating on what has not been done. When indicated, the educator should reassure the parent that the information that has been shared will be helpful. Reassurance to the guilty parent is of considerable help.

*(5) The Disinterested Parent.* This is the parent who presents with an indifferent attitude (or does not present at all). He conveys the attitude of not caring and sometimes says, "I'm not particularly interested in school activities. I think this is a job for the school to do. I don't believe in interfering in school activity." This parent often frustrates the educator who is spending considerable time working with the child (or who simply respects the child).

The reasons disinterested parents may not want to participate in the school program may vary. The parent may be involved in too many programs outside the school, may have too many more pressing obligations, or may not think that he is qualified. The main consideration in working with disinterested parents is not to pressure for school involvement. They should be given an opportunity to participate at their convenience: that is, if they can only help one time during a semester, or once every two weeks as the need arises, this is fine.

Disinterested parents may volunteer to participate on a one-time basis only. This is reasonable. Many people do not want to commit themselves to programs that they do not know anything about or do not know whether they would like to participate in on a continuous basis. The opportunity should be left open that if the parent wishes or has a future opportunity, he can participate. For example: "We appreciate your participation. If in the future you think that you have more time, then please contact us. We'd welcome your help." The parent thinks that the participation he does give, no matter how minimal, is appreciated. If the parent wants to participate more or thinks that he can manage more participation at a later date, then he will be less hesitant to communicate with the school.

It is not uncommon for a disinterested parent to be reflecting his own feelings of inadequacy to handle responsibility.

(6) *The Perfectionist Parent*. This is the parent who thinks the youngster has to do everything perfectly. Unless the youngster does something perfectly (which usually is never to the satisfaction of the perfectionist parent), he does not get that parent's praise or acceptance. This is the parent whose child brings home a 95 and the parent only comments on the 5 percent that is wrong. This type of parent generally does best in a job that requires meticulous work.

Group work with the perfectionist parent (as with most parents) can be significantly helpful because it allows the parent to relax and be less rigid in his general demeanor. No matter what the school does, this particular parent will feel that something has been left out. One way to build a relationship with the perfectionist parent is to accept the parent himself.

Group counseling sessions can be helpful. If the educator and the group accept the parent and are willing to listen, and if the parent feels comfortable in talking with the group members, the parent may gain some insight and techniques that will allow her to modify the "negativism" he may engender in his child. (The other parents will usually come to the rescue of the child.)

*(7) The Positive Parent.* This is the parent who thinks that schools "can do no wrong." Anything the school does is okay. Teachers do not make mistakes, nor do counselors or principals. The youngster could not be accurate in his report of what happened in class because this would not be allowed. The parent may reflect this "positive" approach in an opposite way, saying that his youngster could not do anything wrong: "I know my child couldn't do anything like this and become a behavior problem." Denial is significant.

One approach with the positive parent is to build on the elements of what the parent relates: i.e. accept when possible what the parent says, and develop the relationship via positive interaction. It is very difficult to change attitudes of the positive parent, especially immediately. It often takes two or three group or individual sessions to review the pertinent data in a meaningful way.

*(8) The Optimistic Parent.* The optimistic parent thinks his child is a genius, is absolutely brilliant and should be at least one grade level above his current grade. It is often humorous to observe the optimistic parent relate in a parent discussion group about what his youngster is doing, only to find that other parents can relate similar, or perhaps above-average, performances by their children. It is not infrequent, however, that parents do observe traits and qualities in their children that are significant and that can help to alter the behavior pattern in the classroom. It is important for the educator to reflect on the comments of even the optimistic parent. The teacher might be able to build a successful program,

transferring the approach of the parent to the classroom, using similar rewards and punishments when indicated and applicable.

(9) *The Pessimistic Parent.* The pessimistic parent thinks that his child cannot do anything right, never could do anything right, and probably will never do anything right. The pessimistic parent's child may have to act out considerably in class for attention or may be quite passive because he has never been rewarded at home and feels incapable of performing well. Group counseling ( for the parent) is usually helpful because other parents will not tolerate a continually negative portrayal of the child (even by the child's own parents). Group members will usually "enlighten" the parent that perhaps the child has more qualities than he is willing to recognize. The educator when working with the parent can adopt the attitude of "If this is so, perhaps working together we can develop a program both in the school and at home that might help to stimulate the youngster and to improve his performance." The pessimistic parent is usually asking for support or direction from some responsible person. If the parent thinks that he has this support, he will often be willing to "try" to modify his behavior and to adopt a more realistic attitude.

## SUMMARY

The mechanics of group counseling with parents are the same as with any group. Parent groups usually show more enthusiasm than other interest groups. The parents' cooperation and involvement are for the most part dependent upon how the program is presented, the attitude of the school staff, and the enthusiasm stimulated in the parents and the children. A parent program should be well organized so that the parents know exactly what the school expects. The basic responsibility of most projects should be retained by the school itself. Programs and projects should be so designed that parents are able to handle and to complete their assignments without any embarrassment to themselves, their children, or the school.

Parent participation in the schools is changing in character. Many schools no longer have the classical parent-teachers' associations but are now organizing parents' associations or parent-participation associations. These are organizations in which the parents meet, discuss, and often suggest school projects that they think they are capable of. This should be encouraged by the schools. Many parents, when first forming parent groups, want to revert to the classical parent-teachers' association. This is reasonable and should be encouraged. The parents should start at that level of performance and organization with which they feel comfortable. As the association matures and leadership is organized, the participation of the parents can evolve from a classical PTA to more participation within the school, including participation within the classroom when indicated. In order for this to effectively occur, the school should develop training programs for the parents and teachers involved.

## SUGGESTED READINGS

Devaney, Elizabeth S. and JoAnn P. Milstein. (Apr.1998). Kids+family+school=success: a kindergarten student and family support program. Social Work in Education. 20(2), 131-38.

Duhon, Gwendolyn M. and Tony Manson. (2000). Preparation, Collaboration, and Emphasis on the Family in School Counseling for the New Millenium. E. Mellen Press: Lewiston.

Gordon, Thomas. (2001). Parent Effectiveness Training: The Proven Program for Raising Responsible Children. Three Rivers: New York.

Mathis, Richard D.; Tanner, Zoe. (Mar 2000). Structured Group Activities with Family-of-Origin. Journal for Specialists in Group Work. v25 n1 p89-103.

Metcalf, Linda. (2002). Counseling Toward Solutions: A Practical Solution-Focused Program for Working with Students, Teachers, and Parents. Jossey-Bass: San Francisco.

Morgan, Barbara; Hensley, Laura. (Sep1998). Supporting Working Mothers through Group Work: A Multimodal Psychoeducational Approach. Journal for Specialists in Group Work. v23 n3 p298-311.

Nixon, Charles D.; Singer, George H. (May 1993). Group Cognitive-Behavioral Treatment for Excessive Parental Self-Blame and Guilt. American Journal on Mental Retardation. V97 n6 p665-72.

Springate, Kay Wright and Dolores A. Stegelin. (1999). Building School and Community Partnerships through Parent Involvement. Merrill: Upper Saddle River, N.J.

# CHAPTER XIV

## *GROUP SUPERVISION*

Group supervision can be defined as the direction and training of two or more people at the same time. The group involved may be as small as two or as large as the needs and goals of the program require. It has become evident that the classical, tutorial, one-to-one system of supervision has limited value and can be a limiting factor in training large numbers of personnel.

Group supervision, like any technique used in modifying human behavior, has its advantages and disadvantages. The training supervisor can work with a greater number of people per given hour. A team model can be easily developed. A unified, well-organized, system approach can often be accomplished. The same material is shared by all the participants who can individualize the material to meet their own needs while at the same time attempt to accomplish a unified system effect. The participants can literally have the benefit of a hundred-plus years of experience rather than the experience of one supervisor. It gives the participants an opportunity to test themselves within the "safe" confines of the group with which they have identified. It allows the supervisor or department to develop programs in a systematic way at the level of performance of the trainees.

Group supervision does not allow for continuous individualized supervision. This may be considered by some a major drawback, but the opportunity to observe how different people handle many different situations more than offsets the individualized approach.

Another disadvantage of group supervision is that it does not allow the group leader to defend herself in a one-to-one way. Her ideas have to be presented to a group which should then discuss them. This means that the group supervisor has to be better trained than the supervisor who works on a one-to-one basis. A group will not tolerate what an individual supervisee will tolerate. Group supervisors should be trained to teach the pertinent subject matter and also be trained in how to work with groups of trainees. This demands more sophistication of the supervisor and better programs by the universities and school systems that are training the supervisor. One of the reasons there is not currently much group supervision is that universities have not been training people who can assume the role of group supervisors. Until the large school systems, training universities, and teacher colleges orient themselves to group training, group supervision will continue to be a second choice as a supervision technique.

The fault does not lie only with the teaching institutions. Many administrators (and individual teachers and counselors) who have been working within school systems for many years are also uncomfortable with the "idea" of group supervision. In order to change the training concepts, it is the leadership who will have to take the initiative.

There are many ways to initiate group training programs. The method used depends upon the personality of the school system and its individual personnel. Programs should be initiated that have some general interest and whose goals are not particularly difficult to achieve. It is helpful when the initial group is composed of volunteers who are highly motivated. Most volunteer groups adapt to the idea of group supervision, utilize it, and have some success with it. Another way of initiating a group approach is by a directive from the superintendent of schools or director of the institution outlining well-organized, well-prepared plans to bring people together to accomplish definite goals. This can be a seminar workshop in which half the time is spent presenting didactic material and the other half of the time is spent discussing the material. Another type of group supervision is the consultant type in which a member of the training staff within the department or a consultant from the community discusses and shares ideas about a particular technique, subject, or program. How the consultant works and spends his time depends upon her personality, the goals of the project, the needs of the trainees involved, and the frequency with which she meets with that particular group.

The following is a verbatim transcription of a group supervisory hour, with a consultant, three counselors, and a supervisor. The discussion and supervision are concerned with a group counseling session that Mrs. Counselor had conducted. The group counseling session itself was composed of eight boys from the eighth grade. Composition of the group was made up of youngsters from a lower socio-economic group.

## A SUPERVISORY SESSION

**MRS. COUNSELOR:** Do you want me to start playing the tape or to summarize things, Dr. Consultant?

**DR. CONSULTANT:** I think a summary would be rather difficult.

**MRS. COUNSELOR:** Okay, I will play the tape.

**DR. CONSULTANT:** Okay.

**MRS. COUNSELOR:** The reason I am going to play the tape is that it is concerned with the question of rapport with the children, but I think it could be improved in terms of technique.

**DR. CONSULTANT:** Go ahead.

**MRS. COUNSELOR:** I feel that establishing rapport is not the problem, but the idea of technique is....(I'll play my tape for everyone.)

**(TAPE)MRS. COUNSELOR:** How **about** you, Robert? What do you think about smoking?

**ROBERT:** It is okay right now. You might get cancer later on, but at least by then they should have something to cure it. Even if you don't smoke, you still get cancer.

**MRS. C:** Okay, well, right, you could get different kinds of cancer.

**R:** Yes, ma'am.

| | |
|---|---|
| **MRS. C:** | Okay, it can affect various parts of your body and, like Peggy is saying, maybe they'll have a cure for it. |
| **R:** | They should. |
| **MRS. C:** | Well, why did you begin? |
| **R:** | I don't know. I don't know, I just started smoking. |
| **MRS. C:** | How old were you when you started smoking? |
| **R:** | About eight years old. |
| **MRS. C:** | Okay, so do your parents smoke? |
| **R:** | My stepfather does. |
| **MRS. C:** | Does he smoke a lot? |
| **R:** | No, ma'am. |
| **MRS. C:** | Okay, so your stepfather smokes. Did you get cigarettes from your stepfather or what? How did you get them when you were eight years old? |
| **R:** | My one brother used to give them to me. |
| **MRS. C:** | Do you think your brother likes you very much? |
| **R:** | I don't know. |
| **MRS. C:** | Did anyone else know that you used to run around with smoke when they were eight years old? |
| **R:** | Not too many people. |
| **DR. CONSULTANT:** | The group is becoming defensive and reflecting on the attack by the counselor. When the leader starts "getting on" a member of the group, the other group members start to feel uncomfortable. It may become a threatening situation. Have you ever seen a crisis situation in a movie and said to yourself: "My goodness, what would I do if I were in a situation like that?" The individual has a tendency to identify |

with the person being affected. In part, that is what's happening on the tape. The group leader is pushing and the youngster (the group member) is becoming defensive and feeling somewhat guilty. This is being reflected in the group.

**MR. COUNSELOR:** Feeling that she is getting at the smoking aspect and –

**DR. CONSULTANT:** Well, she is asking "Why? Why? Why?" and when you push it like this, you convey the idea of guilt. The person feels "Well, what have I done wrong?" The youngster obviously is being defensive.

**MR. COUNSELOR:** Would you suggest some other approach? Why are you saying it's all right to go ahead and face the reality?

**DR. CONSULTANT:** Well, I think this is too often what we do. I don't think this is the best approach. I don't think the question of smoking, for example, may be the main issue. These may be good questions: What age did you start smoking? Why did you start smoking? "Well, I don't know." From this point, instead of pursuing the personal questioning, the group leader could take it away from the individual and generalize. For example: "Why do people smoke in general?" Then the leader could get into some of the things that smoking does for the individual and then go beyond that and ask things like, "What leads a person to smoking?" He could generalize the question, perhaps ask about the urge to smoke. You are laying the ground work for alternatives to smoking; you don't necessarily concentrate on the issue presented. In the army it is said, never give an order unless you can be sure it can be carried out. Well, with adolescents in particular, you never give an order or confront them with an issue unless you feel you can follow through. A do-or-don't situation that you create for the child and for yourself is one that few can accomplish.

**MR. COUNSELOR:** Are you saying, don't back him into a corner?

**DR. CONSULTANT:** Yes. You may be the only **one** who can help him out of that corner. Not always, of course. The important thing is how to lead up to an issue. The question isn't whether to smoke or not to smoke. The question should be, what are the alternatives to smoking? After all the reasons are given, for example, why he might be smoking, what leads a person to smoke, what smoking does for a person, and so forth, then the leader could ask: "What are some of the substitutes for smoking that you could suggest?" Well, they may come up with something or they may not. The key is to offer an alternative. The counselor has to lay the groundwork so that the youngsters can understand what the reasons are for the questioning. If you just tackle the question of to smoke or not to smoke, the students will lose the opportunity to learn alternative behavior patterns.

**MR. COUNSELOR:** This is great, but I think that Mrs. Counselor fell into a trap that we all fall into, where the kids begin to individualize what they are saying. The counselor tends to respond to that kind of statement. Rather than to stay on the fringes like you've been telling us here, you tend to say, well, you know, why did you do this? and what age did you start smoking? and this kind of thing.

**DR. CONSULTANT:** There is also an element that we talked

about last time. I think that Mrs. Counselor is getting a "kick out" of this. It's sort of intriguing to her. It's also intriguing to the kids. They're getting a secondary "kick out" of seeing how Mrs. Counselor reacts to the intricacies of life, like smoking at the age of eight. So I think there is a certain secondary gain for everybody here. This is one reason it is being pursued.

**MR. COUNSELOR:** You say, secondary gain?

**DR. CONSULTANT:** Sure, you use everything you can. The group is obviously a cohesive group. They like Mrs. Counselor, and I think this is very important. (Now we're talking about technicalities.) They'll work the problem out, one way or another, because it is a cohesive group.

**MR. COUNSELOR:** I think it's important, because where most counselors get hung up in terms of what they learn in colleges and universities, as we were discussing before we did this tape, is the business of technicalities. Most counselors come in this business looking for technicalities that are going to get them off the hook and get them flowing. What you are saying is that technicalities are important, but they are only supplementary to other aspects like relationships, group dynamics, group cohesiveness, and so forth. I think that's very important.

**DR. CONSULTANT:** I'll take the sincere, hard-working counselor who truly has an interest in the youngsters against the strict technician any day.

**MR. COUNSELOR:** Yes, this is not inconsistent with an earlier statement of yours in which you're – I guess you said, be yourself.

**DR. CONSULTANT:** Right. This is exactly the way I feel. It doesn't make any difference what your personality is; as long as you feel comfortable with it, everybody else will feel comfortable with it too.

**MR. COUNSELOR:** I think that's important.

**MRS. COUNSELOR:** Well, like you said, I can utilize assets I have. I'm young, and students seem to think that – you know, I'm more closely related to their problems. I can understand them better. But I think at the same time your techniques are important because you can be more efficient about that.

**DR. CONSULTANT:** There's no question about that.

**MRS. COUNSELOR:** It takes me such a long time to get to the core of the questions.

**MR. COUNSELOR:** But I have a feeling techniques – you learn. It comes with experience and it comes with your own security. I think Dr. Consultant thinks you work it out –

**MRS. COUNSELOR:** Yes, you can work it out, but if you can work it out sooner you'll be more efficient.

**MR. COUNSELOR:** Well, you run the danger of being impatient and wanting techniques to happen that are going to give you solutions. My experience is, they don't. You've got to stumble, you've got to make mistakes. I think gradually you become more comfortable, which means your techniques are improving.

**DR. CONSULTANT:** This is true up to a point. Counseling and teaching are no different than medicine. You can't afford too many mistakes. There are technical shortcuts that help you and the individual. The second thing is that, whenever possible, if you can get some insight that is technically correct, it will save a lot of learning later on. It doesn't take away from the relationship. Sincerity in your job, however, is more important than any single technique.

**MR. SUPERVISOR:** Because you may be a great doctor, but if you don't know how to suture and how to cut, and all this kind of stuff, you may be great but the patient dies. Mr. Counselor represents one period of university training, Mrs. Counselor another, I another, and you another. So we bring to the counseling office the results of our training. In the very beginning, when you first take a course in counseling techniques, you are trying to respond to textbook responses, and trying to understand the theory of personalities, rather than to bring these things in and smooth them over and let them become part of you. I think this is what I notice in the second-year counseling, where the first few counseling interviews become interrogations, very much like what we hear here – you know, why, why, why. And then we try to move away from that and say, all right, whatever your approach is, whether it's test-oriented or whether it's diagnostic-oriented, or whatever it may be, you're not going to be able to use all of these techniques at a time; you have to be slightly eclectic at times in order to make it go. But in any event, take all these group things you've learned and let them become part of you, then move out and be yourself and enter into a healthy relationship with the kids. If we can get to that point, I think we're doing counseling.

**MR. COUNSELOR:** I certainly agree. I think the denominator is correct that we're going to interchange techniques. I think the thing that troubles us all – this may or may not be true in the physical sciences – is that in the behavioral sciences we are still so loosely feeling our way. You know, we still don't know too much technically. So we keep changing techniques and so on. We've got a long way to go, I'm sure we all admit that.

**MR. COUNSELOR:**    Behavior doesn't fit into any kind of box, you know.

**DR. CONSULTANT:**    This is absolutely true.

**(TAPE)MRS. COUNSELOR:** Did anyone else know that you used to run around with smoke when they were eight years old?

**R:**    Not too many people, no. I used to know a little kid who smoked cigars.

**MRS. C:**    Okay, so you say you've been smoking now for about six years or seven years. Right?

**R:**    Yes, ma'am.

**MRS. C:**    How many cigarettes do you smoke a day?

**R:**    It all depends. If I don't give them away –

**DR. CONSULTANT:**    Mrs. Counselor is a little bit intrigued, which is natural, I think.

**(TAPE) R:**    . . . I can save about half a pack of cigarettes.

**MRS. C:**    So you must smoke about ten cigarettes a day.

**R:**    Sometimes more than that. It depends. Like over where I live. I'm at a pool hall I can smoke about three packs.

**SH:**    How long?

**R:**    In about an hour.

**CB:**    Three packs in an hour?

**MRS. C:**    Wait a minute.

**R:**    You can do it, the way I do.

**JG:**    How do you do it, a pack at a time?

**MRS. C:**    How would you do it if it takes about five minutes to smoke a cigarette?

**DR. CONSULTANT:** This is not a bad technique, because it's a type of buddy approach, or a less-than-formal counseling approach. A great deal is being accomplished, as you can hear. There is a great deal of involvement and attention back and forth. The kids are comfortable.

**MR. COUNSELOR:** Yes, when she said "Wait a minute" she really was with them, and they knew it. Ordinarily you couldn't get away with that, that would be a derogatory kind of thing; but not in this case.

**MRS. COUNSELOR:** Right. It's an unusual group. This is why some of the techniques that you might use in this group, you might get results, whereas in another group you wouldn't.

**MR. COUNSELOR:** Here you're being yourself. You didn't learn that in a textbook.

**MRS. COUNSELOR:** No.

**MR. COUNSELOR:** Anywhere.

**MRS. COUNSELOR:** No.

**DR. CONSULTANT:** Well, at this particular moment the style is more applicable. At a different time, even within this group it may not be applicable. The group itself will change from time to time. The group changes just like you; all the members change. This is adaptation to the group and the subject matter.

**MRS. COUNSELOR:** Right. You see that later in the tape, where I ask one of the boys something. He doesn't respond, and no one else in the group says anything; there's a silence. That's what I wanted to bring out in the group when we played it for the counselors, that the group will guide you if some of your techniques are very effective, or aren't very effective.

**DR. CONSULTANT:** This is good leadership. You will respond to the group just like they respond to you. They will present the questions as they see them. This is fine.

**MRS. COUNSELOR:** I think another reason you can tell that it's a cohesive group is that I feel very free to take people out of the group and see them individually. And yet they can go back into the group and are interested in further discussion of what's happening.

**(TAPE)R:** Well, you can do it, like you're playing pool and you get nervous and when you get nervous you smoke a lot faster.

**JG:** Let's see, a pack an hour.

**SH:** Not one pack but three packs.

**MRS. C:** Wait a minute, he said not one pack but three packs an hour ...

**DR. CONSULTANT:** You see what was happening? You were putting the pressure on the student at that point. You had asked him about smoking three packs in a half-hour or an hour. You challenged him on this. He was saying two things: He was saying, "I know, I smoke more when I'm nervous." He was also saying, "I'm particularly nervous now – you're putting the pressure on me."

**MRS. COUNSELOR:** You could tell.

**MR. COUNSELOR:** Did he light up at that point?

**MRS. COUNSELOR:** I thought it was interesting and I just let it go. I figured the kids had had enough. Then, the group picked it up.

**MR. COUNSELOR:** Wasn't there also an attempt, so far as this kid is concerned, for the limelight? He was bragging at the same time that he was complaining.

**DR. CONSULTANT:** He got a little bit out of it. This is when the leader challenged his bravado.

**MRS. COUNSELOR:** Oh, you know, it's no longer important in this group where they sit. They sit anyplace now. They come in and they just sit down.

**DR. CONSULTANT:** Who sits first?

**MRS. COUNSELOR:** There's something that is interesting. They try to beat each other down to the room. They'll come in sections. One boy came in – I don't know how he got in here so fast.

**DR. CONSULTANT:** Do you sit in the same place every time, or a different spot?

**MRS. COUNSELOR:** It's generally over here some place, because I'm usually the last one to come in.

**DR. CONSULTANT:** Which chairs fill up first?

**MRS. COUNSELOR:** Over here ... and I think one of the reasons is that one of the boys generally offers to help with the tape.

**MR. COUNSELOR:** Mrs. Counselor, let me ask you a technical question. I beat Mr. Administrator's brains out to get this round table. Do you think if you had a square table, or no table, or just chairs around in a group, it would be better? What meaning does this physical fact of a round table have?

**MRS. COUNSELOR:** I think in a way it's a sense of security. You can put your hands there. I think it's a good idea.

**MR. COUNSELOR:** Yes, it was Dr. Therapist who likes to have people sitting around in a circle with nothing in between. I wonder whether this is even better than a round table. For instance, in my narrow office over in the other building, I find this a handicap. We've all got to squeeze together. We're literally sitting on top of each other. I think it would be better if we could expand like this. Would you comment on this aspect of the group counseling?

**DR. CONSULTANT:** I think a physical setting can be used in many different ways. I think it is a handicap when kids are too close together, because then it may be a distraction because of the closeness, but it may also lead to physical interaction.

**MR. COUNSELOR:** Right. It does.

**DR. CONSULTANT:** You have to set more limits. Too much closeness is not good, as you described. Too much physical separation isn't good either, because it tends to emphasize distance between people and topics. I think this type of situation for a small group is – I won't say perfect, but I think it is very, very good. The kids can interact. They feel comfortable when there is enough distance between them, but yet there is enough closeness to emphasize a feeling of cohesiveness. The physical setting can be helpful. For example, if a child pushes his chair away from the table or away from the group, you can say, "Why don't you come in and join us?" This indicates to the youngster that you are willing to support and help him, that you are interested in him. He may want to isolate himself or need more attention or can't get close enough to the group. You can use the physical structure. Also, a group may need to be primed or given explicit direction as they come in. One group you may encourage to accept more responsibility and allow them to sit wherever they want. With another group you may want to start by imposing definite limits and direction. You may indicate to them, "You sit here, you sit here, and you sit here." Depending upon your goals and the group that you are working with, you can utilize the physical setting. The other thing is that this is a relatively good setting because you have little in the way of distractions from the hall. When the meeting place is near an administrator's office, a classroom, and so forth, you may get noise from their activity and it may be distracting.

**MR. COUNSELOR:** Would you advise a counselor's getting up from behind his desk and not use a desk as a home base?

**DR. CONSULTANT:** In general –

**MR. COUNSELOR:** It doesn't matter.

**DR. CONSULTANT:** I would say it doesn't matter, especially if the kids know you; they don't care. If they get used to seeing you there, they will react to you there. I think the key is to sit where you feel most comfortable. Some counselors, because of either lack of experience or other reasons, may not want to sit at the table with the kids. They may elect to use their desk. They may feel uncomfortable getting too close to the kids. If this is the case, I would say, by all means stay at your desk unless you want to recognize and work through the problem. Other counselors want to get close to the kids and would feel uncomfortable with that much physical distance between the students and themselves. So you can use the physical setting as a cohesive factor, but also as a distancing factor. With some youngsters you may not want to get too close, because this may be part of the problem that they have to work through. Other kids may want to have increased cohesiveness in the group. In general, I think a round table is very advantageous. The circle effect gives a feeling of cohesiveness. There is no disunity.

It's all one link. On the other hand, there's enough physical distance between people so that everyone is comfortable.

**MR. COUNSELOR:** You'll see that this is put on your A.R. for every counselor? Round tables?

**MRS. COUNSELOR:** Round tables. [Laughter]

**MR. COUNSELOR:** I'm serious about that.

**MISS COUNSELOR:** I'll tell you, Dr. Consultant, I had an interesting experience. My office is next door but it is not as large as this one. Because of the physical setting I have a desk with a chair beside it. We put the chairs in a in a semicircle in front of the desk. I have noticed the children rush to get down because there is something important about sitting in the chair that's right beside the desk. If someone gets there who is not supposed to be there, the other will bring the chair around. Consequently, they are backing me against the wall. It looks as though – to me – that everybody wants to get as near as possible to me as they can.

**DR. CONSULTANT:** Yes. This is why I asked Mrs. Counselor where she sat and where the students usually sat first. This may be an answer to your question. You notice that there is a difference in the seating arrangement. Well, there may be a difference in the seating arrangement because of the person who arrives first. There may be a consistency in where they want to sit, as in your group. You may see different kids sitting in different places, but not because of random selection. It is influenced by who arrives first and sits down closest to the leader. So there may be a consistency in the seating arrangement. This is not unusual. It's something that inexperienced counselors are often concerned about. Inexperienced counselors are not used to the overwhelming closeness that the kids want. This makes the counselor uncomfortable. They feel a little uncomfortable about handling this initial experience of closeness and overt display of affection.

The more experienced the individual is in counseling, the more he accepts this at face value and lets the kids work it out. If the counselor doesn't become particularly concerned about it, then the kids won't. It'll just be one of the phases that they go through. It may be an indication that you're getting a positive result. There is the other end of the spectrum, too, that is, the students who consistently never want to be next to the counselor. This may or may not be an indication of affection, or wanting to identify with the counselor. For example, it may be that the counselor may have a habit of asking the first person on his right to answer the first question, and the youngsters may be avoiding this. There are many different factors involved. It may have nothing to do with the student. The first key question may always be referred to the left-hand chair. The counselor may be used to doing this. So, there are different things that will influence seating. This is a phenomenon which we repeatedly observe. I think it is something which counselors should take at face value.

| | |
|---|---|
| **(TAPE)MRS. C:** | . . . not a pack but three. |
| **R:** | In about an hour. |
| **MRS. C:** | That's approximately sixty cigarettes. |
| **R:** | It is. |
| **SH:** | It's one cigarette a minute. |
| **MRS. C:** | Okay. |
| **R:** | When you're smoking like that you don't even know you're smoking because you're throwing half of it away, because when you get nervous you smoke about three puffs and throw it away. . . Because you get nervous |

| | |
|---|---|
| | playing pool, especially when you're playing for money. |
| MRS. C: | Okay, so you just smoke in order to calm your nerves. |
| R: | Yeah, but it don't help. |
| MRS. C: | oh, it doesn't help. |
| R: | No. |
| MRS. C: | Have you ever tried anything else? |
| R: | Yeah, I've tried other things, yeah. |
| MRS. C: | What do you think, Charles? |
| CB: | I don't know. |
| MRS. C: | What do you think about him smoking three packs an hour? |

| | |
|---|---|
| MR. COUNSELOR: | At that point, could she have pursued – |
| DR. CONSULTANT: | She asked a key question, which the youngster found difficult because it was a challenging question. She could have referred to the group and got some group interaction going. |
| MR. COUNSELOR: | What was the key question? |
| DR. CONSULTANT: | The key question was, "Had you ever tried anything else?" He had said, "Yeah, I've tried other things." Then somebody else made a small comment and went on to ask somebody else. At the point she could have pursued it. |
| MR. COUNSELOR: | You're suggesting using the group, or a kind of movement from individual to group and back to individual, as either a reinforcing or probing technique – |
| DR. CONSULTANT: | Yes. Plus further insight – |
| MR. COUNSELOR: | - and amplification? |
| DR. CONSULTANT: | Right. And peer identification and support. |
| MR. COUNSELOR: | You're really using your group as a broad base for idea development. |
| DR. CONSULTANT: | This is one of the key advantages of working |

in a group. Especially with adolescents, in which group identification is so important.

**MR. COUNSELOR:** Would you, then – this is an interesting technical aspect – would you keep coming back to the one individual, or would you let somebody else pick up and move off on a tangent from there?

**DR. CONSULTANT:** It depends –

**MR. COUNSELOR:** In other words, how closely do you follow the thread of the individual?

**DR. CONSULTANT:** That thread has already been well laid. There's usually no question about that. What's important from a counseling-teaching point of view is not only cigarette smoking or not cigarette smoking; what's important is, when you develop a habit that is particularly distasteful, or not in your best interest, what are the ways for you to investigate what leads up to it, and what are the ways for you to consider alternatives to that habit. This is the major lesson here, not smoking by itself. When you get an issue, such as smoking, the key as a teacher or counselor is to give a lesson or structure the session so that members of the group together can probe into the question to learn something meaningful that they can use in future situations, whether it's smoking or anything else. If you want to get into smoking *per se*, from a teaching point of view, then you go back to the way tobacco is grown, the physiology of nicotine in the body, investigation and research, etc., with a didactic approach. Some people use this approach; but with this type of discussion something much more meaningful is developing, or could develop.

**MR. COUNSELOR:** Another question, because I want to throw this into another context. You are saying you are saying you have a specific that you'd throw to the group and develop a generalization, is that correct?

**DR. CONSULTANT:** Yes. Cigarette smoking here is just your ticket of admission. Many of these kids are going to be confronted later on not only with cigarette smoking, but also alcoholic beverages, drugs of all types, exposure to abnormalities in the community, and many other things that they may be confronted with later in life. So the question of cigarettes is relatively an innocuous introduction to a much more important lesson.

**MR. COUNSELOR:** Let me pull a classical type of group counseling situation which I am sure the beginning counselor has, and that is, "I hate this teacher," or "I can't get along with this teacher." The idea in terms of the ultimate is not the specific teacher, but in a great sense having the group feedback, namely, either you learn to get along with people as they are, you learn to understand people. You see, I'm relating what happens in the group. Sometimes this is the thread; it's the context that you get from the thread that is presented. Is this what you're saying?

**DR. CONSULTANT:** This is in part what I'm saying. The important thing is that if the child presents the "problem of the teacher," than one possibility is to work through a meaningful exploration of this, both in fact and in general, and then tie it up at the end with, "Do you think this will help you with this teacher and other teachers?" If the answer is yes, "Fine," and if the answer is no, then "perhaps we can take this up in our next session and follow it through." It's very important that you give the students an opportunity to learn to add to their repertoire, i.e., the idea that lessons they learn in one situation may help them in another situation. You don't have to tell them all the time, but it's often helpful to point this out periodically, especially youngsters who may not have the sophistication of being exposed to environments, or opportunities beyond their own close neighborhood.

It starts opening up new perspectives for them. For example, when the youngster does something well in school, the project can be reinforced with the added note, "Well, if you tackle some other kind of job – do you see where this might apply in another opportunity that you may have? You've done well in this job; do you think that you're doing well in this type of situation will help you with other projects?" Take something that he's done well and expand it so that his horizons are opened up to him: "You know, maybe I *can* do something beyond just being a dropout, or just getting a job that is pushing a broom, or something like that. I did well in this, maybe you got something here. Maybe there are horizons that I can accomplish." His peers will help him. This is important, because a youngster is developing his concept learning and utilizing his ability to develop basic principles and concepts in different areas. It is important to make the transfer. This is one of the goals of counseling and of course one of the major goals of education. Counseling is also teaching. It is a very important part of teaching. This is why I consider counselors as teachers. They are teachers of something that is far more important than factual material.

**MR. COUNSELOR:**   You are really saying teachers of wisdom, in a sense. You want to get philosophical, but –

**DR. CONSULTANT:**   In a philosophical way, yes.

**MR. COUNSELOR:**   It is an imparting of wisdom, or how to live, or get along, or –

**DR. CONSULTANT:** Wisdom, or morality, ways of living. There are a million different synonyms, but there is something you are accomplishing. You are accomplishing a certain degree of motivation, or priming motivation. You help the youngster organize the material so that he can use it, something which many of our children don't have.

**MR. COUNSELOR:** You realize this is a revolutionary, practically heretical, concept in the sense that we are not probing continuously –

**DR. CONSULTANT:** Don't you know I'm a revolutionary?

**MR. COUNSELOR:** Great! [Laughter] You know, in terms of what we get taught at university levels, we are not always probing into feelings, or not always holding back; if anything, we're getting involved. We're not holding back.

**DR. CONSULTANT:** The key is involvement, but involvement in a way that is comfortable for both the counselor and the student. You don't have to get into the personal lives or events of the individual in order to help him. As a professional, you may be aware that there are certain things in a child's life that may have influenced his development and which probably have, but you don't have to bulldog your way, to say "name it." This is not necessary. Sometimes it's very dangerous to do this with adolescents.

**MR. COUNSELOR:** I'm going back to your concept of a teacher because, you know, the teacher – Biblically, incidentally, the Hebrew word for counselor, as transliterated in the Bible, is in a sense "advice-giver." If you want to extend that, it isn't advice-giver as much as it is teacher. The great prophetic leaders were teacher-counselors. They did something to people, they motivated them, and – I'm beginning, I think, to understand your concept of teacher, not from the viewpoint of a factual – an imparter of factual data as much as an involver who does something to people so that they are better off because of this inter-relationship.

**DR. CONSULTANT:** Well, I think this is part of teaching, because you are a teacher. In terms of group dynamics, the teacher is a leader. A leader is somebody who directs and handles the events in the environment. We talk about technical things, but there is much more than the techniques. In general, the message is being pursued in this tape.

**MR. COUNSELOR:** I wonder if you could kind of summarize the tape to this point?

**DR. CONSULTANT:** All right. I think, in general, the kids showed involvement and the counselor showed involvement. They're just finishing the introductory phase and ready to move into the first chapter. The counselor is still priming. You now are ready to move into something more meaningful. What do you think about it?

**MRS. COUNSELOR:** Great. I go along with your comments. I think really this tape is serving as an introduction to drugs because, at the end of the tape the topic of drugs comes up – habit forming. One of the girls mentioned "pot." One of the boys comments on a newspaper article that discussed some the dangers of glue-sniffing. One of the other boys in the group makes a comment that "It came to the right house."

**DR. CONSULTANT:** So the lesson to be learned is that cigarettes was just an easy ticket of admission to things which to them were much more disturbing and important; but even beyond that, the questions are that if there are cigarettes, dope, glue-sniffing, and alcohol – which I'm sure there are – what is the issue? How to handle and resolve it? What are the alternatives? You are priming for something much more important than just cigarettes *per se*. As professionals, this is what you've got to be concerned with. From a technical point of view, you have passed the test. You could handle the information as a leader, as a counselor in the group, and are now willing to get into the major issues, which is very good. I think, for this reason, you're passing from the introductory phase into meaningful discussions.

## *SUGGESTED READINGS*

Akos, Patrick. (Dec 2004). Investing in Experiential Training Appropriate for Preservice School Counselors. Journal for Specialists in Group Work. v29 n4 p327-342.

Bernak, Fred; Chung, Rita Chi-Ying. (Mar 2004). Teaching Multicultural Group Counseling: Perspectives for New Era. Journal for Specialists in Group Work. v29 n1 p31-41.

Bleschke, Kathleen J.; Matthews, Connie; Wade, John; Pricken, Paula Ann. (Mar 1998). Evaluation of the Process Observer Method: Group Leader, Member, and Observer Perspectives. Journal for Specialists in Group Work. v23 n1 p50-65.

Browne, Frederick R. (Sep 2005). Self-Talk of Group Counselors: The Research of Rex Stockton. Journal for Specialists in Group Work. v30 n3 p289-297.

Christensen, Teresa M.; Kline, William B. (Dec 2000). A Qualitative Investigation of the Process of Group Supervision with Group Counselors. Journal for Specialists in Group Work. v25 n4 p376-93.

Coe, David M.; Zimpfer, David G. (Mar 1996). Infusing Solution-Oriented Theory and Techniques into Group Work. Journal for Specialists in Group Work. v21 n1 p49-57.

Conyne, Robert K. (Sep 1996). The Association for Specialists in Group Work Training Standards: Some Considerations and Suggestions for Training. Journal for Specialists in Group Work. v21 n3 p155-62.

Conyne, Robert K.; Wilson, R. Robert (June 1998). Toward a Standards-Based Classification of Group Work Offerings. Journal for Specialists in Group Work. v23 n2 p177-84.

Conyne, Robert K. (Mar 1998). What to Look for in Groups: Helping Trainees Become More Sensitive to Multicultural Issues. Journal for Specialists in Group Work. v23 n1 p22-32.

Conyne, Robert K. (Sep 1997). A Developing Framework for Processing Experiences and Events in Group Work. Journal for Specialists in Group Work. v22 n3 p167-74.

Duncan, Dean M.; Brown, Beverly M. (Nov 1996). Anxiety and Development of Conceptual Complexity in Group Counselors-in-Training. Journal for Specialists in Group Work. v21 n4 p252-62.

Emerson, Shirley. (Nov 1995). A Counseling Group for Counselors. Journal for Specialists in Group Work. v20 n4 p222-31.

Falco, Lia D.; Bauman, Sheri. (Jun 2004). The Use of Process Notes in the Experiential Component of Training Group Workers. Journal for Specialists in Group Work. v29 n2 p185-192.

Fleming, Victoria M. (June 1999). Group counseling in the schools: a case for basic training. Professional School Counseling. 2(5), 409-413.

Forester-Miller, Holly; Duncan, Jack A. (May 1990). The Ethics of Dual Relationships in the Training of Group Counselors. Journal for Specialists in Group Work. v15 n2 p88-93.

Fuhrlman, Addie; Burlingame, Gary M. (Jan 1990). Consistency of Matter: A Comparative Analysis of Individual and Group Process Variables. Counseling Psychologist. V18 n1 p6-63.

Furr, Susan R.; Barret, Bob. (Dec 2000). Teaching Group Counseling Skills; Problems and Solutions. Counselor Education and Supervision. V40 n2 p94-104.

Granello, Darcy Haag; Underfer-Baballs, Jean. (June 2004). Supervision of Group Work: A Model to Increase Supervisee Cognitive Complexity. Journal for Spcialists in Group Work. v29 n2 p159-173.

Hulse-Killacky, Diana; Page, Betsy J. (Nov 1994). Development of the Corrective Feedback Instrument: A Tool for Use in Counselor Training Groups. Journal for Specialists in Group Work. v19 n4 p197-210.

Hulse-Killacky, Diana; Robinson, Floyd F. (Sep 2005). An Effective Resarch Team Method to Influence Research and Scholarly Development. Journal for Specialists in Group Work. v30 n3 p241-252.

Kees, Nathalie L. and Nancy L. Leech. (Mar. 2002). Using group counseling techniques to clarify and deepen the focus of supervision groups. Journal for Specialists in Group Work. 27(1), 7-15.

Krieger, Kenin M.; Stockton, Rex (Dec 2004). Technology and Group Leadership Training: Teaching Group Counseling in an Online Environment. Journal for Specialists in Group Work. v29 n4 p343-359.

Kreiger, Kenin M.; Whittingham, Martyn. (Sep 2005). A Review of the Stockton Training Series: Instructor Reports of Current Use and Future Application. Journal for Specialists in Group Work. v30 n3 p283-288.

Lightsey, Owen Richard, Jr. (Sep 1997). Generalized Self-Efficacy Expectancies and Optimism as Predictors of Growth Group Outcomes. Journal for Specialists in Group Work. v22 n3 p189-202.

Merta, Rod J; And Others. (Nov 1993). Five Models for Using the Experiential Group in the Preparation of Group Counselors. Journal for Specialists in Group Work. v18 n4 p200-07.

Miller, Mark J. (Nov 1995). Participants' Perceptions of the Effectiveness of a Three-Part Videotape Series on Group Work. Journal for Specialists in Group Work. v20 n4 p217-21.

Newman, Jennifer A.; Lowell, Madeline. (Sep 1993). A Description of a Supervisory Group for Group Counselors. Counselor Education and Supervision. v33 n1 p22-31.

Newsome, Sandy; Christopher, John Chambers; Dahlen, Penny,; Christopher, Suzanne. (Sep )2006. Teaching Counselors Self-Care through Mindfulness Practices. Teachers College Record. v108-n9 p1881-1900.

Osborn, Cynthia J., Carrie L. Daninhirsch, and Betsy J. Page. (Spring 2003). Experimental training in group counseling: humanistic processes in practice. Journal of Humanistic Counseling, Education, & Development. 42(1), 14-28.

Pedersen, Paul B.; Ivey, Allen E. (Jul 2003). Culture-Centred Exercises for Teaching Basic Group Microskills. Canadian Journal of Counseling. v37-n3 p197-204.

Pierce, Keith A.; Baldwin, Cynthia. (Sep 1990). Participation versus Privacy in the Training of Group Counselors. Journal for Specialists in Group Work. v15 n3 p149-58.

Proctor, Brigid. (2000). Group Supervision: A Guide to Creative Practice. London: Thousand Oaks, CA.

Rivera, Ed II Torees; Wilbur, Michael; Roberts-Wilbur, Janice; Phan, Loan T.; Garrett, Michael T.; Betz, Robert L. (Dec 2004). Supervising and Training Psychoeducational Group Leaders. Journal for Specialists in Group Work. v29 n4 p377-394.

Robinson, Floyd F.; And Others. (Sep 1996). Research on the Preparation of Group Counselors. Journal for Specialists in Group Work. v21 n3 p172-77.

Roland, Catherine Buffalino; Neitzschman, Lynne. (Mar 1996). Groups in Schools: A Model for Training Middle School Teachers. Journal for Specialists in Group Work. v21 n1 p18-25.

Romano, John L. (Jun 1998). Simulated Group Counseling: An Experiential Training Model for Group Work. Journal for Specialists in Group Work. v23 n2 p119-32.

Romano, John L; Sullivan, Brandon A. (Dec 2000). Simulated Group Counseling for Group Work Training: A Four-Year Research Study of Group Development. Journal for Specialists in Group Work. v25 n4 p366-75.

Starling, Paulette V.; Baker, Stanley B. (Mar 2000). Structured Peer Group Practicum Supervision: Supervisees' Perceptions of Supervision Theory. Counselor Education and Supervision. v39 n3 p162-76.

Stockton, Rex; Toth, Paul L. (Nov 1997). Applying a General Research Training Model to Group Work. Journal for Specialists in Group Work. v22 n4 p241-52.

Stockton, Rex; Toth, Paul L. (Nov 1996). Teaching Group Counselors: Recommendations for Maximizing Preservice Instruction. Journal for Specialists in Group Work. v21 n4 p274-82.

Stockton, Rex; Morran, D. Keith; Nitza, Amy Gibson. (Dec 2000). Processing Group Events: A Conceptual Map for Leaders. Journal for Specialists in Group Work. v25 n4 p343-55.

Toth, Paul L.; Stockton, Rex; Erwin, Wesley J. (Mar 1998). Application of a Skill-Based Training Model for Group Counselors. Journal for Specialists in Group Work. v23 n1 p33-49.

Toth, Paul L.; Stockton, Rex (May 1996). A Skill-Based Approach to Teaching Group Counseling Interventions. Journal for Specialists in Group Work. v21 n2 p101-09.

Tyler, J. Michael; Reynolds, Therese. (Mar 1998). Using Feature Films to Teach Group Counseling. Journal for Specialists in Group Work. v23 n1 p7-21.

Werstlein, Pamelo O.; Borders, L. DiAnne. (May 1997). Group Process Variables in Group Supervision. Journal for Specialists in Group Work. v22 n2 p120-36.

Wiggins, James D.; Carroll, Marguerite R. (Mar 1993). Back to the Basics: Perceived and Actual Needs of Group Leaders. Journal for Specialists in Group Work. v18 n1 p24-28.

# GLOSSARY

Acting out (acting up)

The individual translates his conscious (and/or unconscious) thoughts into physical performance or expression. This can vary from normal to abnormal behavior depending upon the place, appropriateness and type of behavior.

Control

The leader is able to direct and/or handle the events in the environment.

Directly

The word is used in this text to denote the relating by a group member of anecdotes and/or thoughts and feelings that are identified by the discussants as personal. (See *Indirectly*.)

Group anxiety

The group is influenced with or overwhelmed by events in the environment (i.e., topics of discussion) that are, or the group members think are, too difficult to be controlled or handled.

Group spontaneity

A high degree of involvement by the group members whereby everyone is attentive to the topic being discussed (whether they are verbalizing or not) and whereby everyone is enthusiastic and unconstrained enough to participate in some way.

Indirectly

The word is used in this text to denote

381

the relating of a group member's own experiences (and/or thoughts and feelings) that are not identified by the discussant as personal. For example, the group member can attribute a personal experience to that of a friend, or if the group member is angry he may talk about angry topics such as war, murder, or robbery instead of relating his own angry thoughts and feelings. (See *Directly*.)

Setting Limits
The group leader established rules or limits for the group members.

Program
To start at the level of performance that the group members are functioning and to allow to progress as they are capable.

Testing
A conscious or unconscious method or process by which a group member investigates whether the leader is capable of handling or directing all the events in the environment.

Working through
(Analytic Ref.) The conversion of unconscious material to conscious thoughts. In counseling, the term can be defined as the resolving of a problem directly (talking about the problem itself) or indirectly (talking about a "similar" problem.)

# INDEX

386